# Anthropology of Development
# and Change in East Africa

# MONOGRAPHS IN DEVELOPMENT ANTHROPOLOGY

Under the General Editorship of
DAVID W. BROKENSHA
MICHAEL M HOROWITZ
and
THAYER SCUDDER

Sponsored by the Institute for Development Anthropology

*Anthropology and Rural Development in West Africa*, edited by Michael M Horowitz and Thomas M. Painter

*Lands at Risk in the Third World: Local-Level Perspectives*, edited by Peter D. Little and Michael M Horowitz, with A. Endre Nyerges

*Anthropology of Development and Change in East Africa*, edited by David W. Brokensha and Peter D. Little

*Anthropology and Development in North Africa and the Middle East*, edited by Muneera Salem-Murdock and Michael M Horowitz (forthcoming)

# Anthropology of Development and Change in East Africa

EDITED BY
## David W. Brokensha
## and Peter D. Little

Westview Press
BOULDER & LONDON

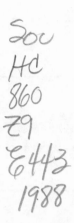

*Monographs in Development Anthropology*

Copyright © 1988 by the Institute for Development Anthropology

Published in 1988 in the United States of America by Westview Press, Inc., 5500 Central Avenue, Boulder, Colorado 80301, and in the United Kingdom by Westview Press, Inc., 13 Brunswick Centre, London WC1N 1AF, England

Library of Congress Cataloging-in-Publication Data
Anthropology of development and change in East Africa/edited by
  David W. Brokensha and Peter D. Little.
    p.  cm.—(Monographs in development anthropology)
  Bibliography: p.
  Includes index.
  ISBN 0-8133-7243-7
  1. Economic development projects—Africa, East—Case studies.
2. Agricultural development projects—Africa, East—Case studies.
3. Community development—Africa, East—Case studies.
4. Anthropology—Africa, East.  I. Brokensha, David W.  II. Little,
Peter D.  III. Series.
HC860.Z9E443 1988
338.9676—dc19                                                              88-16917
                                                                                CIP

Printed and bound in the United States of America

  The paper used in this publication meets the requirements of the American National
        Standard for Permanence of Paper for Printed Library Materials Z39.48-1984.

10    9    8    7    6    5    4    3    2    1

# Contents

# Illustrations

# Acknowledgments

The editors are grateful for the editing and production assistance of a number of IDA staff members, especially Sylvia Horowitz, who copyedited the entire manuscript and supervised its transformation for computer-generated typesetting. Vivian Carlip gave a second editorial reading, Cecily O'Neil helped with production, the manuscript was proofread by Vera Beers-Tyler, and Peter Daly designed the map on the following page.

To the contributors, of course, goes our greatest appreciation, for their gracious cooperation in making requested revisions as well as for the content of their work.

*David W. Brokensha*
*Peter D. Little*

# EAST AFRICA

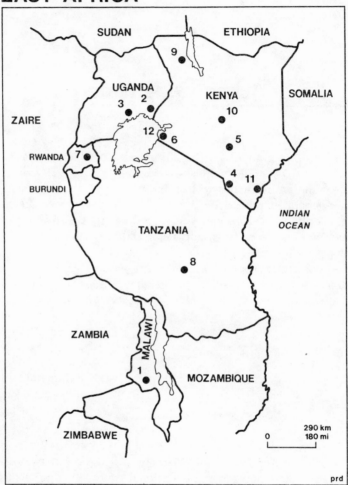

Field Locations Described by Authors.

1. Anita Spring: Malawi (all); 2. Stephen Bunker: Bugisu District, Uganda; 3. Patrick Fleuret: Uganda (all); 4. Anne Fleuret: Taita/Taveta District, Coast Province, Kenya; 5. Joshua Akong'a: Kitui District, Eastern Province, Kenya; 6. Thomas Conelly: Mbita Division, South Nyanza District, Kenya; 7. Angelique Haugerud: Rwanda (all); 8. Benson C. Nindi: Ismani, Iringa Region, Tanzania; 9. Richard Hogg: Turkana District, Kenya; 10. Edward H. Greeley: Meru District, Central Highlands, Kenya; 11. Monica Udvardy: Kaloleni Division, Coast Province, Kenya; and 12. Miriam S. Chaiken: Mbita Division, South Nyanza District, Kenya.

*Source:* From *Premier World Atlas,* © Copyright 1978 by Rand McNally & Company, R.L. 88-S-61, p. 48. Reprinted with permission.

# Introduction: Anthropology, Development, and Change in East Africa

*Peter D. Little and David W. Brokensha*

Current discussions of development and change in East Africa are dominated by themes of stagnant agricultural production, ecological crisis, overextended state enterprise, and a worsening debt situation (Commins et al. 1986; Green 1985; Timberlake 1985). These premises, often only assumed to be accurate descriptions of reality, monopolize the policy dialogue among donor, government, and development planners and shape the development environment within which anthropologists currently work. This environment in certain respects differs from that of the 1970s, when the number of anthropologists involved in development activities—either as consultants, researchers, or project managers—increased exponentially (cf. Hoben 1982). While continuities clearly exist, development anthropologists increasingly will have to be cognizant of the macroeconomic and larger institutional contexts within which rural development activities take place. "Social soundness" analysis, which has been the domain of the anthropologist, will have to be broadened to pay closer attention to linkages between local-level phenomena and the policy and institutional reforms that are taking place at national and international levels.

The realities of East Africa in the 1980s, a period marked by continued armed conflict and famine in certain countries, pose challenges to anthropology, and to development anthropology in particular. They challenge the very theories, methods, and practices of the discipline. What do anthropological method and theory have to say about institutional reform, food aid, agricultural price policy, and hunger (the last of which has received some attention from anthropologists: Scudder 1962 and Torry 1984)? What has been the experience of practicing anthropologists working in East Africa on development issues in the 1980s? How have the new development initiatives of the 1980s, which emphasize "policy dialogue" and "sectoral programs," affected the work of anthropologists in the region? These and other questions with equally dramatic implications for local populations are addressed in this book.

## The Book

This collection of twelve essays, while not representative of all development activities that concern anthropologists in East Africa, does illustrate several main themes. Some clearly represent new emphases in development anthropology in the region—for example, analyses of decision making in regional and national institutions (P. Fleuret, Nindi), political and social assessments of state policies (Bunker, Hogg), and local effectiveness of national food aid programs (A. Fleuret)—while others reflect continuity with earlier topics, although providing new data and different perspectives from earlier analyses. These include the role of anthropologists in agricultural research programs (Haugerud, Conelly, Spring), local response to drought and famine (Akong'a), population and health programs (Chaiken, Greeley), and development of local organizations (Udvardy). All chapters are implicitly or explicitly related to at least one institution or agency, mostly governmental but including international donor agencies and nongovernmental organizations (NGOs).

The authors, anthropologists and sociologists at universities, donor agencies, or NGOs, take different roles in the case studies they describe. Several were employed by the implementing agency or by an organization evaluating a development program, while others conducted research that allowed them to observe and analyze a particular development policy or project. In almost all cases, the authors' studies are based on relatively long-term (at least several months) fieldwork in a particular region, a departure from much of development anthropology, which is based on short-term consultancies. In one case (A. Fleuret), the author was hired by a donor to evaluate a program in an area where she had been conducting long-term field research. While certain development issues can be examined in a relatively brief period of time, the long-term nature of the authors' data enhances their arguments and analyses. To echo Hogg's point, "only such research, carried out over months and years, rather than weeks, can hope to identify long-term economic and social trends. . . ." (p. 194).

The editors of the volume believe that it was important not to restrict contributions to analyses of development projects and programs per se, nor to include only anthropologists who had been employed—either as consultants or staff members—by development agencies. In surveying the current state of development-related research in East Africa, we felt that a number of excellent studies being conducted by independent researchers, with significant implications for policy and development, might have been excluded by a narrow focus on projects and programs. The inclusion of "change" in the title of this volume is intended to emphasize this broader interpretation of development anthropology. Such a perspective places equal attention on analyzing changes with clear development relevance—whether in household structure, population growth, or other social phenomena—as it places on analyzing a particular policy, program, or project.

It was originally our intention to restrict the book to those East African countries defined by the now-defunct East African Community (Kenya, Uganda, and Tanzania). This was not due to our placing any important significance on the Community, but because it defines a region that, in general, shares common historical experiences as well as common social and ecological characteristics. It also was a method of restricting the scope of the book, since a country like Kenya has enough relevant development anthropology experience to justify a volume in itself. Indeed, seven of the chapters in the book do deal with Kenya. Having stated this, however, we were drawn to two examples of development anthropology work in nearby countries, which we felt were too important to exclude from the volume. These were a national agricultural research program in Rwanda, where an anthropologist (Haugerud) was working closely with agricultural scientists in disseminating new techniques and seed varieties to small farmers, and a Women in Agricultural Development Project in Malawi, where the work of the anthropologist (Spring) had played a major role in improving the status of women in national and regional agricultural programs. We feel that the importance of the topics and the work more than compensate for the book's reduced geographical integrity, and complement well the case studies from other parts of the region.

## Importance of Local Production Systems

The majority of chapters deal with local production systems and the contribution anthropology can make toward understanding and improving them. Haugerud, for example, shows how anthropological insights can improve even a successful project, in her case Rwanda's potato-breeding program. By systematically inquiring why Rwandan farmers do—and do not—adopt new potato cultivars, Haugerud points out the central importance of understanding farmers' access to and allocation of land, labor, and capital, in determining cultivar adoption decisions. She goes on to analyze in detail the factors that farmers look for in deciding whether to plant a particular variety. The acceptability of potato varieties depends on taste preferences, starch content, cooking time, market acceptance, blight resistance, yields (in poor rains as well as in good rains), and compatibility with other crops (for intercropping). An understanding of these factors, as well as the local production system, helped researchers to tailor their program more closely to farmer needs, and also to distribute their new varieties more effectively.

Conelly also emphasizes the "farmer first" perspective in his analysis of an integrated pest-management program in western Kenya. Like Haugerud, Conelly was affiliated with one of the international research centers (in this case, the International Centre of Insect Physiology and Ecology) as a Rockfeller post-doctoral research fellow. Conelly looks at a program to reduce infestation of maize by the parasite *striga*, concluding that any successful pest eradication program must consider pests within the whole framework of the farm system, and recommending an integrated pest management approach that would "build on the existing knowledge and practices of farmers and provide solutions that are both technically feasible and appropriate to the circumstances of small-scale farmers" (p. 132). Conelly weaves historical data into his analysis, as do Bunker, Akong'a, Hogg, and Nindi, showing that pest eradication programs were also implemented during the colonial period and that they differ from current attempts in their unwillingness to incorporate local agricultural practices.

Hogg, in his chapter, challenges experts who denigrate the development potential of pastoral production in Turkana, Kenya, and who offer nonpastoral solutions, such as fishing and irrigated agriculture. In analyzing development activities in the area over the past 50 years, Hogg poignantly shows the dismal failure of interventions designed to provide alternatives to pastoralism. These programs were designed with an antipastoral ideology that gained credence from certain "scientific" reports claiming the area to be overpopulated and terribly overgrazed. The theme of peasant rationality also is reflected in Hogg's chapter by his demonstration that seasonal stock and human movements are carefully adapted to the area's meager resource base, and that in certain locations (for example, on hilltops) Turkana have always practiced a form of rotational grazing. The rationality of herders is perhaps best portrayed by their refusal to stop investing in livestock even when they have been settled on irrigation schemes. Hogg concludes his chapter by discussing an OXFAM program to restock Turkana herds, where he was the project manager. In contrast to most development activities, the OXFAM program emphasized the rehabilitation and development of local pastoralism as the most cost-effective, long-term development solution for the district.

## Gender and Household Dynamics

The chapters that examine different aspects of local production reflect certain theoretical and methodological advances that have been made in anthropology. One of the most important of these has been a clearer understanding of household (and intrahousehold) dynamics, with particular emphasis on the role of women in agricultural production and income generation (Guyer 1981; Moock 1986). In her chapter on Malawi, Spring shows how aggregated statistical data on agriculture fail to show the significant contribution of women. Agricultural development programs in Malawi have been designed on the assumption that the household was an undifferentiated unit, and that within it women's contribution to agriculture was minimal and under the control of the male household head. In addition to demonstrating that the assumption is empirically flawed (many households in Malawi, as well as elsewhere in East Africa, are headed by females), she points out the major contribution that women make to agriculture. If anything, agricultural programs should be particularly attuned to the importance of women as laborers and farm managers, since men, who are increasingly involved in wage employment, are becoming part-time farmers while women are emerging as full-time farmers. Spring's analysis had immediate application for women and agriculture in Malawi, resulting in the creation of a government agricultural data base of sex-disaggregated data and the design and implementation of successful demonstration projects for women farmers.

Anne Fleuret also draws on understandings of household dynamics to evaluate the local effectiveness of a food aid program in Taita, Kenya. The program was a Title II Maternal and Child Health (MCH) feeding program, financed by USAID. Her study is one of the first in Kenya to examine the intrahousehold allocation and consumption of relief food, to determine whether commodities were going to the targeted population (i.e., women and children). The study's methodology called for collecting data on food consumption, income and expenditure, and health among 40 households in two different communities (20 in each). Using a household-based model, Fleuret was able to conclude that food aid is used as a substitute rather than a supplement within the household; that the income value of food is not the best criterion for determining food packages; that the nutritional status of the targeted population (women and children) within the household is often only marginally improved; and that well-to-do households often benefit as much as poor households.

In a different context, Chaiken also utilizes household and intra-household units, in her case to examine the effects of a UNICEF-funded rural health program in western Kenya. With the goal of assessing the health and nutritional status of rural households, she collected data on income, consumption, intrahousehold allocation of resources, child rearing practices, fertility, and mortality. Particular attention was given to incidences of child mortality and morbidity. These data were collected and analyzed on a "woman-focused basis, with a woman and her children viewed as the minimal social group, and a woman's own income plus any remittances from the household computed as the household operating budget (rather than father's income or combined income)" (p. 239). The high incidence of female-headed households in the region supported this methodology. Chaiken concludes that improvements in child mortality and morbidity will come primarily from increased public awareness of preventive health and sanitation methods and improvements in health delivery systems. Her suggestions have already had an impact in the area, and an action plan, which includes nutrition-awareness workshops for women, has been formulated that incorporates many of her recommendations.

## Institutional Dynamics

Several of the chapters emphasize the importance of understanding the institutional/organizational context within which rural development takes place. P. Fleuret goes the furthest in arguing for analyses of institutions at local, regional, and national levels. He correctly shows that rural development programs often flounder because of unforeseen organizational problems. He examines an agricultural tool distribution program in Uganda, using his findings to demonstrate the importance of understanding institutional dynamics among local agricultural cooperatives, district officials and elected representatives, the national ministry (in this case, the Ministry of Cooperatives and Marketing), and the donor (USAID). Final distribution outcomes, Fleuret argues, were mediated by interactions between district cooperative unions and cooperative societies, and by the social organization affecting tool delivery at the point of distribution. Fleuret concludes that organizational analysis for development must address several types of institutions, both indigenous and "modern"; relationships among different organizations (national, regional, and local), and how these are changed by the flow of development resources; and the interaction between the organizational context and technical development objectives.

Bunker, also dealing with cooperative societies in Uganda, demonstrates how local institutions can effectively promote the interests of rural producers vis-à-vis national interests. He examines marketing cooperatives in Bugisu, where there has been a legacy of strong and effective local organizations. Because the Bagisu produced a valuable export crop (coffee) and had strong political leadership, their cooperatives were able to expand their autonomy from state supervision. When the central state attempted to increase control of Bagisu cooperatives under the Amin regime, the peasants resisted by retreating into subsistence production and allowing coffee production to decrease precipitously. (See also Nindi's chapter for the theme of peasant resistance to state policies.) Bunker concludes that the state (with donor leverage in some cases) should allow agricultural cooperatives, like those in Bugisu, the political space necessary to promote and defend producers' interests and allow them to participate beneficially in markets, so that export revenues essential for development can be generated.

Udvardy also discusses local organizations, in this case women's groups in coastal Kenya. Like Bunker's and P. Fleuret's, her chapter demonstrates the importance of analyzing institutional linkages at different levels. Investigating the political and economic dynamics of women's groups in Kaloleni Division, Kenya, Udvardy shows that males, who dominate women in local, regional, and national political institutions, have been able to control the activities of women's groups. Because men have stronger political ties to regional and national government organizations, they serve as brokers for women's groups and exert considerable power over their behavior. Udvardy compares this unequal relationship to that of patron-clientelism, with the male as the patron. Udvardy recommends several changes in the structure and organization of women's groups that could enhance the power of women. These include forming producers' cooperatives for women's groups, increasing the flow of information from district and national government organizations to women's groups, and reducing the number of umbrella groups that currently represent women's organizations.

The chapter by Greeley makes a case for involving a special type of local organization—the NGO—in the implementation and management of rural development programs (in his example, a family planning program in Kenya). Greeley argues that it is local NGOs (including private firms) that are in closest contact with rural people and have the most experience in working effectively at the local level. In examining a family planning program in Meru, Kenya, Greeley points out several advantages to utilizing NGOs, including their long involvement in Meru, their role as introducer of Western technologies, their history of involvement with women's activities, and their ability to be experimental and self-sustainable. In addition to examining the potential of NGOs, Greeley shows that fertility regulation was not a concept alien to Meru, and that where appropriate, family planning programs should build upon these indigenous beliefs and practices.

## Local Analysis of Development Policies

Many of the contributions to this volume deal either directly or indirectly with the local impact of state and donor policies. Several contributors mention incorrect assumptions that guide development policies, such as the beliefs about African pastoralists examined critically by Hogg. Greeley shows how population planning activities in Kenya consistently emphasize introduced technologies and approaches while ignoring traditional techniques of fertility regulation. Akong'a, too, argues that government policies on famine relief tend to neglect indigenous adaptive strategies, which still play an important part in helping the Akamba (and others) to survive droughts and famine. In studying state policies and their assumptions, many of our contributors make explicit the links between present and colonial policies. Akong'a, Conelly, Greeley, Haugerud, Hogg, and Nindi all analyze aspects of colonial administrative legacies, which have often resulted in highly inappropriate contemporary structures and approaches to development.

In discussing agricultural cooperatives, P. Fleuret and Bunker examine the degree to which Ugandan peasants have been able to sustain food production in an unfavorable policy environment. Bunker draws attention to the serious social and economic consequences that occur when state policies are enforced from the center with little acknowledgment or participation of rural residents. Nindi presents an even more vivid example of the local effects of state policies, analyzing peasant responses to the implementation of Tanzania's *ujamaa* policy. This policy, which promoted settlement, land reform, and an increased role of government in production and marketing activities, was the basis of one of Africa's most thorough experiments in social transformation. Nindi examines the effects of ujamaa in the context of Ismani, formerly one of the most prosperous maize-growing areas of Tanzania. In presenting historical and economic data on production in the area, he shows how the rush to "villagize" and socialize farmers led to serious technical and social flaws in planning, which served further to alienate peasants from the state. Once ujamaa became defined as government policy, it was turned over to local party and government officials, who often used force to implement the policy. The insensitivity to local historical, ecological, and social conditions led to a form of protest among peasants, resulting in reduced agricultural production and, in the Ismani case, to physical violence. In his conclusion, Nindi notes that Tanzania's economic and agricultural problems are unlikely to be resolved until bureaucrats stop seeing "the solution to those problems in terms of enforcing their policies, in a top-down fashion, on the local peasantry" (p. 178).

Akong'a also explores the local dimensions of government policy, presenting a detailed analysis of how the local populations and government have responded to famine in Kitui District, Kenya. He presents a history of drought and famine in the area dating back to the nineteenth century, and shows that government interventions have mainly been limited to relief efforts rather than development activities. The government's treatment of Kitui as a "famine district," which can be traced to the colonial period, restricted the extent of development initiatives until recently. Only in the past decade have several government/donor-funded programs in forestry, agriculture, and water development been initiated in Kitui. While Akong'a applauds the state's efforts in managing the 1984 drought and thereby avoiding famine on a large scale, he does recommend that the government formulate a national famine relief policy "to be implemented whenever a local or national famine is reported" (p. 117).

## Can Anthropology Make a Difference?

The chapters of this volume demonstrate that while there is no universal way in which anthropology can contribute toward improving development policies and programs, certain common features exist. First is the immediate translation of anthropological knowledge into action programs to benefit low-income populations. Several cases are presented where the anthropologist made an immediate difference in improving a development policy or program. Chaiken, for example, while admitting that not all her recommendations for improving a rural health program were adopted by the Kenyan government, shows that her work did influence programs of local health centers and their personnel. Basing their efforts on her findings, local health workers have initiated campaigns to improve immunization coverage and expand nutritional testing and education programs. Similarly, Hogg has helped to improve the welfare of pastoralists by designing and managing a restocking program in Turkana District that provides an alternative to settled agriculture and fishing for destitute herders. The work of Spring also had relatively immediate applications for helping a particular segment of the rural population, female farmers in Malawi. In challenging the male bias of agricultural programs in Malawi, Spring made significant gains in "putting women farmers into the mainstream of activities whenever possible, without isolating them or neglecting men farmers"(p. 16). She achieved this by assisting project managers to reformulate their projects to include women; by creating a national agricultural data base that was disaggregated by sex; by conducting farming systems research and extension projects proving that women could be used as trial cooperators and that male extension workers could work effectively with female farmers; by increasing the number of women farmers and female extension agents in Ministry of Agriculture training courses; and by implementing action programs at the grassroots level that improved the welfare of women farmers.

A second contribution of the case studies in this volume was the integration of an anthropological perspective into agricultural research programs that hitherto had been dominated by technicians. The work of Spring is one case; Conelly and Haugerud also provide examples. In different contexts, Conelly and Haugerud were able to build anthropological perspectives into agricultural research programs, demonstrating the importance of understanding social relations, indigenous agricultural knowledge, and household dynamics. Their work has not yet had the immediate impact on local populations as have the cases reported above, but it has made a significant contribution toward insuring that future agricultural research programs in their respective areas will incorporate and build upon the knowledge and resources of local farmers, and that anthropologists will play an important role in those agricultural research programs.

A final contribution of anthropology, as reflected in the case studies, is a better understanding of how local populations respond to particular development policies and programs. Nindi and Bunker, for example, show the kind of development stagnation that can take place when state policies are imposed from the center with little farmer participation. Udvardy, in a similar fashion, suggests that the lack of participation of key actors—in particular, women—in making development decisions can inhibit the realization of income and development objectives. A. Fleuret also shows that the effects of national food aid policies and programs on local populations are poorly understood by development planners. In examining the local impact of food aid in Taita, Kenya, A. Fleuret is able to suggest several ways of making national food-aid programs more effective in reaching the most nutritionally at risk segments of the rural population.

The chapters by P. Fleuret and Greeley show that the relationships between institutional factors and outcomes of development projects are also poorly understood. Family planning programs in Kenya, for example, attain only moderate rates of success because NGOs have not been allowed to play a more prominent role. NGOs may better address family planning issues at the local level than can government institutions. Similarly, P. Fleuret shows that many development projects do not meet their objectives because they were designed without a proper understanding of institutional dynamics, and he suggests ways in which development projects can better incorporate the institutional element at local, regional, and national levels.

## A Final Note

The anthropologists in this volume often emerge as brokers, or interpreters, acting between local people and the various agencies and institutions that affect their lives. Some of the contributors have had an opportunity to turn this mediator role into immediate applications for development programs. Others have made less direct contributions, but have demonstrated that anthropological knowledge can help us understand how particular development policies and programs will affect local populations. The analyses presented here build upon anthropological theory and method, showing that anthropology can improve our understanding of contemporary development problems in East Africa, as well as help to design and implement solutions to them.

## References

Commins, Stephen K., Michael F. Lofchie, and Rhys Payne, eds.
    1986    Africa's Agrarian Crisis: The Roots of Famine. Boulder, CO: Lynne Rienner Publishers, Inc.

Green, Reginald H., ed.
    1985    Sub-Saharan Africa: Towards Oblivion or Reconstruction? Department of International Economic and Social Affairs, United Nations. Journal of Development Planning, No. 15.

Guyer, Jane
    1981    Household and Community in African Studies. African Studies Review 24(2/3):87–137.

Hoben, Allan
    1982    Anthropologists and Development. *In* Annual Review of Anthropology. B. J. Siegel, A. R. Beals, and S. A. Tyler, eds. Volume 11. Pp. 349–375. Palo Alto, CA: Annual Reviews, Inc.

Moock, J. L., ed.
    1986    Understanding Africa's Rural Households and Farming Systems. Boulder, CO: Westview Press.

Scudder, Thayer
    1962    The Ecology of the Gwembe Tonga. Manchester: Manchester University Press.

Timberlake, Lloyd
    1985    Africa in Crisis: The Causes, the Cures of Environmental Bankruptcy.

London: International Institute for Environment and Development, Earthscan Paperback.

Torry, William L.
  1984   Social Science Research in Famine: A Critical Evaluation. Human Ecology 12(3):227–252.

# 1

## Putting Women in the Development Agenda: Agricultural Development in Malawi

*Anita Spring*

### Anthropological Input in Development Projects

If anthropologists and their work are rarely used in agricultural and other types of development projects, Cernea asserts, it is because they do not translate "their knowledge into operationally relevant propositions for technical experts" (1986:xi). Another reason for the lack of substantial anthropological input is observed by Hecht (1986): anthropologists are often asked merely to "salvage" the work of the development community, and so they enter the project late or for a short period. Although their short-term assignments on projects and their ability to use secondary sources to supplement field work may give them more freedom than other technical advisers, some development planners consider anthropologists' data sets too small to be used as a basis for planning (Koenig 1986). The ironic danger of an anthropologist knowing the area too well is mentioned as a drawback by Dyson-Hudson, who sees potential problems as the anthropologist translates for others what is happening on a project. He also decries the overuse of such general terms as "tradition," "society," and "culture," with insufficient attention to the idiosyncratic, the predictive, the full range of behavior, and alternative forms of procedures and organization (1985:186).

On the other hand, there are cogent arguments for anthropologists' participation in development projects. Cernea sees the knowledge of social science as assisting in the understanding of households and local organizations, particularly "the centrality of the family-based production unit to any rural development process" (1986:xii). Hecht argues that anthropologists can make such contributions as:

- encouraging broader farmer participation in design,
- identifying farmers' training needs,
- building effective communications channels between farmers and research officials,
- strengthening farmers' local institutions, and
- incorporating socioeconomic research into the larger framework of proposed farming systems research (Hecht 1986:15).

The perspective taken here is that anthropologists can enhance the participation of the intended beneficiaries and can discover mechanisms to incorporate both their participation and other socioeconomic concerns into the new institutions.

This chapter concerns a successful "marriage" between anthropology and technology in the Women in Agricultural Development Project (WIADP) in Malawi, Africa. After describing the Project and giving an overview of the structure of agriculture in Malawi, I will discuss various types of women in development (WID)[1] activities set in motion by the WIADP and other projects. I will offer some comments on strategies for getting women into the mainstream of development projects and proposals. It should be mentioned that although women farmers were the client group of the Project, the WIADP never lost sight of the fact that only some problems were gender related while others related to smallholders (men and women) in general. Data were gathered and presented for both men and women farmers.

## The Women in Agricultural Development Project (WIADP), Malawi

In 1981–1983 a project funded by the Office of Women in Development of the United States Agency for International Development (USAID) entitled "The Women in Agricultural Development Project (WIADP) in Malawi," Africa, was directed by an anthropologist (this author), and in 1985 it was evaluated as the best project that had been carried out in the previous decade to include women in USAID's agricultural projects (Fortmann 1985). The Project was small and its personnel few compared to most AID projects, but it was national in scope and functioned through the Ministry of Agriculture (MOA). What was the nature of this Project, why did it succeed, and what did the discipline of anthropology have to do with it?

### Project Personnel

Academic research projects are usually designed and directed by the same person or persons, while development projects funded by donor agencies often have separate design and implementation personnel. In the WIADP, an anthropologist and an agronomist, both female and principal investigators, designed the original proposal. Because of delay in the initial start-up, the codesigner agronomist was unable to work on the Project, although she later served as a consultant. The position was advertised, and a male agronomist was hired. Because the Project was under way already when he joined the staff, the anthropologist functioned as the Chief of Party rather than having coleadership as originally intended. Nevertheless, there was continuity in design and implementation personnel.

The new agronomist had previously worked overseas in Asia, but had no African experience. He learned Chichewa, the national language, and related well to Malawians. It helped to have a man who was interested in the topic of women farmers and who was able to convey this concern to other male professionals. A female agricultural economist who had anthropological training and extensive experience in southern Africa, including the management of a 600-acre tomato farm in Zimbabwe, joined the Project for ten months. The MOA seconded to the Project one of its Women's Program officers who had a five-year degree from Bunda College of Agriculture and two years of experience in working with extension programs. She came from a farm family and had an avid interest in helping smallholders and women. Finally, because the Project operated through the MOA, the research and extension staff were available for consultation and in many cases were able to provide direct assistance in the various aspects of the WIADP.

As an anthropologist who had research and teaching experience on Africa since 1970, I was knowledgeable about the area. My previous research was in rural northwest Zambia (1970 to 1972 and 1977), where I studied traditional society, particularly indigenous religion and medicine. The village women there had insisted that I learn about their role as farmers; they gave me land and seed and taught me how to cultivate maize and groundnuts. I also looked at how people incorporated biomedical information and agricultural technologies into their lives (Spring 1976, 1978, 1980; Spring and Hansen 1985).

In 1980, as the social scientist on the design team for a large project ($17 million) to build facilities, prepare curricula, and train staff for the National Agricultural University of Cameroon, I became aware of the difficulties in incorporating a social-science perspective into a project that was directed by agricultural scientists. Even though the report I wrote on the impact of the project on women and on smallholder farmers was requested by the AID staff in both Washington and Cameroon,[2] it was largely dismissed by the American team of agricultural scientists. As a result there was little social-science input in the project paper and in the implementation of the project. Hoben (1982) and others have noted the problems of anthropological input in this type of endeavor and the resulting lack of social-science perspective in technical-aid projects. Even where anthropologists are regular members of the teams, discussions and observations show that their work is often believed to be of lesser significance than that of production scientists (see the end-of-project report of Pasley [1986] where the social-science input is negated or overlooked).

These experiences convinced me that an equal footing of social and production scientists was necessary not only for the comfort of the social scientist, but for the success of a project. Consequently, in the WIADP there was never any debate as to whether or not physical/biological information was needed or superior to social/economic information. The underlying assumption was that both types of data and interventions were necessary and that one type might not be complete without the other. The motivation of all the staff was high, and all were in agreement about the goal of the Project, which was to assist smallholder farmers and, in particular, to focus on women agriculturalists at all levels as client groups. The various skills and disciplinary perspectives of the team members combined well, and unlike projects where the social scientist might be brought in only at certain points, on this Project team members worked together on many endeavors.

## Project Methodology and Design

The techniques we used to gain data and people's confidence were anthropological, but our methods and perspectives came from a variety of disciplines. The WIADP worked at all levels of agricultural training and production (from the producer to the policy maker), taking a client-centered (i.e., women agriculturalists)—not an agency—approach, and focusing on putting women farmers into the mainstream of activities whenever possible, without isolating them or neglecting men farmers. General project methodology tended to rely heavily on the social-science techniques in collecting socioeconomic data as well as in affecting policy changes, but methodologies from production scientists in collecting agronomic data and in designing trials were also required. Specifically, standard anthropological techniques of participant observation, individual and group interviews, questionnaires, and survey design were used. Underlying these techniques was the knowledge of the cultural setting including social organization and values, especially as they related to agriculture. Farming-systems research and extension methodologies were used in diagnostic surveys, formal interviews, and on-farm farmer-managed trials (Shaner et al. 1982; Hildebrand and Poey 1985). The perspective was thus interdisciplinary, considering sociological, economic, historical, agronomic, developmental, ecological, and administrative variables; the approach was that of a multidisciplinary team of people bringing their expertise to bear on the subject. My own anthropological perspective broadened to a national view rather than that of a single ethnic group, and I took the perspective of an applied anthropologist who directs change and affects policy (Eddy and Partridge 1978).

The MOA requested that the WIADP work with farmers in all three regions of Malawi, but they did not specify the actors or the methodology. In fact, the WIADP recognized the need to look at the woman's role in agricultural development at a variety of levels. The WIADP worked not only with farmers, but with extension agents, project supervisors, and program managers; the views, training, and programs of all these groups were examined. Simultaneously, planners, policy makers, researchers, and educators/trainers in the MOA were also interviewed and involved in the Project's goals. The Project was aided by the hierarchical organization of smallholder agriculture within the MOA (see below). The WIADP made use of this system to connect the micro-level with the macro-level. That is, as information or techniques that worked were discovered at the local level, they were used in other parts of the system and then implemented at the policy level so they could filter back down to the local level in many areas. In fact, the WIADP showed researchers and development personnel how to collect data on women farmers, then how to reach them with development services and policies using a holistic perspective on the topic.

The Project occurred at the "right" time in Malawi's development plan in that the Home Economics Section of the MOA had been changed to the Women's Program Section six months before the WIADP came to the country. The MOA planned to change from an emphasis on domestic science to a greater emphasis on agriculture, but its approach was limited to putting agriculturally trained women's program officers in a few development projects. In fact, the WIADP came into the country with no prior knowledge of this change and showed the MOA staff as well as the women's officers how to study and target women farmers.

The Project was funded, administered, and evaluated by the Women in Development Office of AID in Washington. It is not possible to say whether local Mission assistance or supervision would have helped or hindered, but the autonomy in planning and budgeting facilitated the ease with which programs could be developed and changed.

## Separate Versus "Integrated" Projects for Women

An issue in the field of Women in Development concerns the benefits of separate or integrated projects for women (Rogers 1980; Charlton 1984). Dixon (1980) examined 32 projects and showed that those that directed attention to women in particular, even if they were small, were more likely to benefit them. Larger projects generally do not target women as a group. Fortmann (1985) notes that agricultural projects may: (1) not have a clear understanding of production systems and therefore hinder women because they increase women's labor or reduce their access to or control of resources, (2) fail to reach women, or (3) be rejected by women because the technologies offered conflict with women's needs. Both Fortmann (1985) and Cloud (1986) note that projects that give funds to women are more likely to benefit them.

Cloud (1986) evaluated a number of development projects and posed two questions: (1) did women receive resources appropriate to their responsibilities in the farming system? and (2) did women receive resources appropriate to what the project gave out? The WIADP was fortunate in that its specific goal was to study women in agricultural development and so all the attention and resources were focused on women, but this is different from giving resources to women farmers or educators. Cloud cautions that targeting women as part of a project helps, but it is not always a guarantee. She and others (e.g., Dixon 1980) suggest that there is a correlation between benefits to women and project success. When women's access to resources is high, project success is high. When women's access to resources is moderate or low, project success is lower. Targeting women does not, however, automatically ensure a successful project, which in fact requires explicit and accurate action.

Dixon (1980) questions how project success is measured and finds that participation is a major indicator. The WIADP did not measure its progress by the number of women farmers we actually contacted, although tabulations were kept of participants in trials and in programs. This was because even though many farmers and virtually all women's program officers and development project staff in the country were contacted, their numbers were less important than the fact that the Project was able to change various policies that would impact on the subject in many places in the country both during and after the Project's duration. The WIADP was fortunate in that it was able to focus on women, rather than to have this client group tacked on as an appendix as is the case in so many projects (Fortmann 1985). The WIADP's goal was to focus on "mainstreaming" women into existing programs, but in carrying out this goal found that it was necessary to combine this mainstreaming effort with separate endeavors for women.

The Project was guided by four major points that had emerged from the literature on women in development (Rogers 1980; Spring and Hansen 1985; Charlton 1984). The first was the importance of the women's contribution to subsistence and cash crop agriculture and livestock in so many parts of Africa (Boserup 1970). Yet the women's contribution was often invisible to development personnel and researchers (Dixon 1985). The second was the increase in women's agricultural and domestic work because of the scarcity of labor as men migrated from their farms in search of wages and as children left to attend school (Kydd 1982; Charlton 1984). The third was the lack of access to resources such as land, capital, and mechanization, either traditionally or because of the development process that prevented women from participating fully in agricultural modernization (Palmer 1985; Rogers 1980; Charlton 1984). Finally, there was women's "second-class" status in relation to donor-funded or government-generated projects that prevented them from receiving agricultural education, extension, and credit services (Staudt 1975–76; Due and Summary 1982; Cloud 1985). The Women in Agricultural Development Project sought to

- research women's contributions and make them visible,
- study women's labor constraints,
- examine women's access to resources, and
- ascertain the types of development services rural women received (Spring 1986c).

## The WIADP Components

The WIADP was initially conceived as a research project that focused on smallholders, but it evolved during its implementation to include training, action projects, and policy components as well as research on various components of the agricultural sector (Spring 1985). There were a number of reasons why this occurred, including the support and encouragement of MOA officials and the WIADP's analysis of what needed to be done to make an impact on women. The WIADP examined the research data collected, the programs, and the services offered to farmers. Special attention was paid to how women as client groups were affected, monitored, and evaluated. The WIADP found that women as farmers were invisible in planning documents because data about their contributions were unknown or nonexistent. In the extension services and in research endeavors nationwide, women had been targeted only for domestic skills training and for organization into women's groups. To remedy the situation, the WIADP had to devise research, training, action, and policy strategies.

*Research.* Research was carried out on the gender roles within various farming systems in the country and within the development context. A number of data sets (both primary and secondary) were studied and disaggregated by gender. Farming systems research and extension methodologies (FSR/E) that included diagnostic surveys, long-term surveys, field trials, and dissemination of information were used (Spring, Smith, and Kayuni 1983b). Women's contributions to the smallholder sector and the types of programs offered to women were described, and the information was made available to the various sections of the MOA.

*Training.* The WIADP worked with the extension service on a variety of training activities. First, a workshop on women in development for all the Women's Program Officers set the stage for focusing on women farmers (Spring 1982b). The female and male extensionists received various training exercises in working with women, including training in preparing work plans, collecting data, and analyzing statistics on small-holders (especially women farmers). Seminars for project management and staff provided methodologies and techniques for targeting women as well as men farmers in development programs.

*FSR/E Action Projects with Farmers.* The WIADP used the methodology of selecting a number of small projects that could serve as case studies. These included: (1) soybean research trials with women that were based on the MOA emphasis on that crop, (2) maize varieties and fertilizer trials with men and women cooperators, (3) work with smallholders doing stall-feeding, and (4) collaborative work on new methods of targeting women for credit.

*Policy and Decision Making.* The WIADP worked with policy makers in the MOA and in each development division (see below) to assist them in: the collection and analysis of data by gender for planning purposes; changing the orientation of project documents to target women for agricultural programs; changing the curriculum for women exten-sionists; and reorienting project personnel to utilize new techniques for working with women farmers. In addition the WIADP staff worked with every manager and section leader in the eight agricultural development divisions to assist them in reformulating their programs and reformatting their reporting efforts to include women.

## The Structure of Agriculture

Malawi, located in southern Africa, is a landbound country with 6.8 million people. Its economy is based on agriculture with an estate sector that contributes about 70 percent to agricultural exports and a smallholder sector that contributes about 30 percent to exports in addition to feeding itself. In 1977 the country embarked on a 20-year National Rural Development Program to increase production in the smallholder sector, which had lagged behind the estate sector. The country was divided into eight contiguous units called Agricultural Development Divisions (ADDs), with each ADD having from two to five Rural Development

Projects (RDPs) under its control. Currently, 28 of approximately 40 RDPs have integrated-development programs that are funded either by donors or by government revenue funds. The programs these projects offer focus on basic infrastructure (roads, markets, schools, and water supply) and agricultural extension services (credit, soil conservation, reforestation, crop production and protection, animal husbandry and livestock development, and women's programs). Each ADD is administered by a program manager, his deputy, and heads of sections (such as the credit or women's programs section) who report to a chief officer in the MOA and who supervise extension staff members that are stationed in the RDPs. Each RDP has a similar structure in that the project officer supervises extension agents who are responsible for each section and who, in turn, supervise grass-roots extensionists residing in the villages. The extension service has approximately 3,000 staff members, with women constituting 7 percent of the total.

## General Themes Concerning Women's Contribution to Smallholder Agriculture

Although there was much recognition that women are active in agriculture, no systematic data that documented their involvement existed in Malawi prior to the WIADP. The Project saw as one of its main activities the need to improve knowledge about the contribution of women to the smallholder sector. To this end, women's and men's contributions to smallholder agriculture in terms of labor and output were studied, and mechanisms for collecting sex-disaggregated data were set up to provide an adequate data base to help distinguish problems that were gender related from those that were not.

An early assumption of the sexual division of labor in African agriculture is that men clear the land and women plant, weed, and harvest (Boserup 1970). The WIADP studies showed, however, that a variety of labor and cultivation patterns existed: (1) men and women cultivated similar crops on separate plots of land and/or had their separate livestock holdings; (2) men and women cultivated different crops; (3) women and men did different farming operations on the same plots or with the same animals; (4) men and women performed the same farm operations on the same plots; and (5) in households that were female headed, women were responsible for all the agricultural production. There was variation by area and by household within each area. The results of this endeavor confirmed that women contributed the majority of labor to Malawi's smallholder agriculture and made many agricultural decisions (Clark 1975; Spring, Smith, and Kayuni, 1983b).

Some of the other major findings concerning women in Malawi small-holder agriculture follow.

*Women Are Becoming Full-Time Farmers as Men Become Part-Time Farmers.* Rural men are increasingly becoming part-time or absentee farmers on their own farms because of salaried employment in urban areas or on agricultural estates. This is reflected in the fact that sex ratios in all rural areas show more women than men in the population of working age. As a result, women have taken over more of the labor and management of family farms (Kydd and Christiansen 1981) and the number of women who have become full-time farmers has increased.

*A Third of the Households Are Headed by Women, and This Number Is Increasing.* Male labor migration appears to contribute to a high percentage of female-headed households. Overall, 30 percent of Malawi's households are headed by women, but some areas have a smaller and others have a greater percentage of female heads (14 percent in the north and 45 percent in the south and central regions) (National Statistical Office 1982). In the Lilongwe Rural Development Project, where there is longitudinal data, the number of female-headed households has increased from 11 percent to 20 percent between 1968 and 1981 (Kydd 1982; National Statistical Office 1982). The sex of the household head is not static, but changes with the movement of men in and out of households in relation to wage labor, divorce, and remarriage. Women have the same number of children whether they are in female- or male-headed households, but female-headed households have one less adult, the adult male. Households headed by women tend to be associated with labor constraints, simpler farming systems, food deficits, and lack of agricultural services such as credit and training. Some of them cultivate slightly less land and hire less labor than households with male heads who either do the work themselves or have money from remittances to pay for labor. Female heads of household often must work as day laborers for other farmers (Spring 1984).

*Women Are Contributing as Much or More Agricultural Labor than Men.* Women spend as much time on farm work as men do, and as much time on domestic activities as on their farm work. Agricultural development projects increase the amount of agricultural work (hours per day and days per year) for both men and women (Clark 1975).

*The Sexual Division of Farming Labor Is Highly Variable and Changing.* Tobacco and cotton production are often considered to be crops that are totally managed by men. In all areas of Malawi, men are in charge of cotton, but women contribute significantly to various operations, and in some areas the cultivation of cotton is dependent on adult female labor. Women and children help in tobacco operations, and in some areas the household head, whether male or female, is responsible for the crop. Rice, groundnut, and smallholder (as opposed to estate) coffee and tea production are more variable in terms of the sexual division of labor. In some places men are responsible for rice production; in others whoever is head of the household takes care of the rice crop. In some areas, groundnuts are grown by both men and women, who do different tasks but contribute equal amounts of work. In other areas, groundnuts are considered a crop that women grow, and women do most of the work. In smallholder coffee and tea production, tasks are shared between the sexes except that men are responsible for pruning. Women are responsible for most subsistence production and contribute the most labor to such food staples as maize, cassava, or rice, depending on the crop grown in an area. In general, women are involved in the full range of cropping patterns in both subsistence and cash crops. They also do many of the farm operations that are commonly believed to be done *only* by men, such as cotton spraying and tobacco nursery planting (Clark 1975; Spring, Smith, and Kayuni 1983b). They are increasingly involved in livestock husbandry in some areas. Traditionally, women cared for small ruminants and poultry while men owned and cared for cattle, but in some areas women are beginning to own cattle, and as the care of large animals moves from the range to the village, women become more important in tending cattle. A number of the RDPs have introduced stall-feeding programs; although women are only a small percentage of the registered owners, they do most of the work feeding the steers that are penned in the village area (Spring 1986a).

*Women Receive Few Agricultural Development Services but Respond Well to Those They Receive.* Women receive fewer agricultural extension services (training, inputs, credit, visits, etc.) than men (Spring, Smith, and Kayuni 1983b) and, as a result, use more traditional farming practices. There are home-economics classes for women that contain some agricultural training, but the usual focus is on domestic subjects. Participants in these classes tend to be married, while female heads of households may not be contacted or may not have the time to attend. The data show that when women are given the opportunity to receive credit, agricultural training, inputs, etc., their agricultural performance increases and differences in farming practices and production output between the sexes decrease. Female heads of households who receive inputs and instruction manage their farms similarly to the male farmers, both on development schemes and in non-project areas, and they obtain similar yields and maintain crop diversity (Spring, Smith, and Kayuni 1982, 1983b; Spring 1986a). These women make good use of credit and rarely default (Evans 1981, 1983; MOA credit officers, personal communication).

## Research on Extension Services

The WIADP examined the various programs and services that RDPs offered to farmers; the curriculum and training of agricultural trainers, supervisors and managers; and the interaction of extensionists with farmers. Special attention was paid to how women as a client group were affected, monitored, and evaluated. It was found that women were considered "farmers' wives" and were invisible as farmers in their own right in planning documents and in project reports; they were generally neglected in agricultural-extension services apart from instruction in home economics. The idea of home-economics training for rural women was introduced in the preindependence period, but the RDPs intensified the effort (Spring 1983; 1986b). Women's responsibilities for fuelwood and water were not noted in reforestation or water programs; women were not targeted in credit, cash crop, livestock, or land-husbandry programs. The pattern was reflected in extension services and in the training of male and female researchers and extensionists. The female extension staff (who are based in the RDPs) consisted of about 150 women, who were expected to deal with women throughout the country. An examination of their training programs revealed their brevity (six months to a year in duration) and a curriculum that dealt mostly with domestic science rather than with agricultural and farm-management subjects that the male extension staff received (Spring 1983). The male extensionists, who were located in development areas, consisted of approximately 1,800 workers whose course of instruction lasted two years and focused on agricultural subjects. The RDP extension services such as credit and farmers' clubs were administered by the male staff, and their contacts with women farmers were few (Spring, Smith, and Kayuni 1982, 1983a, 1983b).

Most supervisors and managers of the extensionists had Bachelor of Science degrees from the country's agricultural college; some senior people had postgraduate training elsewhere. For a certain portion of their training, women students were required to take home economics courses on such topics as family resource management and nutrition, while men took agricultural engineering courses (Spring 1983).

By examining data on extension workers' contacts with farmers, participation in training courses, and participation in farmers' credit clubs, the WIADP concluded that women farmers were not being targeted and reached by development projects. It found that no RDP or ADD recorded farmer contacts or participation by gender, although they counted women's attendance in home economics courses and the number of female extensionists in an area. Accordingly, the WIADP did its own studies, disaggregated data from the National Sample Survey of Agriculture (see below), and asked RDP officers to collect data on participation by sex. The WIADP's analysis showed that contact with extension workers was the primary way that farmers received advice about agricultural inputs and credits; men received many more of those than women. Also, the number of women who belonged to farmers' clubs and who obtained seasonal credit was low. In some areas, only women in female-headed households were eligible; in other areas, some married women were eligible. Women's participation in medium-term credit was sporadic or nonexistent in most areas (Spring, Smith, and Kayuni 1983a, 1983b; Spring 1984).

## Directed Change in the Planning and Implementation of RDPs

Changes were needed at several levels in order for women farmers to benefit from development planning and services. The WIADP set activities in motion that enabled some changes to occur. Its work would not have been successful, however, if the "times were not right" in terms of supportive personnel in the MOA and interest in WID issues by donors, planners, and implementers. In particular, the presence of an active Women's Programs Officer and her staff at the MOA facilitated some of the changes.

Four main factors contributed to changing the situation so that women farmers could be beneficiaries. The first was a genuine interest in and use of the documentation of women's involvement in smallholder agriculture by the MOA that the WIADP and other researchers prepared. The second was cooperation from the government in disaggregating data by gender at national and project levels so that the contributions women made to production and the kinds and levels of agricultural services women received could be ascertained (National Statistical Office 1982). The third was the success of a few "action" or demonstration projects involving women farmers at the grassroots level. The fourth involved creating workable strategies that could be turned into policy decisions for reaching rural women based on the knowledge gained from the research data and the action projects.

### Creating a Data Base of Sex-Disaggregated Data

The WIADP investigated the types of data that were available in the country. Malawi is unique in that some excellent data bases exist on various segments of smallholder agriculture. In particular, each of the ADDs has an evaluation unit that collects data on general farmer practices and occasionally on particular topics. Two large, nationwide surveys had been carried out in 1968–1969 and in 1980–1981. One of them, the National Sample Survey of Agriculture of 1980–1981 (NSSA), had just been completed when the WIADP began. It had surveyed 7,000 households nationwide and was remarkable for its precision, its breadth of topical coverage, and its excellent data collection. Its purpose had been to study the smallholder sector in order to help policy makers decide on priorities and strategies for agricultural development.[3] Analysis of the data was coordinated by the National Statistical Office (NSO) in conjunction with the Evaluation Units of the ADDs. Most of the emphasis was on the collection of data, however, while analysis tended to be rudimentary and limited to aggregated frequency tabulations. The WIADP found a mechanism to determine the sex of the household head that was distinguishable on all surveys, and used the extension survey that contained information about wives. The WIADP convinced the NSO analysts that data on male and female household heads would be useful and would allow the frequency of female household heads in an area to be known. At first, the WIADP manually disaggregated several surveys to show the methodology; subsequently, the NSO rewrote the computer programs so that female heads and male heads could be compared in many of the surveys. This procedure has continued through time (Segal 1985). The initial publication on the NSSA contained the percentages of female-headed households by RDPs and ADDs for the entire country, allowing area-specific and nationwide totals to be seen for the first time (National Statistical Office 1982). As noted above, the data showed that approximately 30 percent of the nation's households were headed by women, ranging from 14 percent in the north to 45 percent in some areas of the central and southern regions. These data could not be ignored by the planners and extension staff of the MOA, as they showed for the first time that women were making farming decisions in household production and for market sales. The WIADP made extensive use of the NSSA to disaggregate data by sex to point out differences in farming practices. Usually these data showed that men and women differed little or that the range of skills overlapped, while there were differences in development services by sex (Spring 1984, 1986a; Spring, Smith, and Kayuni 1983b). Further, the WIADP convinced many of the ADDs to disaggregate the data they routinely collected. Subsequently, several of the ADDs, including those of Ngabu, Liwonde, and Blantyre, collected and published all their data in tables that were disaggregated in terms of gender.

The other secondary data source used by WIADP was the Agro-Economic Surveys (AES) (Ministry of Agriculture 1968–1982). Consisting of approximately 51 reports that had been produced between 1968 and 1982, these surveys contained detailed data on household composition, garden, and yield as well as on soils, labor, and income. The labor data were unique. Enumerators lived in the villages for a year collecting data on labor participation by age and sex of the laborer in terms of crop, cropping operation, and calendar month.

Using AES data for five areas, Clark (1975) showed that women were doing between 50 and 70 percent of the agricultural production labor. Women spent as much (or more) time on agricultural work as on domestic activities; they worked more than men in three of the areas, the same as men in one area, and only slightly less than men in the remaining area. Both men's and women's agricultural work load increased with the introduction of RDPs. The data also showed that women were important in the cultivation of cash crops and that they performed farm operations such as tobacco-nursery planting, cotton spraying, and marketing of cash crops—generally regarded as men's work. The work by Clark and the AES tables showing women's involvement in farming, especially in cash cropping and nontraditional crop operations, were widely publicized by WIADP in workshops, lectures, seminars, and discussions with development personnel (Spring 1982b). The WIADP synthesized the data and found that of the 51 reports produced since 1968–1969, 20 contained sex-disaggregated data of various types (Spring, Smith and Kayuni 1983b: Appendix A). Working with the director and his staff, the WIADP compiled and recalculated the data. The analysis and tables from the 20 reports were presented to the MOA. The director is now aware of the importance of women to the smallholder sector and is interested in designing new questionnaires that will more accurately reflect the farming system and will aid in the assessment of development needs.

In addition to these large secondary data bases that the WIADP helped to disaggregate, the Project undertook a number of surveys of its own. The largest was one carried out in the Lilongwe Rural Development Project (LRDP) in 1982 with the Farming Systems Analysis Section of another USAID project that focused on building agricultural research in the MOA. Fifteen survey instruments were administered to a sample of the same households that had been part of the NSSA sample two years earlier. This survey looked at farming practices and the effects of a development project on smallholders in general and on male- and female-headed households in particular. In addition, women in male-headed households were included, so that comparisons between men and women in the same households could be made. Some of the survey instruments used overlapped partially with five of the NSSA surveys' instruments. These were household composition (including education, migration, and work history), garden (only land-tenure sections), yield (only cultivation practices), and resources. Additionally, the LRDP survey included components on natality, garden labor, farm planning, agricultural knowledge, maize production, anthropometry, change and development, and diet. All the data were presented in tables that disaggregated in terms of female and male heads of households and wives in the male-headed households (Spring 1984).

The results showed that 20 percent of the households were female headed and that there was a range of farmers in the area going from low to high resources. Households headed by women were in all categories, but more of them were lower-resource farmers having fewer innovative crops, less labor, and less access to development services; in general they were less food self-sufficient. There were no differences in terms of the ways in which men and women carried out their farming operations except where interventions had been introduced. Then the men tended to have been the recipients of the new technologies and of capital intensification. Women had less contact with extensionists and with agricultural training, and they knew less about the types of fertilizers, recommended time of planting, plant populations, pest management, and credit. All households required some cash income; sources were differential by gender with men gaining cash from introduced crops (hybrid maize, tobacco, and European vegetables) while women relied on traditional crops (groundnuts and local varieties of maize) and on beer brewing. Men and women perceived development differently, with women noting the absence of services to them (Spring 1984).

The end result of the WIADP's exercises in data disaggregation was a change in policy and procedure. Currently, most of the survey data collected on farmers and on agricultural personnel are disaggregated by sex (Segal 1985; Manda et al. 1985; Kathy Desmond, personal communication).

## Conducting Farming Systems Research and Extension Projects

In 1981–1983, farming systems research was just getting started in the MOA. Subsequently, it became institutionalized and termed "adaptive research" (Nyirenda et al. n.d.). Up to this time it was fairly standard procedure to use farmers' fields and sometimes the farmers themselves as cooperators in trials or for demonstration purposes. Usually, women farmers were not contacted and did not participate. Host country and expatriate researchers tended to ignore the women in the fields during rapid reconnaissance surveys. In terms of on-farm farmer-managed trials and demonstrations, only male cooperators were selected. Sometimes the male cooperators carried out trial work themselves. Other times their wives and female relatives assisted or did much of the work. This produced errors in the way the trials were conducted because these women had not received the instruction and the male cooperators did not pass on the information. In order to understand the problem, the WIADP asked the male trial cooperators to tell them who actually performed each operation. The information obtained showed that wives and female relatives carried out many of these tasks (Spring's notes from Kawinga and Phalombe FSR surveys). Data analysis from the NSSA had shown that very few wives received agricultural information from their husbands. The presumed transfer of technology from husbands to wives and from men to women in the household did not take place. The assumption that if men are trained or assisted, then other family members will learn or be assisted was not confirmed by the data (Spring, Smith, and Kayuni 1983b; Spring 1984, 1986a).

The WIADP conducted FSR/E surveys and trials and studied the ways in which research and extension personnel were utilized to identify and to work with farmers. The WIADP participated in several attempts to remedy the way in which surveys and trials were conducted. Concerning surveys, the WIADP conducted its own FSR/E surveys in three different regions of the country and worked with a German team in Central Region (Spring 1982a; Spring, Smith, and Kayuni 1982, 1983b). In each case, there was a tendency for male extension workers who accompanied the teams to direct attention to the most successful male farmers. In order to remedy the situation, the necessity of examining a range of environments, family types, and economic situations was explained to staff members. The WIADP prepared guide sheets that detailed the types of households and families that needed to be considered, and requested that a variety of categories of farmers be sampled by teams doing diagnostic surveys and trials (Spring 1982a). These included: (1) low resources farmers, including those who must work for others; subsistence farmers; and wealthy farmers who grow cash crops and hire laborers; (2) a diversity of household types with differing family compositions such as nuclear, polygynous, and female-headed families; and (3) a diversity of ages and life-cycle situations. It also helped to have women researchers and extensionists on the teams, and subsequently it became fairly standard practice to have women on FSR/E teams. (The new program of FSR/E using adaptive research teams in the country specifies that there should be a woman on each team.)

The WIADP conducted its own trials and worked with the Farming Systems Analysis Section (FSAS) of another USAID project on its research trials (Hansen 1986). Two examples of trials that included female farmers illustrate the problems of obtaining women cooperators as well as the lessons learned by considering them. The first example focuses on trials conducted in the Phalombe Rural Development Project, a low resource area with a land shortage and a drought-prone climate where 37 percent of the households were headed by women. The average holding size was one hectare, but more than 60 percent of the households cultivated less than a hectare and almost a third cultivated less than half a hectare. Male out-migration was pronounced and women and children remained to work family farms. The trials consisted of comparing an improved cultivar with a local variety with "a simple non-replicated 2 × 2 factorial arrangement with two maize varieties and two levels of fertilizer (0 and 30 kg N/ha)" (Hildebrand and Poey 1985:127–128). Since area farmers intercrop, all the treatments had a mix of maize, cowpeas, and sunflowers (Hansen 1986).

The WIADP and the FSAS specifically requested of the village headmen and the extension workers that half of the cooperators be women. In fact, only 40 percent of the farmers selected in one village and 30 percent in the second village were women. It was later discovered that the women and men farmers selected were not comparable as farmers; the men tended to be vigorous individuals in their middle years, and many were high-resource farmers who owned cattle. Most of the women tended to be low-resource, older individuals at the end of their life cycle. They were probably selected because age is revered and it was considered an honor to be selected, perhaps more so for women than for men. Therefore, comparisons between male and female farmers in terms of management and yields are not valid for showing gender differences and abilities. However, the data do show differences between high- and low- resource farmers and that more women are in the latter category because of selection procedures. A modified stability analysis was carried out on these data by Hildebrand and Poey (1985:126–134) and by Hansen (1986). Because of the inclusion of a range of farmers, young and old and male and female, an evaluation of the types of environments could be made where "environment . . . becomes a continuous quantifiable variable whose range is the range of yields from the trial" (Hildebrand and Poey 1985:126). The analysis showed that the same area encompasses a range of environments in terms of farmer management, soils, rainfall, and the like, and that the cultivars respond differently. The local cultivar was superior in "poor" maize environments while the improved maize was superior in "good" maize environments. Both cultivars did better with fertilizer in both types of environments. The data showed that there were two different recommendation domains in the same geographical area: a group of low-resource and a group of high-resource farmers. Although each domain included both men and women, more women farmers were in the poorer environment, most likely because they were low-resource farmers in the first place. Further analysis, using confidence levels, allowed the high and low environment farms to be compared. The results showed that only farmers in the better environments should choose the improved variety (a composite variety of maize), and that they should fertilize the crop. In the poorer environments, the local variety of maize was better. Fertilizer helped, but should only be recommended to farmers who could afford it, or the farmers could not recover production costs. The final recommendation was "to fertilize the local maize variety in the poorer environment and to use the composite maize with fertilizer in the better environment" (Hildebrand and Poey 1985:132). Farmers who owned cattle and used the manure on their fields were in the better environment. All but one of the farmers in the better environment were men. Women usually did not own cattle, although the single high-resource female farmer did. Most of the farmers in the poorer environments were women, but there were some men. The data showed that recognizing different segments of the population, including those at particular risk, resulted in the delineation of two domains and technology solutions within one micro area. The female-headed households constrained by labor and cash would find it difficult to use fertilizer. This, coupled with their smaller holdings and lack of extension advice, would make their use of the improved cultivar and the standard extension recommendations disastrous (Spring 1988a, 1988b).

The second example of using women as trial cooperators concerns demonstrations and trials with soybeans (Spring 1986b). In this situation, women were targeted through their home economics classes to learn recipes for using soybeans. The MOA determined that this crop would improve the rural diet, which was deficient in fats and proteins. However, only the female staff members were used to reach the women, and they could teach only the recipes, not the methods to cultivate the crop. (The female extensionists did not know how to grow the crop and lacked training on inoculation of the crop and the use of fertilizers.) In a test of whether the male extension staff could work with women farmers, the WIADP held demonstrations one year and gave inputs and instruction to 59 female cooperators. There was a range of environments, and it was possible to compare the performance of women farmers. The better farmers had better management and used viable inoculum. The poorer farmers had problems with pests and unviable inoculum because they failed to reinoculate after late rains and delayed planting. As a result of these demonstrations and of surveys of both men and women farmers involved in soybean production in a number of areas, the problem of how to get viable inoculum to the rural areas was identified as a general problem affecting both men and women. In addition, gender-specific smallholder problems were found, such as the lack of training and the limited amount of seed given to women. Trials were held the following year with 20 female cooperators selected by the male extension staff.

Besides trying to solve the technical problems, we asked two other questions. Could women do on-farm research with precision? Could the male extension staff work with women? The answers to both questions were affirmative. The women were able to learn the procedures for the trials with precision. Special techniques were used to instruct them and to test their knowledge of the techniques before they planted their trials. Second, the male extension staff experienced no difficulty in identifying and instructing the women or in monitoring the trials (Spring 1986b).

### Some Other Projects with Farmers

A British researcher documented that the low-resource households in Phalombe Rural Development Project, discussed above, were being ignored by extension and credit programs (Evans 1981). To remedy the situation, first, the cooperation of male extensionists and male village leaders was required to bring women into the extension arena and to enable them to articulate their problems. Second, the notions of who was creditworthy had to be changed. Finally, the actual credit packages had to be modified.[4] The WIADP used this work by Evans as a case study and helped the MOA disseminate the methodology nationwide in 1983 by means of the National Workshop on Credit (Evans 1983; Spring, Smith, and Kayuni 1983b).

In studying a stall-feeding enterprise in the Lilongwe Rural Development Project, the oldest RDP in Malawi, the WIADP worked with farmers who were fattening steers provided on credit by the Livestock Section. The work showed that although only 13 percent of the participants were women, women often did much of the feeding and care of animals that were assigned to men. The methods of recruitment were different for men and women: the male extensionists sought out male farmers while the women farmers had to "prove" their agricultural fitness. Male participants were given more advice and were visited more frequently; they therefore knew more about constructing the pens and grading the animals (Spring 1986a).

The WIADP was able to distinguish differences that were gender specific and related to extension contacts from those that were not. Both men and women could do the work to the same level, a fact reflected in the lack of differences in the finished steers. Differences were found in the outcome of the enterprise. Women sometimes had higher feeding costs and had to finance the enterprise through nonagricultural work. Women tended to use the generated income for household and family necessities while men used it for improving the farms and purchasing prestige items. As a result of the WIADP's work with farmers, it was asked to give seminars to staff and to prepare a document as to how the ADD could involve women farmers in the various sections' programs (Spring, Smith, and Kayuni 1983a). In the space of one year, the number of women in the stall-feeder program increased from 13 to 17 percent, and male extensionists were less reluctant to choose women for the program (Spring 1986a).

## Training, Policy, and Decision-Making Changes

The WIADP worked with the research, extension, and planning units of the MOA to change policies so that women could be targeted in development planning and implementation. To this end, training exercises and documents were written for various units. The WIADP also worked with the Women's Program Officer at MOA headquarters and with her staff in each of the ADDs to encourage the retraining of female extensionists in agricultural subjects. Work plans and reporting formats of these women's programs' officers, and of the female extensionists they supervised, were rewritten to focus on women farmers for training, credit programs, and the like. The emphasis on domestic science was lessened. Subsequently, the Lilongwe ADD set aside 30 percent of the places in agricultural training classes for women farmers. Concomitantly, female extensionists were allowed for the first time to take refresher courses on agricultural topics alongside male extensionists.

The WIADP visited all the ADDs and met with management and those responsible for RDP services and data collection. The programs, reporting formats, and work plans (annual, quarterly, and monthly) of each section or project were discussed. Strategies for incorporating women farmers into the various programs and unit activities were devised. In particular, the WIADP helped to restructure work plans that form the "charters" or guides to what particular personnel or units are supposed to do. Generally, once these are approved, the accomplishments are measured in terms of the targets stated there. The WIADP determined that if women were not targeted or if the strategies to reach them were unrealistic, then not much could be accomplished to assist women. Often work plans contained such phrases as "encourage women to participate," without being able to translate this notion into any concrete or feasible actions. The WIADP worked with each officer to discern usable methods. The WIADP was asked to present its findings to each ADD and to discuss potential changes. In addition to restructuring work plans, the WIADP suggested the disaggregation of reporting formats (which each ADD, section, supervisor, and extensionist uses for tabulating its contacts with farmers and participation in its programs) and creation of appropriate strategies to contact and interest women farmers (Spring, Smith, and Kayuni 1983a is an example of a report written for the Lilongwe

Agricultural Development Division; separate reports were done for each of the eight ADDs). The WIADP also convinced various sections in the MOA that its sections and development personnel should disaggregate their reporting formats. For example, the credit section redesigned the form in the "National Credit Manual" that its officers use for listing the farmers who take credit, so as to include the gender of participants.

The WIADP prepared a set of technical recommendations in the form of an Extension Aids Circular that was based on the discovery that male extensionists could work with women on agricultural instruction, credit programs, visits to give technical advice, monitoring of trials, and the like. The general belief in Malawi and elsewhere is that female extensionists can work only with women and that male extensionists can work only with men. The problem, of course, is that here and elsewhere there are few female workers, and they have little agricultural training and are not plugged into mainstream agricultural services. The circular was unique in that it was issued by the MOA rather than by the WIADP. Extension Aids circulars from the MOA are regarded as technical recommendations to be distributed to the entire extension staff and to be heeded by them. Although the general policy for the delivery of extension services is "non-discriminatory," the data showed that women were not being contacted, as too few received credit and other services. There was need all over the country to legitimate male extensionists' working with women as well as with men farmers in their areas. The circular, entitled "Reaching Female Farmers Through Male Extension Workers," was published in August 1983 (Ministry of Agriculture 1983). An article in the national newspaper marked its distribution to all grass-roots workers and to agricultural project management. Prior to this circular, some male extensionists included women farmers in their programs, but in general the inclusion of women was neither consistent nor reflective of women's contributions and needs in an area. Most male extensionists believed that women farmers were to be contacted by female extension workers and that rural women should study home economics. The circular both legitimated and mandated the entire male extension staff's working with women farmers in the smallholder sector.

The circular presented methods for improving the delivery of extension services to women and for getting women into extension and research activities. Techniques were developed to encourage women to attend village meetings and agricultural training courses and to increase their participation in credit programs and farmers' clubs. The male extensionists were directed to include women at their demonstrations, trials, and field days. They were also told to keep records of contacts and program involvement in terms of the number of women and men participating. Detailed suggestions were offered for recruiting women farmers, for using leadership training so that women might learn to express their problems, and for using various techniques to increase participation in credit and soil conservation programs. The circular noted that household types vary and that women, both as wives and as heads of households, needed to be targeted.

Finally, the MOA asked the WIADP to undertake a review of the Women's Programs in the country and to suggest a five-year plan. The consequent report included a review of all programs for women starting with the colonial period, an examination of curriculum for women and men extensionists at all levels, new job descriptions for female staff (that focused on agricultural rather than on home economics topics), and a five-year plan of activities (Spring 1983). The Project was asked to present this document and the results of the other research data (Spring, Smith, and Kayuni 1982, 1983a, 1983b) that it had accumulated to two groups: top level MOA officials and Women's Programs' Officers nationwide. The goal for the former group was to gain the information and perspective they needed in order to use these materials in planning RDPs and in preparing proposals to international donors. The goal for the latter group was the restructuring of the section.

As a result of these endeavors, most senior officials of the MOA have been made aware of the need to incorporate women agriculturalists (farmers and MOA staff members) into development planning of programs and training. For example, the current USAID project (Malawi Agricultural Research and Extension) incorporated a technical assistance position to work with the Women's Program's Section on women in agriculture that was based on the WIADP's success. The MOA officials who carried out site visits and selected the institution to fulfill the contract focused on the importance of both WID and FSR/E. The institution selected (Oregon State and Consortium for International Development) not only contacted this author to conduct its orientation for the entire team of technical experts going to Malawi, but insisted on specific lectures on women's roles in agricultural development.

## Conclusion

Anthropological expertise in knowing the area, using appropriate methodologies, taking a holistic approach, and using an applied perspective aimed at changing policy all contributed to the WIADP's success. The Project had a clear understanding of production systems, smallholders' access to resources, necessary technologies, and methods to deliver interventions. The Project did not attempt "overinnovation," but built on the existing strengths in the organization of development services to the smallholder sector. The types of interaction with farmers and with MOA officials were appropriate for generating data and suggesting interventions. The cultural traditions were recognized and utilized to enhance participation of the intended beneficiaries.

The documentation of women's agricultural contributions and their participation in development services provided information to planners and to implementation teams. Much of the data was quantified to demonstrate women's importance to the smallholder sector and the extent to which they were bypassed by development services. The WIADP did not attempt to change people's values or attitudes concerning the nature of women's place in society—Malawi is still male dominated in many aspects of life. The aim was to begin to change development planners' and workers' behavior regarding policies and services offered, data collection, and data analysis. For example, designing sex-disaggregated formats for data collection and rethinking the design of work plans involved MOA staff members in the process of thinking about the need to create better methods of reaching women and men farmers. It should be mentioned that in many ways it was easier for some Malawians to collect sex-disaggregated data or to target women participants as part of their job than it was to change their ideas about the importance of women's contributions to production or to society.

Although the WIADP worked nationally and on various levels, its scale was smaller than most other USAID projects in Malawi. Dixon (1980) cautioned that women-specific projects tended to be on a small scale, and the WIADP was in fact small as measured by the number of its staff and its overall level of funding. Yet it was able to make an impact because of good design and implementation and its flexibility to consider new avenues to accomplish its goals. Dixon (1980) and Fortmann (1985) found that it was important to include women in project decision making either as project staff or in the target group. In the WIADP, the need to have female trainers and supervisors participate and learn about the issues was critical. Dixon found that when women's programs were affiliated with larger, male-dominated institutions, decision making on major policy issues tended to be transferred to men in the parent institutions. The WIADP was affiliated with the MOA, a larger, parent— and predominantly male—organization. In this case, however, rather than resenting this agency's taking over the decision making, WIADP in fact desired and utilized that strategy. Only by having the MOA make policy that targeted women, could women benefit from the mainstream of development activities. For example, the shortage of trained female staff was addressed by legitimizing the male staff's work with women farmers. Joining with the other USAID project on research was only possible through the Farming Systems Analysis Section in some collaborative research. Autonomy would not have been possible within the confines of that project.

In terms of access to the benefits of the project, Dixon (1980) found that women have more direct access when planners explicitly recognize the prevailing sexual division of labor (and build on women's work in order to enable women to control their earnings) as well as when the project fits prevailing cultural norms and recognizes cultural and legal limitations to women's direct access to project goods and services. Unlike many of the projects that Dixon and Fortmann evaluated, in the WIADP, women were the client group and the ones who received the direct benefits. The WIADP provided information to planners about the prevailing sexual division of labor, women's household and remunerative activities, and cultural and legal constraints that affect women. The data showing that women were extensive contributors to household production and national food security helped to acquaint planners and development staff with the significance of women's contributions to smallholder production and with the need to target women in development planning.

## Notes

1. See List of Acronyms that follows these Notes.

2. I was hired to prepare the Social Soundness Analysis that is required of all large USAID projects.

3. The NSSA was intensive in terms of the amount of data collected (there were 10 survey instruments), the length of time involved (the data were collected over an entire year), and the local specificity (its ability to assess production at the RDP project level as well as at divisional and regional levels).

All sample households received the NSSA survey instruments on household composition (education and employment history), garden usage, yield, resources, livestock, and nutrition. Thirty-five percent of the sample were questioned on extension, energy, and crop storage. Twenty percent were given the income and expenditure survey. Four of the surveys were administered once (household composition, yield, resources, and extension); another four were given twice (garden, crop storage, nutrition, and energy); the livestock survey was given three times; and the income and expenditure survey involved weekly accounts. A household was defined as all members who make common provision for food and who eat together from a common pot. The household head was defined as the person making day-to-day decisions (especially concerning agriculture).

4. To do this, male village leaders were asked to designate women farmers for leadership training. The women were taught leadership skills by both male and female extension personnel in order to enable them to speak about their problems in farming. They noted the lack of extension services such as credit and training. It also became clear to the male staff members that because of the women's small landholdings and because of their risk-averting practice of intercropping, the standard credit packages of improved seed and fertilizers that

were offered in multiples of one acre were too large. The solution to the actual credit package itself was the creation of smaller, half-acre packages of fertilizer and seed. The solution to credit services' bypassing women was to instruct the male staff members to target women, but a new method of determining credit-worthiness (usually defined by collateral or membership in the mostly male farmers' clubs) had to be devised. A new idea was promoted in which male village headmen were able to recommend ("certify") certain women for credit (Evans 1983). With the assistance of the male extension staff, the number of women receiving credit increased from 5 percent to 20 percent of the recipients in a single year. There also was concern as to how the women would pay back the loans, since these households would not have cash sales (because the inputs were helping them to attain food self-sufficiency), but it was known from other credit programs that women are particularly conscientious about repaying loans. The women, much to everyone's surprise, began paying back their loans prior to the harvest, using income from the sales of beer and crafts (Evans 1983). These households went from food deficient to food self-sufficient. Nonstandard techniques had to be used, however, and the male extension staff members were important to the success of the endeavor.

## Acronyms

| | |
|---|---|
| ADD | Agricultural Development Division |
| AES | Agro-Economic Surveys |
| AID | See USAID |
| FSAS | Farming Systems Analysis Section |
| FSR/E | Farming Systems Research and Extension |
| LRDP | Lilongwe Rural Development Project |
| MOA | Ministry of Agriculture |
| NSO | National Statistical Office |
| NSSA | National Sample Survey of Agriculture |
| RDP | Rural Development Project |
| USAID | United States Agency for International Development |
| WIADP | Women in Agricultural Development Project |
| WID | Women in Development |

## References

Boserup, Ester
    1970    Women's Role in Economic Development. New York: St. Martin's Press.
Cernea, Michael
    1986    Foreword: Anthropology and Family Production Systems in Africa. *In* Anthropology and Rural Development in West Africa. M. Horowitz and T. Painter, eds. Pp. ix–xiii. Boulder, CO: Westview Press.
Charlton, Sue Ellen
    1984    Women in Third World Development. Boulder, CO: Westview Press.

Clark, Barbara
  1975    The Work Done by Rural Women in Malawi. Eastern Journal of Rural
          Development 8(2):80–91.
Cloud, Kate
  1985    Women's Productivity in Agricultural Households: How Can We Think
          About It? What Do We Know? *In* Women as Food Producers in
          Developing Countries. J. Monson and M. Kalb, eds. Los Angeles: UCLA
          African Studies Center and African Studies Association.
  1986    Comparative Analysis of Women's Access to Project Agricultural Re-
          sources in Asia, North and West Africa, and the Middle East. Paper
          delivered at the Conference on Gender Issues and Farming Systems
          Research and Extension, Gainesville, FL, February 26.
Dixon, Ruth
  1980    Assessing the Impact of Development Projects on Women. AID Program
          Evaluation Discussion Paper No. 8. Washington, DC: USAID.
  1985    Seeing the Invisible Women Farmers in Africa: Improving Research
          and Data Collection Methods. *In* Women as Food Producers in De-
          veloping Countries. J. Monson and M. Kalb, eds. Pp. 19–36. Los
          Angeles: UCLA African Studies Center and African Studies Association.
Due, Jean, and Rebecca Summary
  1982    Constraints to Women and Development in Africa. Journal of Modern
          African Studies 20(1):155–166.
Dyson-Hudson, Neville
  1985    Pastoral Production Systems and Livestock Development Projects: An
          East African Perspective. *In* Putting People First: Sociological Variables
          in Rural Development. M. Cernea, ed. Pp. 157–186. New York: Oxford
          University Press.
Eddy, Elizabeth, and William Partridge, eds.
  1978    Applied Anthropology in America. New York: Columbia University
          Press.
Evans, Janis
  1981    Rural Women's Agricultural Extension Programmes in Phalombe Rural
          Development Project: Report on Baseline Survey of Phase 1. Blantyre
          Agricultural Development Division, Malawi. Mimeo.
  1983    Women's Involvement in the Seasonal Credit Programmes in the
          Phalombe Rural Development Project. National Credit Seminar, Chin-
          theche, Malawi. February. Mimeo.
Fortmann, Louise
  1985    A Matter of Focus: The Incorporation of Women into Agricultural
          Projects 1976–1984. USAID Evaluation Section. Unpublished manu-
          script, July.
Hansen, Art
  1986    Farming Systems Research in Phalombe, Malawi: The Limited Utility
          of High Yielding Varieties. *In* Social Science and Farming Systems
          Research. J. Jones and B. Wallace, eds. Pp. 145–170. Boulder, CO:
          Westview Press.

Hecht, Robert
    1986    Salvage Anthropology: The Redesign of a Rural Development Project
            in Guinea. *In* Anthropology and Rural Development in West Africa.
            M. Horowitz and T. Painter, eds. Pp. 11–26. Boulder, CO: Westview
            Press.
Hildebrand, Peter, and Fredrico Poey
    1985    On-Farm Agronomic Trials in Farming Systems Research and Extension.
            Boulder, CO: Lynne Rienner Press.
Hoben, Allan
    1982    Anthropologists and Development. *In* Annual Review of Anthropology.
            B. Siegel, A. Beals, and S. Tyler, eds. Pp. 349–375. Palo Alto, CA:
            Annual Reviews, Inc.
Koenig, Dolores
    1986    Research for Rural Development: Experiences of an Anthropologist in
            Rural Mali. *In* Anthropology and Rural Development in West Africa.
            M. Horowitz and T. Painter, eds. Pp. 27–60. Boulder, CO: Westview
            Press.
Kydd, Jonathan
    1982    Measuring Peasant Differentiation for Policy Purposes: A Report on
            a Cluster Analysis Classification of the Population of the Lilongwe
            Land Development Programme, Malawi, for 1970 and 1979. Zomba,
            Malawi: Government Printer.
Kydd, Jonathan, and Robert Christiansen
    1981    The Distribution of Income in Malawi in 1977. Working Paper No. 1,
            University of Malawi. Zomba: Centre for Social Research.
Manda, D., Benjamin Dzowela, and William Johnson
    1985    Agricultural Research Resources Assessment in the SADCC Countries.
            Volume II Country Report: Malawi. Southern African Development
            Co-ordination Conference: USAID and Devres.
Ministry of Agriculture (MOA)
    1968–1982  Agro-Economic Survey Reports. (51 reports) Lilongwe, Malawi.
    1983    Reaching Female Farmers through Male Extension Workers. Extension
            Aids Circular, August. Lilongwe, Malawi.
National Statistical Office (NSO)
    1982    Preliminary Report of the National Sample Survey of Agriculture for
            Customary Land 1980/1981. Zomba, Malawi: Government Printer.
Nyirenda, F., H. Mwandemere, and G. Mkamanga
    n.d.    A Review of Results of a System Based on Farm Research Approach
            in Malawi. Lilongwe: Ministry of Agriculture. Mimeo.
Palmer, Ingrid
    1985    The Nemow Case: Case Studies of the Impact of Large Scale Devel-
            opment Projects on Women: A Series for Planners. West Hartford, CT:
            Kumarian Press.
Pasley, Kay
    1986    Malawi Agricultural Research Project. End of Project Report, University
            of Florida. Manuscript (draft).

Rogers, Barbara
   1980   The Domestication of Women: Discrimination in Developing Societies.
          New York: St. Martin's Press.

Segal, Marcia
   1985   Land and Labor: A Comparison of Female- and Male-Headed House-
          holds in Malawi's Small Holder Sector. Paper presented at the African
          Studies Association, New Orleans, November 23.

Shaner, W., P. F. Philipp, and W. R. Schmehl, eds.
   1982   Farming Systems Research and Development: Guidelines for Developing
          Countries. Boulder, CO: Westview Press.

Spring, Anita
   1976   An Indigenous Style and Its Consequences for Natality. *In* Culture,
          Natality, and Family Planning. J. Marshall and S. Polgar, eds. Pp. 99–
          125. Chapel Hill, NC: Carolina Population Center.

   1978   Epidemiology of Spirit Possession Among the Luvale of Zambia. *In*
          Women in Ritual and Symbolic Roles. J. Hoch-Smith and A. Spring,
          eds. Pp. 165–190. New York: Plenum.

   1980   Traditional and Biomedical Health Care Systems in Northwest Zambia.
          *In* Traditional Health Care in Contemporary Africa. P. Ulin and M.
          Segal, eds. Syracuse University: Maxwell School African Series 35:57–
          80.

   1982a  Adopting CIMMYT's Farming System Survey Guidelines to the Ma-
          lawian Situation. Report No. 5. Lilongwe: Women in Agricultural
          Development Project.

   1982b  Proceedings of the National Workshop on Women in Agricultural
          Development. March 9–10, 1982. Lilongwe: The Women in Agricultural
          Development Project.

   1983   Priorities for Women's Programmes. Lilongwe: The Women in Agri-
          cultural Development Project and the Ministry of Agriculture.

   1984   Profiles of Men and Women Smallholder Farmers in the Lilongwe
          Rural Development Project, Malawi. Final Report. Washington, DC:
          Office of Women in Development, USAID.

   1985   The Women in Agricultural Development Project in Malawi: Making
          Gender Free Development Work. *In* Women Creating Wealth: Trans-
          forming Economic Development. R. Gallin and A. Spring, eds. Pp.
          71–75. Washington, DC: Association for Women and Development.

   1986a  Men and Women Participants in a Stall Feeder Livestock Program in
          Malawi. Human Organization 45(2):154–162.

   1986b  Trials and Errors: Using Farming Systems Research in Agricultural
          Programs for Women. *In* Social Sciences and Farming Systems Research.
          J. Jones and B. Wallace, eds. Pp. 123–144. Boulder, CO: Westview
          Press.

   1986c  Women Farmers and Food in Africa: Some Considerations and Sug-
          gested Solutions. *In* Food in Subsaharan Africa. A. Hansen and D.
          McMillan, eds. Pp. 332–348. Boulder, CO: Westview Press.

1988a    Using Male Research and Extension Personnel to Target Women Farmers. *In* Gender Issues in Farming Systems Research and Extension. S. Poats, M. Schmink, and A. Spring, eds. Pp. 407–426. Boulder, CO: Westview Press.

1988b    Agricultural Development in Malawi: A Project for Women in Development. Boulder, CO: Westview Press.

Spring, Anita, and Art Hansen

1985     The Underside of Development: Agricultural Development and Women in Zambia. Agriculture and Human Values 2(1):60–67.

Spring, Anita, Craig Smith, and Frieda Kayuni

1982     Karonga Farmer Survey. Report No. 12. Lilongwe: The Women in Agricultural Development Project. Mimeo.

1983a    An Evaluation of Women's Programmes in LADD: How LADD's Sections and Projects Can Incorporate More Women Farmers in their Programmes. Lilongwe: The Women in Agricultural Development Project. Mimeo.

1983b    Women Farmers in Malawi, Their Contributions to Agriculture and Participation in Development Projects. Washington, DC: Office of Women in Development, USAID.

Staudt, Kathleen

1975–1976   Women Farmers and Inequalities in Agriculture Services. *In* Rural Women: Development or Underdevelopment. A. Wipper, ed. Rural Africana 29:81–94.

# 2

# Lineage, District, and Nation: Politics in Uganda's Bugisu Cooperative Union

*Stephen G. Bunker*

## Introduction

The cooperative ideology espoused by the Uganda government stresses that cooperatives are apolitical and egalitarian. In fact, they are neither, and lamenting or criticizing this fact does very little to advance our understanding of how they work or why they fail. The national state, the district administration, the professional staff, the elected committee, and the members at large are all prone to use cooperatives for political ends, and the prizes that they can gain from such uses are not of a nature that favors egalitarian distribution. The reasons are clear. Uganda's economy is overwhelmingly agricultural,[1] and most of its production occurs on small plots owned by freeholding peasants. This means that the major sources of revenue, whether for the state or for the accumulation of individual wealth, rest in the collection and marketing of the crops grown by numerous dispersed households. For historical reasons described by Wrigley (1959), Brett (1973) and Mamdani (1976), the colonial state acted to impede the emergence of a powerful commercial class. From the mid-1940s, it increasingly devolved the complex and costly task of coordinating crop collection to locally based cooperatives, which eventually grew to control most of the major export crops. Because these cooperatives control its primary source of revenues, the national state has attempted to control the cooperatives. Because the cooperatives control the major local sources of wealth, individuals and groups at the local level have also sought to control them. The result has been an unending political struggle between district-level and national-level power groups and officeholders (Bunker 1983a, 1983b, 1987). The state's revenues and the local leaders' wealth can only emerge from differences between prices paid to farmers and prices gained on the world market, minus costs of collection, processing, transport, and marketing. Thus, the state's interests and the local leaders' attempts to gain personal wealth create a downward pressure on farm-gate prices and on cooperative services to members. State and local leaders compete with each other for the surplus generated, and peasants compete with both by trying to keep prices higher.

## The Struggle over Markets and Prices

Cooperative politics revolve around this three-way struggle. The state controls cooperative legislation, and so can dictate the powers and rewards of the local leaders. The local leaders, however, control the cooperative, which coordinates the collection and marketing on which the state's revenues depend. The peasants themselves control production, the essential element in the entire equation. Because they own their plots in freehold, they can determine what crops they will grow. If the prices they receive for cash crops are insufficient, they can exercise their "exit option,"[2] that is, they can retreat from the market into subsistence farming. Their exit from the market would leave both the state and local leaders without income, and thus without power. The peasants clearly prefer to stay in the market, however, because it provides them with valued goods they cannot produce themselves. Their best strategy is to learn how to use their exit option as a threat to bargain for better prices.

Effective bargaining with the state to ensure better prices, however, requires spokesmen who can articulate the threat and voice peasant demands. This requirement provides an opportunity for local leaders to gain positions of power within the cooperatives. If they can effectively represent the peasants' demands, they can count on peasant support in their own contest with the national state. Their power is precarious, however. The more strongly and effectively they present the demands for higher prices, the less wealth is available from crop marketing. In this sense, they are under pressure to act against their own financial interests. Moreover, the state controls the conditions of cooperative office—primarily through national cooperative legislation and other policy instruments executed through the Ministry of Cooperatives and Marketing and the Commission for Cooperative Development. The state has the power to remove leaders from their positions if they are too successful in reducing the margin of surplus from which the state extracts its own revenues. The state, however, is itself constrained, because popular and effective local leaders can use the threat of crop reduction or market exit when the state attempts to reduce local cooperative (and therefore the leaders') autonomy and power. Furthermore, the cooperatives in which these leaders hold office control the administrative resources necessary to collect and process crops cultivated by numerous smallholding producers.[3]

The state, the local leaders, and the peasants all have opposing interests, but each controls resources or can offer services that the others need. These different resources give each a very different kind of power.[4] Their conflicting interests within a situation of interdependence and differential control of essential resources explains why cooperatives in Uganda are necessarily political, and why the struggles to control them lead to unequal, though fluctuating, distributions of the benefits they provide. Many studies have attempted to evaluate the efficiency of cooperatives in terms of whether or not politics predominate over an ideal model of business management,[5] but if politics are inevitable, it makes more sense to explain them, rather than assume them away or condemn them. In the rest of this chapter, I will describe how politics worked in the Bugisu Cooperative Union (BCU) and try to assess some of their beneficial and deleterious effects.

The BCU is particularly interesting, because it controls one of Uganda's most lucrative crops. Coffee has provided over 50 percent of Uganda's foreign revenues since the early 1950s. Most of the coffee exported is Robusta, which is easy to cultivate and inexpensive to process, but does not command high prices. The slopes, fertile soils, and rains on Mount Elgon on the Kenya border, however, allow the Bagisu[6] to cultivate the much more valuable Arabica coffee. For many years, even though they grew only about 5 percent of the nation's coffee by volume, they accounted for nearly 10 percent of coffee revenues. The importance of the price differential they enjoyed was enhanced when Uganda joined the International Coffee Association, which sets export quotas by volume rather than market value. The national state therefore had good reason to want to control the marketing of Bugisu coffee, but it had equally good reason not to offend the Bagisu coffee growers. The result has been a long series of delicate negotiations that have frequently broken down in stormy recriminations, with control over the cooperative fluctuating between the central state and the local leaders, and no permanent resolution possible (Bunker 1983a). Understanding these politics involves accounting for the complex interplay of power, authority, and interests at the national, district, regional, local, and lineage levels. The BCU is very much part of the national and international economy, but it is deeply rooted as well in a lineage organization whose basis was established long before the British introduced coffee into the area. The BCU collects and processes coffee for an entire district, but it is made up of over 90 growers' societies whose boundaries are closely tied to kinship divisions.

The establishment of cooperatives in Uganda reflected in varying degrees local demands to control crop marketing (Brett 1970; Mamdani 1976), but local initiative was more aggressive and sustained in Bugisu than it was in many other areas. Coffee and cotton were introduced into Bugisu in 1912, the same year British rule was firmly established, and nine years after the long military conquest of Bugisu began. The British had coopted local lineage heads to serve as colonial chiefs, and these authorities were made responsible for ensuring that the Bagisu grew the crops and tended them properly. Many chiefs exploited their crucial economic function to expand their own landholdings and commercial cropping.

The coffee crop grew rapidly, from 11 tons in 1915 to 50 tons in 1925, 260 tons by 1930, and 4,000 tons in 1940. Coffee trading was at first in the hands of private traders, mostly Asians, but the Bagisu soon learned that threatening to neglect their crops was a sure way to provoke an official response to their complaints against low prices and dishonest rates of payment. The administration failed in its first attempts to control the buyers. In 1930 it was authorized to start buying directly, and by 1933 the Bugisu Coffee Scheme (BCS), an official agency established for this purpose, was the sole authorized buyer of coffee in the district. As the coffee crop grew, so did the need for trained personnel in the BCS. Bagisu with technical formal education, primarily the sons of chiefs, were hired for these positions, but they soon discovered that their possibilities for promotion were directly limited by European control of the higher posts. They began a campaign for greater and more responsible participation, first using the influence of their fathers, but soon afterwards appealing to the growers themselves.

They discovered that the best means to bring pressure on the colonial administration was by mobilizing the peasants behind claims that they were not receiving a fair return for their crops, and the promise that greater Bagisu employment in the BCS would help to protect their interests. This tactic led to gradual expansion of the positions open to Bagisu. With each victory, the Bagisu civil servants strengthened their demands. Their call for even greater local control found a new focus in the 1946 legislation that authorized cooperatives throughout Uganda, and they made common cause with the leaders of lineages who were attempting to organize new local growers' cooperative societies. In 1954, after a long organizing campaign and a bitter struggle to move forward the date at which the Bagisu could formally take cooperative control of the crop (Bunker 1983b, 1984), the BCU was formally established as a union of the many local growers' societies (GCSs). Most of the newly elected BCU committee was drawn from the local organizers.

These organizers were exceptional men who had emerged from positions of trust and influence within their own lineages, but who had managed to coordinate the mobilization effort across lineages (Bunker 1983a). In doing so, they had both benefited from and contributed to a growing sense of ethnic identity among the Bagisu. Originally organized in territorially distinct lineages with no overarching authority, and prone to feuding across fairly narrowly defined boundaries, the Bagisu had been incorporated within a British-imposed administrative district under the governance of men whose authority was rooted in individual lineages. These chiefs, however, had soon realized their common interests and the opportunities for collaboration within the externally imposed, unified administrative system in which they now served. As the administration expanded to include their sons, and as they themselves extended traditional strategies for forming alliances through marriage across their areas of influence, the idea of common ethnic identity became stronger (La Fontaine 1969). The need to define the entire ethnic group as a political and economic unit with its own local rights and powers was a key part of the campaign for the cooperative, not only to help mobilize the Bagisu and persuade them to join the local growers' associations, but also to affirm to the colonial government their collective rights (Bunker 1984).

The GCSs themselves, however, were firmly rooted in the lineage system. The need to turn over the crop without immediate payment and to delegate the handling of accounts and the disbursement of coffee payments meant that it was much easier to organize around already existing bases of solidarity and trust. The Bagisu were extending their own idea of themselves past the old lineage divisions, but old distinctions between trust and cooperative endeavor within the lineage, and danger and suspicion beyond it, persisted.

## Lineage Structure and Cooperative Organization

The dependence on lineage organization enhanced the Bagisu's willingness to entrust their crops to a new institution, but it engendered a series of organizational and political problems. There are considerable cultural and dialectal differences between Bugisu's different regions, and the distrust across these divisions is strong. In the north, on the mountain itself, lineage organization corresponds directly to territory and space. As La Fontaine (1959) has described it, each of a series of maximal lineages contains a number of major lineages, each of which in turn contains a number of minor lineages, each of which contains a number of minimal lineages. Each of these levels, except the smallest, is identified with a particular territory, so its members all live together. The bonds of solidarity and the acceptance of common authority are strongest at the lower, or smallest levels, and diminish at each higher level, but there is a clear common identity throughout, within an organization that is tightly knit in both kinship and territory but has few natural ties with units outside of itself. Both its unity and its isolation are simultaneously social and spatial.

The mountain has the richest land, but the close identity of lineage with territory means that population growth leads to strains within lineages, and especially to intergenerational conflict over land. When these strains become too great, erupting in frequent or severe violence, there is no solution except outmigration. As a result, various groups left their own lineage areas and migrated down the mountain, first onto the southern plains, and then around the mountain to the north. These groups took their lineage identities with them, but different groups from different lineages settled near each other, giving rise to a territorial organization far less structured than the original one on the mountain. Small groups of migrants from one maximal lineage might therefore settle next to members of several others, while other members from their maximal, or even major, lineage might settle much further away. This meant that small migrant groups had to learn to live with close neighbors with whom they shared no kin identity, while they did share kinship with groups in distant locations.

With the formation of the local growers' societies, the farmers in the migration areas in the south had to learn to collaborate with non-kin, while those who had remained on the mountain were able to use more traditional organizational bases. Throughout the history of the cooperative, the mountain societies have been noteworthy for their ability to solve their own internal differences themselves, with few appeals to the Department of Cooperative Development. This has had a number of positive results, but it has also meant that the officeholders of each society were relatively immune to criminal proceedings if they embezzled funds or in some way mismanaged their business. The societies in the south have had far more difficulty maintaining internal peace. Contests for office have pitted unrelated rivals against each other, and the continuing distrust across lineage boundaries has often led to violent outbreaks over election to GCS office. These divisions, however, have also meant that members were not at all reluctant to denounce dishonesty, corruption, or incompetence to the state authorities. As a result, many of the southern societies have had healthier financial careers, even though the volume and quality of their crops cannot compete with those of the more fertile mountain.

These differences of lineage organization in the different regions have directly affected the politics of the BCU itself. Representatives from all of the GCSs meet to elect the BCU committee. All seven of the men who have served as BCU president between 1954 and 1983 were from migrant groups, five from the much poorer south, and two from the groups who had migrated north around the mountain. The wealthy northerners have complained frequently about the political dominance of the less numerous southerners, but they are unable to do anything about it. The northerners are too bound into their territorially tight lineage organizations to form effective alliances and coalitions across the entire northern region, while the southerners and other migrants, though they fight much more within the small areas of the GCSs, are able to exploit the fact that groups from the same lineages are scattered all across the southern region. Aspiring leaders of the BCU can call on close relatives who live far away, and who have had to learn to deal politically and economically with other non-kin groups. The resulting alliances are more tenuous than those on the mountain, but they cover a far wider area and include many more people. So the loosely united southerners win the general elections against multiple tightly knit groups of northerners.

The result of these differences has been a number of attempts by the northerners to secede and form their own cooperative union. Their discontent has twice given rise to significant dissident movements, one of which lasted for nearly four years in the early 1960s and led to considerable violence and destruction of coffee trees (Bunker 1985b). Even secessionist movements, however, have been narrowly localized and have therefore failed.

The other persistent conflict in the Union has been between the professional management and the elected committee. The cooperative serves both groups as an avenue to power and wealth, but in different ways. Both groups depend on relative autonomy from state control, and as long as the BCU was subject to direct control under the colonial administration, they made common cause against the state. After independence, however, different political parties, vying for control of the national state, attempted to win the support of local politicians (Leys 1967). One of the ways that they could do so was by granting greater autonomy both to the district councils and to the cooperatives. In Bugisu, this allowed the BCU's elected committee to increase greatly its influence on the day-to-day running of the cooperative. The professional staff responded by questioning both the honesty and the management skill of the elected committee, whose members defended themselves by claiming that the measures they were proposing would increase benefits to the farmers. The Department of Cooperative Development also opposed many of the measures that the committee proposed, and did so in part because the committee was directly challenging the state's ability to determine what prices should be paid to the farmers and what should be done with the resulting revenues.

The farmers largely supported the elected committee, as they had tended to do in the committee's earlier campaign to increase its autonomy from the state. The professional staff made common cause with the state's representatives. By appealing to the state, the staff collaborated in the reduction of the committee's power, but at the same time contributed to the BCU's loss of autonomy as a local organization capable not only of representing the growers' demands to the state but also of encouraging them to increase their production (Bunker 1983a).

The committee, because it was elected, was far more sensitive to peasant demands than the staff or the state. While it is true that BCU autonomy provided committee members with opportunities to increase their personal wealth and political power, it also allowed them to present the growers' case for higher prices and less onerous marketing conditions strongly to the state. The fact that committee positions were personally advantageous meant that there was considerable competition to hold them, and committees that were not sensitive to the growers' needs were likely to face dissident movements to replace them, either in elections or through separation from the union itself. I have shown elsewhere (Bunker 1987) that the two most significant increases in coffee production occurred in association with the two most successful campaigns—from 1954 to 1957 and from 1964 to 1966—to increase committee autonomy (see Table 2.1). The Commissioner for Cooperative Development intervened in both cases, citing mismanagement and criticizing high prices to farmers, and appointed Supervising Managers in 1958 and in 1966 to run the union. The state's strong reaction to undercut local autonomy in both instances indicates that its primary concern has been to assure that it maintains sufficient control to be able to extract revenue, and will promote crop increases only under conditions that do not threaten its ultimate control over sales.

## State Attempts to Centralize Control

The central state's need for political control actually increased after independence. In the first years after independence, the national competitors for power found it convenient to woo local support, but once the major contest was resolved by Obote's coup of 1966 and the subsequent formation of a one-party state, Obote's primary concern was to sustain the political coalition that kept him in power. This required channeling funds to political supporters and to the bureaucracy at the national, rather than at the local, level. The national bureaucracy grew enormously after independence, far in excess of the rate of expansion in the economy.[7]

TABLE 2.1
Coffee Production and Sale in Bugisu, 1939–1968

| | Estimated Acreage[a] (thousand acres) | Exports[a] | | Production (in thousand long tons)[b] | Value to Growers (thousand shillings)[c] |
|---|---|---|---|---|---|
| | | Volume (thousand tons) | Value (thousand shillings) | | |
| 1939 | 20 | | | 1.82 | |
| 1945 | 14 | | | 2.70 | |
| 1950 | 18 | 2.5 | 1,000 | 2.85 | |
| 1954 | | | | 3.02 | 1,232 |
| 1955 | 24 | 6.7 | 2,800 | 6.17 | 2,016 |
| 1956 | | | | 4.10 | 1,350 |
| 1957 | | | | 5.17 | 1,435 |
| 1958 | | | | 4.80 | 1,209 |
| 1959 | | | | 4.91 | 775 |
| 1960 | 36 | 7.5 | 2,200 | 5.79 | 1,037 |
| 1961 | | | | 5.15 | 972 |
| 1962 | | | | 8.80 | 1,962 |
| 1963 | 42 | 8.6 | 2,300 | 4.40 | 1,066 |
| 1964 | | | | 9.52 | 2,376[d] |
| 1965 | | | | 4.52 | |
| 1966 | 52 | 17.3 | 5,300 | 13.89 | 3,395[d] |
| 1967 | | | | 7.93 | 2,482 |
| 1968 | | | | 13.13 | 3,004 |

[a]Jameson 1970:191.
[b]Bugisu Cooperative Union.
[c]Uganda Statistical Abstracts 1963, 1967, 1969 (series cannot be continued because of aggregation of Robusta and Arabica accounts after 1970).
[d]Includes Arabica coffee grown outside of Bugisu.

The single party was transformed into the major conduit of local development funds, and the central state arrogated to itself control over much of the nation's economy.

Cooperatives were directly affected. New laws passed in 1968 and 1970 gave parastatal marketing boards (and the Minister of Cooperatives and Marketing under whom they operated) specific authority over prices and monopoly rights to sell export crops. These rules were particularly injurious in Bugisu, because the BCU was the only organization in Uganda with experience in the processing, storage, and sale of the delicate Arabica coffee. Arabica coffee brings high prices, but it also requires extra work. The Coffee Marketing Board allowed delays in shipment and inadequate storage to reduce the coffee's quality and appeared reluctant to grant the price differentials necessary to compensate for the extra work in cultivation and processing. As a result, the BCU

TABLE 2.2
Operating Balance in the Bugisu Cooperative Union (in shillings)

| Financial Year | Profit (Loss) | |
|---|---|---|
| 1969–1970 | 4,781,971 | Profit |
| 1970–1971 | (1,143,849) | Loss |
| 1971–1972 | (1,306,561) | Loss |
| 1972–1973 | 1,008,056 | Profit |
| 1973–1974 | (19,003) | Loss |
| 1974–1975 | (978,078) | Loss |
| 1975–1976 | (817,776) | Loss |
| 1976–1977 | (3,224,818) | Loss |
| 1977–1978 | (3,607,401) | Loss |
| 1978–1979 | (5,648,261) | Loss |

*Source:* Bugisu Cooperative Union. Accounts for subsequent years have not yet been approved, but have also entailed losses. Prior to 1970–1971, the BCU had recorded losses in only two financial years, 1954–1955 and 1958–1959.

incurred, in 1970, what was to become a long, nearly unbroken run of operating losses (see Table 2.2).

In Bugisu at least, the new measures to increase central control actually reduced the market value of the crop. Amin's coup in 1971 occurred too soon for anyone to know how the peasants would have responded to the BCU's loss of autonomy and its subsequent inability to sustain farm prices. What happened during the Amin regime, however, indicates that when prices fall too low, and there is no political association through which they can protest, Bagisu peasants carry out their previous political and symbolic threats to withdraw from the market.

Under Amin, active protest was physically dangerous. The BCU committee, which for years had challenged the state, could only very cautiously voice mild protests over low prices and over the fact that central state control, coupled with inefficiencies and corruption in the Coffee Marketing Board, left the BCU so few operating revenues that it could not even maintain its equipment or pay the peasants such low prices as were authorized (Bunker 1985a). As raging inflation after 1975 further undercut the coffee prices the farmers received, they neglected their coffee trees, smuggled whatever coffee they did harvest into Kenya, and increasingly turned to other crops, primarily for subsistence. The BCU was caught in the double bind of a narrowed operating margin and a swiftly declining volume.

Because payments for coffee were often late, opportunities for theft and embezzlement in the GCSs grew. The GCS members in any event had little means of knowing whether the BCU had sent the money for their coffee or not. As a result, suspicion and resentment developed among minor lineages, as everyone suspected that the GCS authorities were favoring themselves and their closest kinsmen. Many GCSs split into smaller units, either between separate lineages that had previously cooperated in the south, or along the lines of minor lineages in the northern GCSs, which had included entire maximal lineages. The proliferation of small GCSs increased overhead and also required more personnel trained in accounting, precisely at a time when neither the BCU nor the Department of Cooperative Development had the staff to train or to supervise them.

The BCU fell into disarray. Significantly, instead of the old fierce competitions for committee office, some committee members tried to resign and were told by the Commissioner for Cooperative Development that they could not. The further the BCU declined, the more farmers turned to other crops, and the worse the BCU's predicament became.

Amin was finally overthrown in 1979, and Obote established a new regime in 1980. Hopes ran high for a change in the economy, and many Bagisu brought out coffee that they had stored, so 1982 saw a large increase in the crop. The cooperatives were cited in Obote's economic reconstruction plan as a central vehicle for recovery, but again, the state maintained low prices to the farmers and even lower operating margins for the cooperatives. Various development agencies made several attempts to provide basic implements such as hoes to the farmers, but the cooperatives were not adequate any longer even to the distribution of these goods, and much of what was available was resold. The greatest bulk of the considerable World Bank, International Monetary Fund, European Economic Community, and U.S. Agency for International Development funds available for reconstruction went either into urban and infrastructural projects or into expensive attempts to expand crop processing facilities. Remarkably little attention was paid to assure that the peasants, the basic producers on whom the economy's revenues ultimately depended, would receive adequate stimulus to return to and increase their production for the market.

To some extent it is possible to see Obote's willingness to ignore the peasants as the result of his access to international credits and grants (see Bunker 1985a). It is also clear, however, that Obote's position was extremely precarious, and that a great part of the revenues his regime controlled went to the military, either for its long and fruitless battle with an armed opposition, or through special favors and privileges to the military officers who controlled much of the economy, including the Coffee Marketing Board. The overall result in Bugisu was that market production continued to decline (see Table 2.3).

TABLE 2.3
Total Coffee Purchased and Processed
by the Bugisu Cooperative Union, 1970–1982 (in tons)

| Financial Year | Coffee Purchased | Coffee Processed |
|---|---|---|
| 1970–1971 | 12,955 | 12,300 |
| 1971–1972 | 12,076 | 11,103 |
| 1972–1973 | 15,097 | 15,217 |
| 1973–1974 | 11,421 | 12,787 |
| 1974–1975 | 12,312 | 10,762 |
| 1975–1976 | 11,634 | 11,084 |
| 1976–1977 | 2,315 | 4,416 |
| 1977–1978 | 652 | 623 |
| 1978–1979 | 5,760 | 4,007 |
| 1979–1980 | 6,965 | 6,055 |
| 1980–1981 | 2,661 | 3,886 |
| 1981–1982 | 19,388[a] | 10,764 |

[a]This figure reflects the purchase of coffee stored by farmers and Growers Cooperative Societies from three previous seasons. Export data for 1983 and 1984 indicate a sharp drop in these years.

*Source:* Bugisu Cooperative Union.

## Discussion

The Bagisu fought for and won the right to establish a locally controlled cooperative, and then to expand its autonomy from state supervision. In the process, different lineages and regions either fought each other or made common cause against the state; factions collaborated or competed for election to the committee; and the committee and the staff passed from essential cooperation to open opposition and back. Many of these struggles were costly to the BCU's efficiency, and much of the collaboration was at least partially corrupt; but until 1970, the BCU was an active political arena in which the state, local officeholders, and peasants could compete and search for at least temporary compromises. Because the cooperative provided an arena within which the peasants' voice, and their threat to withdraw from the market, could be heard, it was possible to restrain the state's requirement of greater revenues sufficiently to encourage the peasants to continue producing cash crops. Average coffee income per household fluctuated between US $80 and US $150 (author's rough estimates) between 1965 and 1970. When, desperate to gain more revenues to keep its flimsy hold on power, the central state tried to reduce local autonomy, the combination of low prices and political repression started the long process of market withdrawal that now makes it much more difficult to resuscitate the economy. By 1980, prices for

Arabica had fallen to less than 25 percent of their 1970 levels in real terms. As peasants withdrew from coffee production, household revenues from coffee dropped to as little as 10 percent of their 1970 levels (another rough estimate). It is precisely because the cooperatives were able to function politically until 1970 that they allowed for essential communication between the national state and the lineage organization that controlled actual production. Bargaining over coffee prices was a crucial part of this communication. The state broke this line of communication in order to heighten its own political and economic power, and in the process lost both.

Uganda's political condition remained highly unstable during Obote's second regime. Control over the central state was therefore precarious, so holders of central state power tended to extract as much revenue as they could from peasant production to satisfy short-term political obligations and dependencies. They therefore attempted to suppress local autonomy and the power of the cooperatives to represent peasants' interests. Low coffee prices and the organizational inefficiency of bankrupt cooperatives drove peasants away from the market. World Bank, European Community, and International Monetary Fund policies concentrated resources on infrastructural development rather than on price supports and agricultural inputs to farmers; the state planners were insulated from peasant demands, at least in the short run, because they were more interested in gaining foreign loans and grants than they were in boosting agricultural production. The actions of various international development agencies thus, paradoxically, undercut the peasant production on which the Ugandan economy depends (see Bunker 1987, Chapter 8, for a fuller discussion of this process).

As long as agriculture remains central to the Uganda economy, development programs must focus on incentives to the producers of crops. Development planners must recognize both the economic and the political functions of the cooperatives if they hope to use them as vehicles of development. International agencies in particular may have the leverage necessary to make assistance programs conditional on the central state's allowing the cooperatives the political space necessary to defend peasant interests and thus encourage their participation in the markets that provide revenues essential for development.

## Notes

The data for this chapter were gathered during field work in 1969–1971, supported by the Rockefeller Foundation and the Shell Foundation, and in 1983, supported by the Hewlett Foundation.

1. See Wrigley (1959), Young (1971), Brett (1973), IBRD (1982) for agriculture's position in different periods.

2. See Hirschman (1970) for a general discussion of this term; see Hyden (1980) and Bunker (1983b, 1987) for its application to freeholding peasants.

3. See Bunker (1987) for a full discussion.

4. See Blau (1964) on control over resources, bargaining, and power.

5. See Hyden (1970, 1973), Kasfir (1970), Brett (1970), and Saul (1969) for examples of this management ideal, and for further criticism of this approach, see Bunker (1984).

6. The District is called Bugisu; its inhabitants are called Bagisu.

7. The Uganda Public Service, excluding teachers and military, grew from 16,896 to 25,603 between 1962 and 1969 (Uganda 1970).

# References

Blau, Peter
  1964    Exchange and Power in Social Life. New York: John Wiley and Sons.
Brett, E. A.
  1970    Problems of Cooperative Development in Uganda. *In* Rural Cooperatives
          and Planned Changes in Africa. R. J. Apthorpe, ed. Pp. 95–156. Geneva:
          UNRISDP.
  1973    Colonialism and Underdevelopment in East Africa. New York: Nok
          Publishers.
Bunker, Stephen G.
  1983a   Center-Local Struggles for Bureaucratic Control in Bugisu, Uganda.
          American Ethnologist 10(4):749–769.
  1983b   Dependency, Inequality, and Development Policy: A Case from Bugisu,
          Uganda. British Journal of Sociology 34(2):182–207.
  1984    Ideologies of Intervention: The Ugandan State and Local Organization
          in Bugisu. Africa 54(3):50–71.
  1985a   Peasant Responses to a Dependent State: Uganda, 1983. Canadian
          Journal of African Studies 19(2):371–386.
  1985b   Property, Protest, and Politics in Bugisu, Uganda. *In* Banditry, Rebellion,
          and Social Protest in Africa. Donald Crummey, ed. Pp. 267–285.
          London: James Currey Publisher.
  1987    Peasants against the State: The Politics of Market Control in Bugisu,
          Uganda, 1900–1983. Urbana: University of Illinois Press.
Hirschman, Albert O.
  1970    Exit, Voice, and Loyalty: Responses to Decline in Firms, Organizations,
          and States. Cambridge: Harvard University Press.
Hyden, Goran
  1970    Cooperatives and Their Socio-Political Environment. *In* Cooperatives
          and Rural Development in East Africa. Carl Gosta Widstrand, ed.
          Uppsala: The Scandinavian Institute of African Studies.

1973    Efficiency vs. Distribution in East African Cooperatives: A Study in Organizational Conflicts. Nairobi: East African Literature Bureau.

1980    Beyond Ujamaa in Tanzania: Underdevelopment and an Uncaptured Peasantry. Berkeley: University of California Press.

IBRD/World Bank
1982    Uganda, Country Economic Memorandum. Washington, DC: World Bank.

Jameson, J. D., ed.
1970    Agriculture in Uganda, 2nd edition. London: Oxford University Press.

Kasfir, Nelson
1970    Organizational Analysis and Ugandan Cooperative Unions. *In* Cooperatives and Rural Development in East Africa. Carl Gosta Widstrand, ed. Pp. 178–208. Uppsala: The Scandinavian Institute of African Studies.

La Fontaine, Jean S.
1959    The Gisu. *In* East African Chiefs. Audrey Richards, ed. Pp. 260–277. London: Faber and Faber.

1969    Tribalism Among the Gisu. *In* Tradition and Transition in East Africa: Studies of the Tribal Element in the Modern Era. P. H. Gulliver, ed. Pp. 177–192. Berkeley: University of California Press.

Leys, Colin
1967    Politicians and Policies: An Essay on Politics in Acholi, Uganda, 1962–65. Nairobi: East African Publishing.

Mamdani, Mahmood
1976    Politics and Class Formation in Uganda. New York: Monthly Review Press.

Saul, John S.
1969    Marketing Cooperatives in Tanzania. Paper presented at the Institute of Development Studies, University of Sussex.

Uganda, Republic of
1963, 1967, 1969, 1970    Uganda Statistical Abstracts. Entebbe: Government Printer.

Wrigley, C. C.
1959    Crops and Wealth in Uganda: A Short Agrarian History. Kampala: East African Institute of Social Research.

Young, M. Crawford
1971    Agricultural Policy in Uganda: Capability and Choice. *In* The State of the Nations. Michael Lofchie, ed. Pp. 141–164. Berkeley: University of California Press.

# 3

## Farmers, Cooperatives, and Development Assistance in Uganda: An Anthropological Perspective

*Patrick Fleuret*

### Introduction

Action agencies must repeatedly work their way through a difficult three-step process. Effectiveness depends on accurately identifying legitimate problems, conceiving feasible remedial actions, and finding ways to implement the actions needed. Anthropologists tend to focus their principal energies on the first step, although many know that the second step is critical too. Here I look at the vital but often unrecognized third step. Sound plans to deal with legitimate human problems too often go astray because poorly conceived implementation arrangements deflect, distort, or stop the flow of development resources. More importantly from an anthropological perspective, an analysis of what happens during program implementation constitutes a powerful test of our understanding of organizational action and the behavior of organizational systems. A problematic implementation experience can reveal weaknesses not only in development planning but also in social theory.

### Organizations and Development

The organizational dimension of development is receiving increased attention. The World Bank has made a major assessment of problems of organizational performance and management (World Bank 1983), and the U.S. Agency for International Development (AID) has prepared policy statements on institutional development and local organizations in development (USAID 1983, 1984a). A wide range of organizational issues has been explored in recent analyses, including the comparative strengths and weaknesses of alternative organizational formats (Esman and Montgomery 1980), methods of increasing the learning capacity and adaptability of bureaucracies (Korten 1980), structural and processual factors influencing organizational effectiveness (Paul 1982), decision making within development organizations (Moris 1981), and linkages among complementary organizations (Leonard and Marshall 1982). A recent review of rural development strategies views organizational improvement as an integral element of improvement in production and consumption (Johnston and Clark 1982).

For the most part, the growing debate on organizations in development is framed in terms of single organizations.[1] But propositions derived from the study of single organizations are unsatisfactory, because all development interventions involve more than one, and often very many, organizations. A few observers have recognized this complexity (Uphoff and Esman 1974; Esman and Uphoff 1982; Paul 1982); multi-organization analysis has probably been carried furthest by Leonard (1982), but even his discussion is primarily of a two-organization model. Moreover, Leonard implies that most interactions are one-way, from a superordinate entity to a recipient entity. But two-way or multiple interactions are probably characteristic, and must be accounted for fully to understand the performance of single organizations or systems of organizations. Moris (1983) has given greater attention than others to subtle features of organizational systems, noting that systemic interactions are often unobserved, and that rational and apparently "correct" behavior by actors in an organizational system may have perverse outcomes because of interaction within the system (cf. Simon 1969; Katz and Kahn 1966; Katz 1972).

Neither do the dominant conceptual schemes effectively encompass what are often referred to as "traditional" or indigenous types of organization, such as those based on descent, affinity, or neighborhood. Johnston and Clark speak for many when they write that

> [Traditional groups] stand in radical contrast to "modern" groups. . . . The relevant questions for policy have become, "when is a transition from traditional modes of organization desirable and feasible? and, How, and to what extent is that transition to be effected?" (1982:166).

Other analysts have suggested that indigenous organizations might, instead of being overlooked or changed, be incorporated substantively into planned programs of development (cf. Cernea 1981; Rogers, Colletta, and Mbindyo 1980; Uphoff, Cohen, and Goldsmith 1979). Most such discussions view these groups as agents of planned development, and usually assume their importance will decline. Some recent materials indicate, though, that indigenous, local associations may persist not simply because they have not yet been replaced by modern organizations, but because they work better (see in particular Coward 1982). Other assessments (cf. Hyden 1980, 1983) suggest that indigenous modes of integration not only persist, but may have major effects on formally superordinate organizations. Hence any discussion of the organizational dimension of development that fails to include a dynamic, interactive role for indigenous modes of organization is likely to be deficient.

Our understanding of organizations in development is thus flawed. The dominant conceptual frameworks have not addressed the multi-organization problem with any great facility; the treatments of inter-organizational linkages are relatively simple; there is little recognition that the connection between organization-level action and system-level outcomes might be indirect; and there is a tendency either to discount indigenous organizations entirely or view them as passive—and passing—agents of superordinate interests.

This chapter shows how some of these weaknesses can be overcome by employing an anthropological perspective in the analysis of an organization-intensive development project sponsored by AID in Uganda during the period 1979–1983.

## The Uganda Background

In January 1979, Tanzanian troops crossed into Uganda on a punitive expedition that grew into a liberation war and ultimately put an end to Idi Amin's military regime. The war and a subsequent period of civil disorder resulted in widespread looting and destruction throughout the country (Seers et al. 1979). The damage done was severe, but would not have been insurmountable, had Uganda's economic and institutional framework not been previously weakened by eight years of idiosyncratic and corrupt manipulation at the hands of the military regime (World Bank 1982).

In rural areas peasants responded to the collapse of Uganda's national-level political and economic structure by retreating into subsistence production, as happened in other parts of Africa that were caught up in conflict or economic depression, e.g., Ghana in the 1970s and early 1980s. But even in the subsistence sphere repercussions were felt, because basic production tools began to grow scarce. The hand-held, short-handled hoe, the principal agricultural implement, became unavailable except at high cost on the parallel market. Families without hoes were forced to borrow from neighbors. The hoes in use were often badly worn, to the point that they were suited only for light weeding, and of little value for the heavy work of ground preparation prior to planting.

As international donors reentered Uganda in 1979, hoes were widely identified as an immediate need. Most plans called for imports of the manufactured blades from factories in England; by contrast, AID planned a longer-term effort to rebuild Ugandan manufacturing capacity and foster an indigenous supply. Thus what took shape was a capital-intensive industrial rehabilitation project, but in an industry with direct ties to the rural economy, and with the potential to meet vital needs of peasant farmers (USAID 1979, 1981). But prevailing scarcities, a thoroughly instituted parallel market, and widespread corruption made it difficult to find a way to distribute the hoes that would ensure that most of them reached peasants at affordable prices. The Uganda cooperative movement emerged as a potentially effective distributional structure.

After being produced at implement-manufacturing plants at Jinja and Lugazi, the hoes were held by the Uganda Cooperative Central Union (UCCU). District cooperative unions were responsible for collecting the commodities from UCCU. Unions distributed the hoes to selected primary societies, where (to guard against loss) they were ideally sold to farmers on the day of delivery. Representatives of the primary society, the union, the Ministry of Cooperatives and Marketing (MCM), local chiefs, and other staff witnessed the sales. Four roving monitor teams were also present on days when hoes were distributed to help protect the integrity of the distribution scheme.

## Organizational Interactions and Program Outcomes

This section examines the results of the hoe distribution program at regional and community levels, and also looks at the effects of the program on Uganda's cooperative movement.

### Distributional Outcomes at the Regional Level

The allocation of hoes to various parts of the country was in principle done on the basis of population estimates, with each administrative district receiving equal numbers of hoes on a per capita basis. But district unions and district cooperative officers reallocated hoes on their own when MCM allocations did not suit them. This was done partly to move hoes from areas of weak demand to areas of high demand, and partly for personal gain or in response to local political pressures. Parliament[2] also took a close interest in the distribution of these scarce, valuable tools. Records were kept on the numbers of hoes going into parliamentary constituencies, a step taken at the request of the Cabinet, and the MCM sent letters to members of Parliament to notify them when hoe sales were to take place in their constituencies, so that they could attend and take some credit. Some constituencies received one hoe for every 14–

16 residents, while others received one for every 30–40 residents. There is no question the nation's politico-administrative institutions had a measurable impact on distributional outcomes at a regional level. But this ought not be seen in an entirely negative light, as will become clear in reviewing the response of the distribution program to variations in Ugandan agricultural patterns.

Agricultural production patterns in Uganda may be summed up in terms of the distribution of predominant staple food and cash crops, since these largely determine needs for labor and tools. In northern areas, annual crops dominate. Cereals (mainly finger millet and sorghum) are the staple foods, supplemented to varying degrees by root crops such as sweet potatoes and cassava. Cotton is the main commercial crop. In the south, where rainfall is higher and soils generally more productive, perennial crops play a large role. Bananas and root crops are the staple foods, apart from some areas in the east and west, where agriculture is very diverse and cereals (especially maize) enter into the banana-root crop patterns. In all these places coffee is the primary cash crop.

The difference betweeen annual and perennial crops is critical, because requirements for agricultural labor—particularly hoe labor—are greater in the north than in the south. Northern agricultural patterns require extensive land clearance, seedbed preparation, and weeding for all major crops. Although southern agricultural patterns include some cereals and significant amounts of root crops, the total amount of hoe labor required is likely much lower than in the north because of the prevalence of perennial banana/coffee regimes. It is difficult to assess the situation in the areas of mixed agriculture, but they could be expected to occupy an intermediate position between the north and south in this regard.[3]

Annual crop rainfall requirements also have a bearing here. Land clearing and seedbed preparation should take place before the onset of the rains, so that planting may be done either just before or coincident with the first rainfall. A delay of even a few days, once the rains have begun, will mean substantial yield reductions in cereal crops. Cotton too is sensitive to variation in the timing, amount, and distribution of rainfall. Throughout East Africa, these factors have stimulated the formation of complex labor exchange relationships, by means of which farmers seek to ensure that their own fields are prepared and planted in timely fashion (cf. Gulliver 1971; Vincent 1971). Such relationships are most important in annual cropping zones, where rainfall is most problematic.

The general lack of hoes during the 1979–1981 period made farmers in the north extremely reluctant to share their scarce, worn-out, and fragile tools, even among close agnatic kin, or to use them in the fields of another. People were more willing to lend hoes after their own land was ready, but by then the rains were imminent or in progress and it was usually too late for those without their own hoes to get much seed in the ground. Those borrowing hoes usually could not do an adequate job of land preparation before planting, nor could they, after the crop had germinated, weed as often and as completely as they ought.

In the south, on the other hand, the predominance of perennial crops allows labor inputs to be spread somewhat more evenly through the year. Bananas and coffee demand less labor than annual crops. Moreover, the root crops grown are not as sensitive to delays in planting as are cereal crops, and do not require as much weeding. Perhaps as a consequence, people there were much more willing to share hoes among relatives and neighbors, and the result was that a community's hoes met the needs of more people than was possible in the north.

These variations in patterns of agricultural production and hoe utilization suggest that patterns of hoe distribution should also vary—more hoes should go to the north on a per capita basis than to the south. Because the MCM compiled figures on the district-by-district allocation of hoes during 1980 and 1981, it is possible to determine whether there was a response to variation in regional needs. The incomplete correspondence of administrative districts with agroecological zones makes it difficult to be certain, and the picture is further confused by undoubted political distortions, but it seems that the allocation of hoes responded at least partially to regional variation in need for hoes. The annual cropping areas received more hoes than the perennial cropping areas in the ratio of about 1.3:1 (Fleuret 1981). Zones of mixed perennial/ annual crop production received intermediate numbers of hoes, apart from the Mt. Elgon area, which received considerably more than its share.[4]

The significance of this should not be understated. No one in AID or the Uganda government took agricultural diversity into account when the project was initially planned, and no mechanism for achieving differential rates of distribution was set in place. On the contrary, and in common with most development projects, the possibility that there might be local variations in need was overlooked, and overt planning statements called for uniform distribution around the country on the basis of "average family size" (USAID 1979:24).

That the hoe allocations aligned themselves roughly with agricultural needs was due primarily to cooperative officials and agricultural staff at the district level, who assisted in planning hoe allocations, and who, by lobbying for greater access to the tools, were able to translate agricultural needs into allocative decisions. Local cooperative representatives in particular had much incentive for doing so, because their positions are held at the pleasure of cooperative members, and they cannot remain in office without distributing external resources. It is vital to remember the thorough-going political character of the hoe distribution; in the past, allocation of resources distributed through the cooperative structure constituted an important aspect of local political action, and there is no question that hoes were treated in the same way. The political character of hoe distribution, which AID sought unsuccessfully to minimize, enabled the distribution program to respond to differential need at the regional level.[5]

## Distributional Outcomes at the Local Level

Final distributional outcomes were mediated by two further types of organizational interaction: between district unions and constituent primary societies, and through the social organization of distribution at the actual place and time of delivery. In reviewing these data, special attention is given to the effect of organizational interaction on distributional "equity," an elusive concept and an elusive goal.

District unions selected the primary societies that would receive and sell hoes; typically, about one-third of the primary societies in any one union were chosen. Although district-level officials made these decisions, the criteria for selecting societies were laid down by senior MCM officials in Kampala and included accessibility, good management, and safe storage facilities. These criteria were derived primarily from AID's legal obligation to preserve accountability in the disposition of public funds. The chosen societies had to be accessible by lorry, for the hoes were heavy and other forms of transport were not feasible. This clearly biased the distribution toward populations relatively nearer to towns and transport arteries. The high cost and scarcity of fuel also swayed distribution in the direction of nearby places. Hinterland areas, where the poorest and most needy groups are found, were therefore relatively unlikely to be served.

Good management was also an essential criterion; it would have been senseless to provide hoes to societies incapable of responsible book-keeping and careful supervision, for the hoes would then have simply disappeared into the parallel market, to be purchased at higher prices by wealthy farmers, traders, and smugglers. The necessity for safe storage facilities was also evident. Again, these criteria tended to favor wealthier, more successful societies over poorer ones. Central officials tried to surmount this difficulty by ruling that farmers whose own primary societies were not receiving commodities could obtain them at neighboring societies, but the long distances to be covered on foot limited the effectiveness of this idea.

Once primary societies were selected by the union, they were allocated hoes in proportion to membership, this being taken as a rough indication of the size of the total needy population (members and nonmembers alike) in the area served by the society. This convenient procedure tended to give greater numbers of hoes, on a per capita basis, to commercial farming areas where large proportions of the population are cooperative members. Subsistence areas received fewer hoes because cooperative membership is much lower there.

Thus AID's project to help poor farmers in Uganda was significantly influenced by unforeseen organizational interactions. The need for hoes dictated commodity assistance, in an environment where commodities were under great diversionary pressure; this led to a need for rigid accountability at all levels. Accountability in turn led to the imposition of administrative controls that biased the system in favor of relatively wealthy communities and households, thus substantially modifying the original commitment. Rational and sound judgments made by officials at international, national, and local levels cumulated to affect significantly the distributional impact of the Uganda assistance program.

## Community-Level Social Organization of Hoe Distribution

To minimize local political influences, AID and MCM officials directed that all local residents, cooperative members and nonmembers alike, were to be sold hoes on a first-come, first-served basis. But local administrators around the country made adjustments to meet more particular needs within the broad outlines of this central plan. These local adaptations illustrate the difficulty of defining, much less ensuring, equitable outcomes for planned development activities.

Some adaptations were based on primary cooperative membership. In such communities members stood in one line, nonmembers in another. Hoes were sold to the person at the head of each line alternately. The result was that members waited for shorter periods of time to receive their hoes, and were also more certain to get one when supplies were short. The rationale for this was that members had built up the society through past investments, while nonmembers had not; members were therefore thought to have a prior claim on cooperative services. Elsewhere this same logic was applied to the distributional problem, but to a greater degree: members were served first, followed by nonmembers. The first procedure was accepted by AID and MCM officials, although it constituted a distortion of the "first-come, first-served" model, but the second was judged too discriminatory. Both should be seen as efforts by local organizations to expand the administratively convenient but unacceptably unidimensional AID/MCM concept of "equity" by adding economic and historical dimensions.

In other places, a variety of household-level factors took precedence over cooperative membership in shaping distribution procedures. In one place, women stood in one line, men in another. The person at the head of each line was sold a hoe alternately. Usually, the women's line was shortest, since many women expected that hoes received by their husbands would in fact be given to them, and so did not attend the distribution on their own. The rationale for separate lines was that women could be bruised if required to compete with men for places in line. The location of the place where this system was used, however, makes it likely that many of the women in line were widows of men recently killed; they had to stand in line themselves. Throughout the country, unmarried mothers and women whose husbands were absent working were similarly disadvantaged, but their equally great need for hoes apparently did not generate an adjustment at any level of distribution.

Family size and structure did, however, influence the program in other ways. In some locations, adults with large families and many mouths to feed received two hoes, while adults with smaller or no families received one. The decision that a particular person should get two hoes was made by parish and subparish chiefs. This procedure was an adaptation to variation in need stemming from the household developmental cycle, introducing yet another dimension to the equity question; but it also magnified the opportunity for local political processes to influence commodity distribution. The decision about who was to get more than one hoe was made by political leaders, who could be expected to regard this resource as currency in the system of patron-client relationships that defines political networks in rural Uganda. The inherent susceptibility of assistance programs to political manipulation can be reduced, but only at a cost. To illustrate, it is useful to consider a close variant, observed elsewhere, of this family-based hoe distribution procedure: each man received one hoe, and as many additional hoes as he had wives. Because in this case the decision to allocate extra hoes was linked to numbers of wives, the opportunity for political relationships to influence allocation was diminished. At the same time it became more difficult to respond to legitimate variations in need; for instance, two-wife households with four children would receive two hoes while a single-wife household with the same number of children would receive just one.

In sum, cooperative managers and government administrative officers at district and subdistrict levels were able to evolve a wide range of local hoe-delivery procedures within the national distribution scheme; a different procedure was observed in virtually each location where hoe deliveries were taking place. This impressive systemic flexibility was achieved in part because local leaders had considerable decision-making authority—a circumstance due more to the difficulty of communication in postwar Uganda than to any official intent for events to be influenced by local considerations.

These cases illustrate the difficulty of ensuring that any particular development intervention, even one so apparently straightforward as the hoe distribution program, has an "equitable" outcome. The concept of equity is not unidimensional; the universalistic definition of equity formulated by AID and MCM needed to be augmented through consideration of social, economic, and historical dimensions. But it would have been difficult or impossible to design and administer a program responsive to this more sensitive definition, even assuming that all legitimate claims of competing groups could be satisfied simultaneously. Perhaps the most that can be achieved is to allow considerable discretion to the small-scale organizations involved in the intervention, so that some of the myriad dimensions of "equity" can be effectively addressed. But even this involves difficult trade-offs: placing decision-making power at local levels increases the flexibility of the organizational system to respond to human considerations, but it also increases the opportunity for complex local political dynamics to influence the result. To maintain local flexibility while eliminating politically inspired diversions requires direct national oversight, which is expensive or even impossible in difficult administrative environments. Also, such direct oversight can easily lead to excessive control of the local organizations involved, thus reducing the systemic flexibility that made the local organizations attractive in the first place.

### System-Level Outcomes

To this point the discussion has centered on the effect organizational interactions had on the access of farmers to hoes. But the organizational system examined here did not simply influence program results; it also changed in response to the program. As with distributional outcomes, however, the system-level outcomes derived from interactions that were not evident beforehand and that would in any case have been difficult or impossible to direct. Two system-level outcomes are considered: rapid growth in primary society registrations, and the emergence of an administered input-pricing scheme.

Many new societies were registered by the MCM after the AID program began in 1979 (see Table 3.1). These were often labelled "family cooperatives" because they barely met the requirement of the cooperative act for a minimum of ten members, and because they often consisted almost exclusively of close relatives.

TABLE 3.1
Increase in Registrations of Primary Societies, 1977–1983

| Event | Year | Number of Registered Societies | Increase | |
|---|---|---|---|---|
| | | | No. | % |
| | 1977 | 2,852 | — | — |
| | 1978 | 2,905 | 53 | 2 |
| CIP[a] Begins | 1979 | 2,941 | 36 | 1 |
| | 1980 | 3,136 | 195 | 7 |
| FPSP[b] Begins | 1981 | 3,434 | 298 | 10 |
| | 1982 | 3,949 | 515 | 15 |
| | 1983 (as of July) | 4,325 | 376 | 10 |

[a]Commodity Import Program
[b]Food Production Support Project

*Source:* Fleuret et al., 1983.

A dramatic surge in registrations occurred when donor-financed commodities began to move through the cooperative system. The rate of growth increased sevenfold within the space of just a few months in 1980, and early figures for 1983 showed that the rate had increased again (10 percent growth in the first six months of the year). In all, over 1300 new societies were registered between 1979 and 1983. This seemed encouraging; one could say the cooperative movement had emerged as one of Uganda's leading rural development institutions in the postwar period. The growth in cooperative membership, however, brought many problems of its own. The cooperative movement had difficulty absorbing so many new, untrained members, and the commodity distribution program was forced to expand its coverage prematurely, outrunning the capacities of central and local administrators. More disturbingly, many of the new societies were apparently formed solely to gain access to scarce commodities, and there were intimations that the commodities often were not used by members themselves, but rather resold for private profit. All this was generally thought to be eroding the moral basis of the cooperative movement.

Thus a number of so-called "second-generation" problems were caused by the program itself; inability to foresee such systemic responses weakens development planning and significantly alters the impact of development resources. A more subtle but equally serious example of this process is discussed below.

Throughout sub-Saharan Africa governments control the prices and distribution of agricultural commodities. These controls persist despite clear evidence that they do not contribute to stated objectives of increased production and welfare (cf. Eicher 1982; World Bank 1981). Bates (1981) has documented the macro-level political and economic factors responsible for this. The Uganda data suggest, however, that such controls may also grow out of rather minor administrative decisions, made to facilitate the implementation of development programs by accommodating immediate weaknesses of participating organizations.

In the early stages of the hoe program it was apparent that a special effort would be required to monitor the distribution process and ensure that hoes actually reached those for whom they were intended. The monitoring operation was expensive, requiring vehicles, petrol, maintenance, and a monitoring staff with associated salaries and per diems. The MCM had no funds for such extraordinary expenditure, so AID agreed to provide the vehicles and allow local costs to be met out of the revenue generated through hoe sales. The need to collect a "monitoring mark-up" (at levels administratively determined by MCM officials) at once ensured an important role for the ministry in setting retail prices and handling the funds generated through retail sales.

Other seemingly inconsequential factors solidified the MCM role in setting prices and regulating hoe distribution. AID expected quick, accurate reporting on shipments and related financial transactions; MCM was much better at this than the cooperative organizations. The two implement-manufacturing plants, when asked to submit estimates of the cost of producing hoes from AID-financed steel, provided suspect figures; the understaffed AID mission relied on the MCM to prepare counter-proposals. District unions, weakened by loss of staff and bewildered by rapid inflation and currency shifts, were generally unable to plan sensibly for the expenses of transport and distribution; the MCM stepped in. Farmers and members of Parliament were complaining about unpredictable variations in hoe prices, caused by variable quality, variable transport costs, variable source costs, and variable exchange rates; MCM advocated and partially instituted a nationwide uniform price to quell this discontent.

The administered price system thus came together piece by piece, with outcomes familiar from elsewhere in sub-Saharan Africa. Uniform transport margins penalized distant unions and peripheral populations. Uniform retail prices meant the hoes were underpriced in some places and overpriced in others, which created an opportunity for large profits through resale on the parallel market; this possibility in turn justified the continuation of controls on prices and distribution. District cooperative unions were expected to operate at cost, which kept them dependent upon government subventions, prevented the emergence of proper cost accounting and management, and perpetuated the need for government involvement. In sum, a short sequence of administrative actions, each initiated to meet legitimate needs of particular organizations, cumulated to an unintended and unfortunate outcome, but it would have been difficult to identify before the fact which actions would lead to such undesirable results, and even more difficult to identify alternative procedures.

## Conclusion

In this chapter I have sought to understand the effects of a commodity-import program in Uganda by exploring the actions and interactions of organizations involved in the program. Conventional organizational analysis, stressing the behavior of single organizations, was rejected in favor of an anthropological approach based on the concept of the organizational system. Organizational analysis for development must consider the objectives and behavior of many different organizations, indigenous as well as "modern"; the performance of organizational systems, which transform and are themselves transformed by the flow of development resources; and relationships among organizational and other systems. The difficulty of specifying this broad context before it actually emerges in operations may help explain why so many development activities founder on unforeseen organizational obstructions, and thus fail to achieve technical, economic, and social objectives.

Anthropology is characterized by a concern for the analysis of whole systems, by a recognition that relations among people and among human organizations are multiplex and systemic, by an awareness of the vitality and significance of social behavior at the level of the community and household, and by a sense that most human events are the result of subtle processes that are not readily apparent to outside observers. This paper has drawn upon these fundamental anthropological strengths to identify and more fully understand the effects of the Uganda hoe program, and to broaden the set of concepts used to analyze the roles of human organizations in development.

The paper has also tried to surmount some characteristic weaknesses of the anthropological approach. Chief among these is a continuing reluctance to expand the field of analysis beyond community-level human organizations to include more formal organizations at the regional, national, and international levels. But this needs to be done for at least three reasons: because it is within such organizations that major decisions about resource allocation are made; because current understanding of these organizations can be improved through anthropological insights; and because the true significance of much that anthropologists see happening within communities can only be discerned when events are viewed within a broader organizational context. As this paper shows, developmental outcomes that are unsatisfactory at the community level are rarely caused by exclusively local events or processes. Thus it seems necessary to adopt a more general frame of reference, one that can encompass not only the circumstances surrounding the final impact of a development activity but also the circumstances surrounding its conception, design, and implementation.

On a different level, this paper argues for a certain humility in the application of anthropological knowledge. Anthropologists played key roles in the Uganda program, helping to focus AID's attention on a worthy group (small farmers), a genuine need (hoes), and a sound distributional mechanism (the Uganda cooperative movement). The program has definitely succeeded in getting large numbers of needed hoes to farmers in rural Uganda (Fleuret et al. 1983; USAID 1984b). But much of what was good resulted from the compounding of organizational actions without planning, or even in spite of bad planning. Other more ambiguous outcomes were not foreseen and probably were not foreseeable; in fact, much of this would not have come to light had not an anthropologist been selected to head a crucial midterm evaluation. The point is that organizational systems, once "interconnected and resonant" (Moris 1983:18), may be relatively impervious to conscious efforts at planning and direction. If so, our theoretical understanding of organizational behavior has very low predictive power—a grave deficiency. It is important to note, however, that such lessons can only emerge in applied settings where the need is not merely to find meaning in what has passed but to influence the shape of events to come. Thus anthropological theory and application are interdependent; neither can be advanced far without knowledge of the other. This argues for a much increased two-way flow of ideas between anthropological theory and the world of application.

## Notes

In January-February 1980 the author travelled widely in rural Uganda to assess community-level, socioeconomic conditions for the then-nascent AID program (Fleuret 1980). A second field trip took place in August-September 1981, to assess the rural impact of the AID agricultural-commodity import program and to assist in the design of the follow-on Food Production Support Project (Fleuret 1981). In October-November 1983 a third field trip was undertaken to evaluate the Food Production Support Project (Fleuret et al. 1983). During the first field trip the cooperative movement was one of several areas of investigation. Special attention was directed at the cooperative structure during the second and third field trips. Over 300 officials and private individuals were interviewed during this work, but the continued delicacy of the sociopolitical environment in Uganda makes it difficult to acknowledge their essential contribution. The views expressed in this paper are those of the author alone and do not necessarily represent those of the U.S. Agency for International Development or any unit thereof.

1. Most attempts to define organizations relate to particular types, for instance, bureaucracies or voluntary associations. Overarching definitions are too vague to retain much analytic utility. Bryant and White, in an authoritative text, consider that "organizations are clusters of people, each with its own needs and interests, interacting to accomplish certain tasks and operating within resources and constraints in the environment" (1982:42). Somewhat different formulations can be found in Uphoff and Esman (1974) and Esman and Uphoff (1982).

2. This paper was written prior to the 1985 military coup, which removed the second Obote administration from power.

3. Overviews of labor requirements for African staple food crops are available in Miracle (1966), Jones (1959), Cleave (1974), and Anthony et al. (1979).

4. Some senior managers in concerned organizations have their homes there.

5. There is not space here to consider the sociological and political aspects of cooperative development in Uganda, without which it is difficult fully to understand the genesis of many of the issues discussed in this paper. Important background may be found in Agricultural Cooperative Development International (ACDI) (1973), Bunker (1983), Kasfir (1970), Mamdani (1976), Okerere (1970, 1974), Mason et al. (1962), Young (1971), and Young et al. (1981).

## References Cited

Agricultural Cooperative Development International
  1973    Ten Years of Cooperative Development in Uganda. Washington, DC: ACDI.
Anthony, Kenneth R. M., et al.
  1979    Agricultural Change in Tropical Africa. Ithaca, NY: Cornell University Press.
Bates, Robert H.
  1981    Markets and States in Tropical Africa. Berkeley, CA: University of California Press.
Bryant, Coralie, and Louise G. White
  1982    Managing Development in the Third World. Boulder, CO: Westview Press.
Bunker, Stephen G.
  1983    Center-local Struggles for Bureaucratic Control in Bugisu, Uganda. American Ethnologist 10(4):749–769.
Cernea, Michael
  1981    Modernization and Development Potential of Traditional Grass Roots Peasant Organizations. *In* Directions of Change: Modernization Theory, Research, and Realities. M. O. Attir, et al., eds. Pp. 121–139. Boulder, CO: Westview Press.

Cleave, John H.
   1974   African Farmers: Labor Use in the Development of Smallholder Agri-
          culture. New York, NY: Praeger.

Coward, E. Walter, Jr., ed.
   1982   Irrigation and Agricultural Development in Asia. Ithaca, NY: Cornell
          University Press.

Eicher, Carl K.
   1982   Facing up to Africa's Food Crisis. Foreign Affairs 61(1):151–174.

Esman, Milton J., and John D. Montgomery
   1980   The Administration of Human Development. *In* Implementing Programs
          of Human Development. Peter T. Knight, ed. Pp. 183–234. Washington,
          DC: The World Bank.

Esman, Milton J., and Norman T. Uphoff
   1982   Local Organization and Rural Development: the State of the Art. Ithaca,
          NY: Center for International Studies, Cornell University.

Fleuret, Patrick C.
   1980   Draft Background Paper: Community-level Conditions and Develop-
          ment Assistance Needs in Uganda. Report prepared for USAID/
          Kampala.

   1981   Uganda Agricultural Sector Support Project: Social Analysis. Report
          prepared for USAID/Kampala.

Fleuret, Patrick C., et al.
   1983   Midterm Evaluation of Uganda Food Production Support Project. Report
          prepared for USAID/Kampala.

Gulliver, Philip
   1971   Neighbors and Networks. Berkeley, CA: University of California Press.

Hyden, Goran
   1980   Beyond Ujamaa in Tanzania: Underdevelopment and an Uncaptured
          Peasantry. Berkeley, CA: University of California Press.

   1983   No Shortcuts to Progress. Berkeley, CA: University of California Press.

Johnston, Bruce F., and William C. Clark
   1982   Redesigning Rural Development: A Strategic Perspective. Baltimore,
          MD: The Johns Hopkins University Press.

Jones, William O.
   1959   Manioc in Africa. Stanford, CA: Stanford University Press.

Kasfir, Nelson
   1970   Organizational Analysis and Uganda Cooperative Unions. *In* Coop-
          eratives and Rural Development in East Africa. Carl Widstrand, ed.
          Pp. 178–208. New York, NY: Africana Publishing Corporation.

Katz, Daniel, and Robert L. Kahn
   1966   The Social Psychology of Organizations. New York, NY: John Wiley
          and Sons, Inc.

Katz, Saul
  1972 The Institution Building Model: A Systems View. *In* Institution Building
       and Development: From Concepts to Action. Joseph W. Eaton, ed.
       Beverly Hills, CA: Sage Publications. *Quoted in* Institution Building:
       A Sourcebook. M. G. Blase. P. 23. East Lansing, MI: Midwest Universities
       Consortium for International Activities, Inc.
Korten, David C.
  1980 Community Organization and Rural Development: A Learning Process
       Approach. Public Administration Review 40(5):480–511.
Leonard, David K.
  1982 Analyzing the Organizational Requirements for Serving the Rural Poor.
       *In* Institutions of Rural Development for the Poor. David K. Leonard
       and Dale R. Marshall, eds. Pp. 1–39. Berkeley, CA: University of
       California Institute of International Studies.
Leonard, David K., and Dale Rogers Marshall, eds.
  1982 Institutions of Rural Development for the Poor. Berkeley, CA: University
       of California Institute of International Studies.
Mamdani, Mahmoud
  1976 Politics and Class Formation in Uganda. New York, NY: Monthly
       Review Press.
Mason, Edward S., et al.
  1962 The Economic Development of Uganda. Baltimore, MD: The Johns
       Hopkins University Press.
Miracle, Marvin
  1966 Maize in Tropical Africa. Madison, WI: University of Wisconsin Press.
Moris, Jon R.
  1981 Managing Induced Rural Development. Bloomington, IN: International
       Development Institute.
  1983 What Do We Know about African Agricultural Development? The Role
       of Extension Performance Reanalyzed. Report prepared for USAID/
       Washington.
Okerere, Okoro
  1970 The Place of Marketing Cooperatives in the Economy of Uganda. *In*
       Cooperatives and Rural Development in East Africa. Carl Widstrand,
       ed. Pp. 153–177. New York, NY: Africana Publishing Corporation.
  1974 The Economic Impact of the Uganda Cooperatives. Kampala: East
       African Literature Bureau.
Paul, Samuel
  1982 Managing Development Programs. Boulder, CO: Westview Press.
Rogers, Everett M., Nat Colletta, and Joseph Mbindyo
  1980 Social and Cultural Influences on Human Development Policies and
       Programs. *In* Implementing Programs of Human Development. Peter
       T. Knight, ed. Pp. 235–210. Washington, DC: The World Bank.
Seers, Dudley, et al.
  1979 The Rehabilitation of the Economy of Uganda. Commonwealth Sec-
       retariat.

Simon, Herbert
   1969    The Sciences of the Artificial. Cambridge, MA: Massachusetts Institute
           of Technology Press.
United States Agency for International Development
   1979    Uganda Commodity Import Program (617–0101), September. Wash-
           ington, DC: USAID
   1981    Uganda Food Production Support Project (617–0102), September. Wash-
           ington, DC: USAID
   1983    Institutional Development. Washington, DC: USAID.
   1984a   Local Organizations in Development. Washington, DC: USAID.
   1984b   Auditor's Report: Uganda Food Production Support Project. Wash-
           ington, DC: USAID.
Uphoff, Norman T., John M. Cohen, and Arthur A. Goldsmith
   1979    Feasibility and Application of Rural Development Participation: A
           State-of-the-Art Paper. Ithaca, NY: Rural Development Committee,
           Cornell University.
Uphoff, Norman T., and Milton J. Esman
   1974    Local Organization for Rural Development: Analysis of Asian Expe-
           rience. Ithaca, NY: Center for International Studies, Cornell University.
Vincent, Joan
   1971    African Elite: The Big Men of a Small Town. New York, NY: Columbia
           University Press.
World Bank
   1981    Accelerated Development in Sub-Saharan Africa. Washington, DC: The
           World Bank.
   1982    Uganda Country Economic Memorandum. Washington, DC: The World
           Bank.
   1983    World Development Report. Washington, DC: The World Bank.
Young, Crawford M.
   1971    Agricultural Policy in Uganda: Capability and Choice. In The State of
           the Nations. M. F. Lofchie, ed. Pp. 141–164. Berkeley, CA: University
           of California Press.
Young, Crawford M., Neal P. Sherman, and Tim H. Rose
   1981    Cooperatives and Development: Agricultural Politics in Ghana and
           Uganda. Madison, WI: University of Wisconsin Press.

# 4

## Food Aid and Development in Rural Kenya

*Anne Fleuret*

### Introduction

Little is currently known about intrahousehold allocation of food—the inequitable or disproportionate division of foodstuffs at the household level, or the effects of an individual's age, sex, or life condition on access to the total food supply or particular components of it. With reference to programs of food aid, knowledge of any aspect of recipient utilization of foodstuffs received through distribution programs is quite limited, and planners and policymakers have little data upon which to base important decisions about the composition and size of ration packages provided.[1] There is clearly a role for anthropologists in conducting field studies of actual household-level utilization of commodities received through project food aid. The use of appropriate ethnographic methods, including interviews, observation, and surveys, can provide information on food-consumption patterns, dietary preferences, food-preparation techniques, socioeconomic characteristics of food-aid recipients, and other variables critical to making decisions on the targeting of food aid as well as the types of commodities provided. Such studies can also help in establishing whether food aid actually meets its implicit and explicit objectives. In 1985 I conducted such a study of a food-aid program.[2] In this chapter I will discuss the nature, origins, and objectives of project food aid and use data from the anthropological study to assess the extent to which these objectives are met. I will also discuss the relevance of the findings to food-aid programming in Kenya.

The focus of the field study was on actual utilization of food-aid commodities provided to rural residents of Taita/Taveta District. Issues directly addressed included determination of the net income value of the ration and its significance vis-à-vis total household income and investment capacity; the supplementary or substitutive effects of the food provided; the effectiveness of both geographical and intrahousehold targeting; sales or exchanges of donated foods, and interhousehold patterns of sharing; and sources and quantities of non-food-aid items ordinarily consumed. In order to make some judgment of the effects of food aid on the usual consumption patterns of households in this part of Kenya, comparisons are made with similar households in the same area that do not have access to the feeding program.

## United States Food Aid

United States government provision of food aid had its origins with the Marshall Plan after World War II, and became a permanent feature of U.S. foreign assistance with the enactment of the Agriculture, Trade and Assistance Act, commonly known as PL 480, in 1954. As currently amended, this law calls for the provision of U.S. agricultural commodities as food aid in three categories (titles), of which Title II, outright donations through Private Voluntary Organizations (PVOs) or international agencies, is the concern of this paper. The original legislation identified as the objectives of food aid the following:

- expansion and stimulation of international trade,
- promotion of American agriculture,
- disposal of surplus U.S. agricultural commodities,
- furtherance of U.S. foreign policy (see Tarrant 1980, Austin 1981, Shepherd 1985).

These initial objectives remain a central concern of U.S. food-aid programming today, but more recently humanitarian and development-related objectives have also entered the picture. In 1966, the Food for Peace amendment identified combating hunger and malnutrition as an explicit goal of the food-assistance program. In addition, 75 percent of Title II aid is by law directed to countries with the lowest per capita incomes, and is to be targeted to the poor majority or the "poorest of the poor." Field and Wallerstein (1977:236) argue that ". . . food aid can make a meaningful contribution to development if it is targeted explicitly against protein-calorie malnutrition," regarding malnutrition itself as a barrier to development; their view is endorsed by Schuh (1981:88) who recommends that "as large a proportion of food aid as is possible should be shifted to the formation of human capital."

Title II programs donate commodities free of charge through such intermediaries as CARE, the Red Cross, and Catholic Relief Services (CRS). In FY 1984, 1.9 million metric tons of food valued at over $500 million were distributed under the auspices of Title II and benefited an estimated 56 million recipients. Commodities available and distributed in recent years include bulgur, whole wheat, wheat flour, maize, sorghum, nonfat dry milk, rice, and soybean oil. Some processed and/or fortified foods are also available. The size, composition, and nutritional value of the package of food ("ration") provided to recipients varies from country to country, and the ration designated for a particular country varies also. There is no real rationale for the size and composition of these ration packages. The actual delivery of food aid under Title II is accomplished in four principal ways: through clinics or maternal and child health programs (MCH); in school feeding programs (SFP); as compensation for labor (FFW, or food-for-work); and as emergency relief to famine victims. Each of these methods of distribution singles out a specific group or groups in the population as its principal beneficiary, or target. MCH programs target pregnant/lactating women and children under the age of five years; SFP, the school-age (and, importantly, school-attending) population; FFW, un- or underemployed adults and their households. The organizations that actually distribute Title II food aid, such as CRS, themselves often wish to meet quite different objectives with food aid than those embodied in law and bureaucracy. Their motivations are principally humanitarian in nature: the alleviation of hunger, the improvement of nutritional status, and economic development, particularly among the poorest. As Reutlinger notes, "In the case of project food aid, there is a . . . widespread consensus that its primary objective is the alleviation of malnutrition and hunger, and that this noble objective is achieved best if the recipients are given the proper foods and consume them in addition to the foods in their existing diet" (1984:254).

Much of the Title II food aid provided by the U.S. to countries of sub-Saharan Africa is actually delivered by Catholic Relief Services. CRS programming in Africa is firmly rooted in the premise that the objectives of food aid are both the direct improvement of nutritional status and the delivery of economic aid to recipients in the form of food. The bulk of the foods provided under the auspices of CRS is delivered through MCH clinics, and the recipients take it away with them to prepare and consume as they wish in their own homes. CRS believes, given appropriate nutrition education, that making additional resources available to the household and thereby giving that household more flexibility in the allocation of all of its resources will ensure that food consumption, especially among vulnerable members, will increase, and their health and nutritional status will improve. A crucial condition of such an approach is that the economic value of the food provided be sufficiently large to have significant impact at the household level, since it is assumed that the food will be shared by all household members rather than reserved for the exclusive use of just some of those members. Nutrition education, primary health care, and the involvement of the recipients in other development-oriented social and economic activities are additional components of CRS MCH programs.

Beneficiaries' views of food aid often remain unexplored. Both the United States Agency for International Development (USAID) and PVOs have made some attempts to ascertain what program elements encourage participation (see, for example, evaluations of Title II food-aid programs in Senegal, Burkina Faso, and Cameroon), but most evaluations leave aside any consideration of the desires and preferences of recipients. This is at least partly because many decisions, particularly those concerning what foods can be provided, are beyond the control of the organization. CRS regards its relationship with food-aid recipients as contractual, each partner having specific obligations vis-à-vis the other, but studies have shown that there is often mutual misunderstanding of the nature of these obligations, which can lead to mutual dissatisfaction with the relationship (see Cook and Csete 1983).

While food aid has a number of laudable objectives, it has been criticized for its unanticipated negative consequences. The most frequently cited of these are that the provision of free or cheap food functions as a disincentive to local agricultural production, depresses local food prices, creates food dependence, and encourages the development of inappropriate food preferences and patterns (see Austin 1981).

In sum, over the past 30 years U.S. government food assistance has served many masters and has been expected to meet a number of distinct and potentially contradictory objectives, and it has been accused of deleterious impacts. In the following pages I will use ethnographic data from the Taita MCH program to describe the household-level impact of the food provided, in an effort to see to what extent nutritional, economic, development, foreign policy, and other objectives—from USAID, CRS, and beneficiary perspectives—actually are being met.

## The Study Area

Taita/Taveta District is a rural area located in the inland portion of Kenya's Coast Province. In the 1979 census the population of the district was 147,597 people, in a total area of 16,975 sq km. The rural population is concentrated in Wundanyi Division, which comprises only 15 percent of the total area of the district but includes most of the fertile and well-watered Taita Hills. These hills rise abruptly from the surrounding arid plain and reach maximum altitudes of 2,200 m above sea level. As the altitude rises, so do the average annual rainfall, the potential for intensive agricultural production, and the population density. Most of the people live in the hills at elevations of 1,000 m or above, and support themselves through a combination of food production, cash-crop production, temporary and permanent wage labor, and sales of craft items, forest products, and livestock. The principal crops include maize, beans, other legumes, sweet potatoes, bananas, taro, vegetables, and coffee. Many households raise cattle, sheep or goats, and keep poultry as well. All of the hills' residents belong to the Taita ethnic group and speak Taita (Kidawida) as their first language.

Traditional Taita agriculture was based on the exploitation by individual households of multiple fields in different soil, rainfall, and temperature zones. At least until the 1920s this strategy permitted self-sufficiency in food production and the development of a substantial export trade in vegetables. By the 1930s, however, food deficit years began to exceed years in which food production within the district satisfied internal demand, and labor migration developed as a significant income-generating activity (see Harris 1972, A. Fleuret 1985).

## The Title II Program

The Title II MCH feeding program in Mbuvhenyi[3] began in 1971 and currently serves 1,200 recipients. Mothers may enroll themselves plus one child under the age of five years, or two under-five children. Most of the current (1985) recipients originally enrolled in 1983. At that time the sole criterion for admission to the program was first-come, first-served. Neither a nutritional nor an income criterion was applied to determine eligibility.

The recipients are provided with food once every four weeks. Villages in the program's effective catchment area are divided into a dozen groups, and recipients in each group of communities are assigned a particular day of the week and week of the month for collection. Distribution operates on a first-come, first-served basis. Women arrive as early as they choose and place their containers in line in the order that they came. Clinic personnel distribute numbered chips to the women according to this order. The index child is weighed, questions are dealt with, and the mother proceeds to collect her ration. After that she is free to return to her home. Although some of the women live near the distribution point, most live quite a distance away. A woman may leave her home at first light, receive her rations at 11 a.m., and not reach home again until the afternoon.

There are other components of the program besides the distribution of food aid, principally nutrition education and participation in income-generating activities. Efforts are made to instruct recipients in the proper preparation of the foodstuffs and to impart some nutrition education knowledge, but the groups of women and children assembled at any one time are quite large and much of the teaching is minimally effective. Attempts are also made to reinforce the nutrition education messages and create permanent bonds of cooperation by the creation of income-generating projects. Every food-aid recipient is required to belong to one of these groups: rabbit, chicken, goat, or pig production, and handicrafts. In mid-1985 membership fees of Ksh 30 to 50 per participant had been collected, but no further progress had been made in forming the groups, organizing their activities, or providing breeding stock or manufacturing materials.

## Ration Size and Composition

The size and composition of the ration have varied. When the program began in the 1970s, the commodities provided included maize flour and nonfat dry milk (NFDM). In 1983, bulgur and soybean salad oil were available. NFDM was later added to this, so that by mid-1983 the package consisted of 4 kg bulgur, 4 kg NFDM, and 2 liters soybean salad oil per household per month. This package remained essentially the same through most of 1984, although on a month-to-month basis alterations were sometimes made because particular items in the package might be in short supply. During the study period a special "drought ration" was provided, containing a full bag of bulgur (22.68 kg or 50 lb), 6 kg corn-soy milk (CSM, a blended food intended for infants), and 2 liters soybean salad oil. Shortly thereafter, CRS and the Kenya Government agreeing that the drought emergency had been alleviated, the ration was reduced to 6 kg bulgur, 3 kg CSM, and one liter oil per mother-child pair per month.

## Economic Value of the Ration

A number of considerations enter into calculations of the net income value of the ration. For the research period, the value was arrived at in the following way:

Bulgur:    22.68 kg at Ksh    4.15/kg = Ksh   94.12
CSM:          6.0 kg at Ksh    4.15/kg = Ksh   24.90
Oil:             2.0 kg at Ksh  27.43/1  = Ksh   54.86

Total Gross Value:                              Ksh 173.88
    N.B.   16 Ksh = $1.00

The prices used to calculate these values were the current retail prices of the same or functionally similar items in local shops and markets.

Against this gross value must be calculated costs to the recipient of obtaining the ration package. Recipients paid a collection charge of Ksh 16 for their ration. The cost of lost female labor time must also be added in. The cost, or value, of one day of labor is based on the current cash remuneration paid for one day of unspecialized agricultural or domestic labor: Ksh 15 to 20. During the study period this is calculated at 1.5 days per recipient, because extra help was needed to transport the large quantity of food provided under the drought ration. Therefore, net value to the consumer of the ration package was as follows:

| | |
|---|---|
| Gross value | Ksh 173.88 |
| Less service charge | Ksh 16.00 |
| Less labor costs | Ksh 26.25 (1.5 days @ 17.5/day) |
| Net value | Ksh 131.63 ($8.23) |

The net value of the package dropped sharply when the drought ration was discontinued. Its gross and net value can be arrived at as shown below. Labor costs are calculated on the basis of one day at Ksh 17.50; due to the decrease in package size, adult assistance probably is not required. Moreover, these new values apply after the service charge was increased to Ksh 22 per mother-child pair.

| | |
|---|---|
| 6 kg bulgur @ 4.15/kg | Ksh 24.90 |
| 3 kg CSM @ 4.15/kg | Ksh 12.45 |
| 1 l oil @ 27.43/l | Ksh 27.43 |
| Gross value | Ksh 64.78 |
| Less service charge | Ksh 22.00 |
| Less labor costs | Ksh 17.50 |
| Net value | Ksh 25.28 ($1.58) |

Since not all eligible women manage to appear at the distribution centers at the right time each month, a correction for absence at a rate of 10 percent is made to reach an annual value of the ration of Ksh 273.02 ($17.06).

### Sample and Sample Selection

In order to understand the impact and utilization of this commodity package at the household level, intensive examination of particular households on a day-to-day basis was necessary. Accordingly, I selected 20 households randomly from among the recipients, 5 each on 4 preselected distribution days, and recruited local research assistants to assist in data collection. Census data on all household members were collected, and each of the 20 houses was visited daily to collect information on the types, quantities, and sources of the foodstuffs eaten within the household since the previous day's visit. The amount of each of the Title II foods remaining was measured each day. Additional data on farming practices, income and expenditure, health, housing and personal possessions, and income-generating activity were collected. The same data were simultaneously collected from 20 households in an otherwise similar community, none of whose members receive any Title II foods. The comparison community, Msidunyi, is about one and a half hours by foot from Mbuvhenyi. The ecological situation and economic opportunities and constraints are similar in these two areas.

## Social and Economic Characteristics of Sample Households

The households studied in both areas are quite heterogeneous, but mean household size, proportion of female-headed households, maternal age, parity, education, and school attendance figures are comparable in the two communities.

Although all households studied are farming households, owning land and producing food and cash crops, nonfarm employment provides much of their cash income in the majority of cases. Men absent as labor migrants pursue varied occupations, including skilled (tailoring, clerical, carpentry) and unskilled work. Even for adult men who are full-time household residents, farming is a secondary economic activity for most. Locally resident males engage in such diverse occupations as tailor, butcher, photographer, and shopkeeper. Only two of the households in Mbuvhenyi and six in Msidunyi are primarily dependent on farming for both cash and kind income. The households are also highly stratified as regards income and investment. Actual weekly cash income ranges from a low of about Ksh 50 to a high of over Ksh 500. Cash was received from sales of agricultural commodities, from regular salaried employment, in the form of remittances from family or household members working elsewhere, and from illegal activity such as beer brewing, charcoal burning, and illicit prospecting for gemstones. Several households received intermittent lump-sum payments for coffee, vegetables, and gemstones.

The variability in access to cash is reflected by diversity in the extent of investment. The traditional Taita house, round and thatched, can be built using cooperative labor and local materials, but in addition to purchased materials, construction of the newer rectangular house requires skilled, cash-remunerated labor. By assigning point values to purchased improvements such as iron roofing, cement for floors, and glass windows, an index showing investment patterns was created. House index values range from 0 points to 580 points.

A similar procedure was used to derive a scale of investment in consumer durables, none of them used traditionally but all of them now available for cash purchase. The items recorded include flashlight, hurricane lamp (kerosene wick lamp), pressure lamp, iron bedstead, radio, kerosene wick or pressure stove, bicycle, wristwatch, wooden cupboard for clothes or dishes, sewing machine, and manual maize-grinding machine. Points assigned to each item are 10 percent of current retail price. Point totals obtained for these material possessions range from 0 to 627.

In the case of livestock, cattle are by far the most valuable as well as the preferred animal, and their value far exceeds that of other beasts. Stock holdings are therefore calculated in cattle equivalents, derived from the relative purchase price of a healthy animal. One cow or bull is equivalent to 5 sheep or goats, or 20 poultry or rabbits.

Compilation of house, wealth, stock, and cash-income measures yields the following results:

| Msidunyi | House | Wealth | Stock | Cash income/week |
|---|---|---|---|---|
| Range | 0–415 | 0–317 | 0–7.45 | Ksh 57–400 |
| Mean | 140.5 | 84.5 | n/a | n/a |
| Mbuvhenyi | | | | |
| Range | 0–580 | 17–627 | .05–7.1 | Ksh 50–500 |
| Mean | 255 | 214 | n/a | n/a |

The comparison of the means and ranges in wealth and house indexes shows a greater range of variation and a higher mean value in Mbuvhenyi than in Msidunyi. Thus, there is a more diverse and generally higher level of investment among the food-aid recipients; people in the comparison community, although their cash incomes are comparable, have less capacity—or desire—to invest in a more comfortable dwelling or in expensive consumer goods.

Cash income and investment figures do not provide the whole picture, however, because all of these households are farming households, and food produced for home consumption also constitutes income. Some of the households sell farm products, especially coffee, vegetables, and milk. Most of the food consumed is produced by women farmers. All of the cultivation is manual, the short-handled hoe being the principal tool. Every household cultivates the two principal staple foods, maize and beans. Other crops cultivated on one or more of the farms include bananas, Irish potatoes, sweet potatoes, taro, cassava, tanias, green vegetables (principally kale and cabbage), commercial vegetables (tomatoes, onions, carrots, peas), coffee, pumpkins, pigeon peas, cowpeas, sugar cane, millet, oranges, guavas, lemons, avocados, papayas, tangerines, mangoes, pineapples, and passion fruits. The maize grown is of both improved (hybrid and composite) and traditional varieties.

Data on yields are difficult to obtain. Some crops are planted two or three times in an annual cycle; different portions of the same field are planted in particular crops at different times; and all crops, even maize, tend to be harvested as needed rather than harvested all at once and stored in a granary. All of the households satisfied at least part of their staple food requirements from their own production, but the irregularity of planting and the peripatetic nature of harvesting make it difficult to determine the quantities. To determine the income value of foods produced for home consumption I measured the quantity of a particular food item consumed at a typical meal, and used the number of meals containing that item over a given period of time as a basis for calculating the quantity of the foodstuff consumed. Its income value can then be determined on the basis of the retail price (replacement price) of the commodity. In order to find out how much of the important foods is generally consumed at mealtime, the raw components of meals being prepared in the homes were weighed. The weighing instrument used was an Ohaus D1001-CA digital electronic balance accurate to the nearest gram. Over 150 observations were made in homes of various sizes and relative wealth and income, and the results of the observations were averaged to generate a figure for the "typical" meal. Items weighed include maize flour, whole grain maize, beans, greens, tubers, other vegetables, milk, cooking fats, sugar, and condiments. The table below summarizes the results of the weighing exercise.

|                        | Maize | Tubers | Beans | Greens |
|------------------------|-------|--------|-------|--------|
| Amount eaten/meal, g   | 1280  | 1897   | 530   | 553    |
| Meals per week         | 9.0   | 1.5    | 4.8   | 6.4    |
| Total weekly quantity, kg | 11.5 | 2.8  | 2.5   | 3.5    |
| Retail price Ksh/kg    | 4.15  | 3.00   | 12.00 | 6.00   |
| Replacement price/wk   | 47.7  | 8.5    | 30.0  | 21.0   |

Taking into account the home production of food, total monthly household income ranges from a low of around Ksh 650 in the poorest households to over Ksh 2,500 in the most affluent (weekly cash income plus home production for about 4.3 weeks per month). Title II foods in the quantities provided during the months of June and July 1985 augment total income by 5 percent in the highest income households, ranging up to 20 percent in the poorest.

## Food Consumption Patterns

Detailed food consumption records were maintained for all 40 house-holds over the period of observation. Recall data on the composition of all meals and other foods and beverages consumed in the household each day, and on the provenance of each ingredient of dishes and beverages prepared and snacks eaten, were collected. Information was also obtained on the preparation of special foods for young children and sick household members, and on any food items stored in the home, including their sources.

Taita generally consume two substantial meals each day, one at midday and one in the evening. Morning intake is often limited to heavily sweetened tea, and occasionally thin maize gruel (especially for children). If foods are consumed, they are generally cold leftovers of maize porridge or other carbohydrate staples from the previous evening's meal, or sometimes ripe bananas. Very rarely special foods may be prepared or purchased for morning consumption, particularly potatoes, bread, or fried sweetened wheat cakes. Almost half of all morning intake consisted solely of tea.

Midday and evening meals are larger and more elaborate affairs. The most important element in such a meal is a dish high both in bulk and in carbohydrates. Foods from which the principal dish may be prepared include maize, wheat, rice, cassava, potatoes, bananas, taro, millet, or pumpkin. Such a dish is usually, though not always, garnished with a sauce or relish prepared from vegetables, beans or other legumes, or animal protein. Tubers such as potatoes or taro are often served without a garnish. Whole maize/bean or tuber/legume combination dishes in which the two principal ingredients are cooked together in one vessel are also eaten. The relative frequency with which different staples and relishes were eaten by the sample households during the period of observation is presented in Table 4.1.

The table shows that maize occupies the central place in the diet. It is the principal source of both calories and protein. The average pot of porridge (*mswara*) prepared for a family meal contains about 1,280 gm of maize flour, yielding approximately 4,500 calories, and is shared among all household members and guests. The relishes are eaten in much smaller amounts and provide additional calories in varying amounts; greens provide about 240 additional calories to the meal, beans nearly 1,800, and meat about 1,000, when used. Only rarely will more than one relish ingredient be served per meal.

## Utilization of Title II Foods in Mbuvhenyi

*Substitution vs. Supplementation.* The foods provided in the ration package are, with the partial exception of CSM, utilized by all household

TABLE 4.1
Relative Frequency with Which Different Staples and Relishes Were Eaten by the Sample Households During the Period of Observation (in percent)

| | Garnishes | | | | |
| | Vegetables | Beans | Meat/fish | Nothing | Total |
|---|---|---|---|---|---|
| **Mbuvhenyi** | | | | | |
| *Staples* | | | | | |
| Maize | 42.3 | 15.3 | 6.5 | 1.7 | 65.8 |
| Bulgur | 3.5 | 10.6 | 0.8 | 1.8 | 16.7 |
| Wheat flour/ | | | | | |
| rice | — | 3.5 | 1.3 | 0.8 | 5.6 |
| Tubers | — | 4.3 | — | 5.4 | 9.7 |
| Other | — | — | — | 2.3 | 2.3 |
| Total | 45.8 | 33.7 | 8.6 | 12.0 | 100.0[a] |
| **Msidunyi** | | | | | |
| *Staples* | | | | | |
| Maize | 49.3 | 16.3 | 5.6 | 0.3 | 71.5 |
| Wheat flour/ | | | | | |
| rice | — | 4.2 | 1.0 | 0.3 | 5.6 |
| Tubers | 1.0 | 9.4 | 0.3 | 8.7 | 19.4 |
| Other | — | — | — | 3.5 | 3.5 |
| Total | 50.3 | 29.9 | 6.9 | 12.8 | 100.0 |

[a]Discrepancies due to rounding errors.

members and serve a principally substitutive rather than supplementary role in the diet. For the most part, bulgur was used to prepare major meals and was served with a garnish of beans or vegetables. Bulgur was the principal ingredient of about one-sixth of all major meals consumed in the sample households during the period of observation. Soybean salad oil took the place of various packaged and tinned vegetable fats, including shortening, vegetable ghee, and margarine, in all cooking tasks.

*Palatability.* Recipients regard the bulgur as palatable, but since they feel that the daily consumption of maize is absolutely essential for health, they much prefer maize and do not use bulgur very frequently. Because other dishes are preferred, even if their consumption requires cash outlays by the household, only 6 of the 20 households completely consumed the total quantity of bulgur. The best-liked commodity in the package is the soybean salad oil. There was universal complaint that the amount provided is insufficient and that more should be given. All but one of the households had completely consumed the two-liter allocation, generally two to three weeks after receiving it.

CSM caused many complaints. Its yellow color leads many women to believe it is merely yellow maize flour, popularly regarded to be animal food or to be actually harmful to people. Every mother in the sample complained that the CSM causes diarrhea in her children. In only eight of the households was the entire quantity of CSM (6 kg) used to prepare special foods for young children. In most of the rest a portion of the CSM went to young children, but the 6 kg provided was not completely utilized. Several households used it to prepare gruel for the entire membership, for mothers as well as children, or for sick members, children and adults. In most cases all or some of the CSM was given away to friends, neighbors, or relatives rather than being fully utilized by the intended recipients.

*Intrahousehold Allocation.* The bulgur and oil are used in the preparation of dishes that are consumed by all members of the household except children under the age of one year. There is nothing to suggest preferential allocation of Title II or any other foods to particular household members. The only item in the ration package reserved for young children is the CSM, but this occurs in very few of the households because of mothers' concerns about its effects on their children.

*Sources of Other Foods Consumed.* While most of the staple food items are home grown, and the majority of the households were able to satisify the demand for maize, beans, and tubers from their own production, many other items have entered the Taita diet that can be purchased only with cash; in shops and in markets both, barter, or the trade of one food commodity for another, has completely disappeared. Most of the items ordinarily sold in the local shops have standard, government-controlled prices. Every household purchases sugar, salt, tea leaves, wheat flour, cooking fat, and meat. Other items purchased include fruit, milk, rice, potatoes, vegetables, bread, eggs, fish, coffee, cookies, soft drinks, and cakes. Relatively little of a given household's food needs is satisfied by non-cash-mediated interhousehold exchanges.

## Calorie and Protein Values of Title II Foods

Analysis of household records shows that, on average, each household actually consumed 16.3 kg of the bulgur it received, or 3.4 kg per household per week. Each bulgur meal on average contains 1.4 kg (1,400 gm) of bulgur; household calorie value of bulgur per meal is 4,650 kcal, with added oil 5,650 kcal. A garnish of beans adds 1,900 kcal to the family meal, greens 400 kcal, and meat about 1,000 kcal. The mean calorie value of a bulgur meal is 6,985 kcal; mean calories per household per week from bulgur meals, 16,765 kcal. Analysis of the comparative data from Msidunyi has already shown that bulgur replaces tubers and

TABLE 4.2
Percent Distribution of Expenditures on Food Budget

|                   | Mbuvhenyi | Msidunyi |
|-------------------|-----------|----------|
| Sugar             | 28.8      | 28.8     |
| Maize flour       | 10.0      | 38.0     |
| Wheat flour       | 7.8       | 9.5      |
| Cooking fat       | 11.2      | 6.6      |
| Condiments        | 6.8       | 4.5      |
| Meat/fish/eggs    | 18.5      | 8.6      |
| Milk              | 6.5       | 0.5      |
| Fruit/vegetables  | 6.6       | —        |
| Bread             | 2.8       | 3.5      |
| Other foods       | 1.2       | —        |
| Total             | 100.0[a]  | 100.0    |
| Mean food expense/household/week | Ksh 49.97 | Ksh 51.93 |

[a]Discrepancy due to rounding errors.

to a lesser extent maize in the local diet. The calorie values of the meals that bulgur replaces provide an aggregate total of 9,615 kcal per week, so that bulgur consumption gives a calorie increment of 7,150 kcal per household per week. The increment supplies 169 additional calories and 17 gm of protein per person per household per day.

CSM is directly substituted for porridge prepared with maize meal, and in similar quantities (up to 1/2 kg per preparation, making an amount that often lasts through the day and is reheated when needed). Since maize meal and CSM have the same calorie values (353 vs. 354 kcal per 100 gm edible portion), there is no discernible calorie advantage to CSM consumption. Even if CSM were targeted in its entirety to young children, the calorie result would be the same, because of the total substitution effect. CSM does, however, provide a protein advantage. An equivalent quantity of maize gruel would provide fewer than 5 gm of protein per child per day, while CSM provides over 10.

## Food Expenditure Patterns

Data on cash expenditures for food and non-food items were collected on a 24-hour recall basis for one week in each household. Analysis of these data reveals that in Mbuvhenyi over 70 percent of all available cash is spent on food, and that food expenditures average about Ksh 50 per household per week. In Msidunyi over 90 percent of money spent went for food purchases. Table 4.2 shows the comparative proportions of cash spent on different categories of foodstuffs per week.

Sugar consumes almost 30 percent of the food budget in each community. It is used mainly in the preparation of tea, but sugar is also added to the thin gruel made for young children more frequently than any of the other additives (e.g., salt, lemon juice, eggs, etc.). Soft drinks and sweets are also popular, although only two instances of the consumption of soft drinks were reported. Every household reported the consumption of heavily sweetened tea once or twice per day. The social and dietary importance of the beverage cannot be overstated. The large quantity of sugar consumed (over two kg per household per week), in addition to taking cash away from more nutritionally positive food purchases, undoubtedly contributes to the rising incidence of rampant dental caries in both children and adults. Since bulgur is substituted for tubers rather than for cereals, differential expenditure on maize cannot be attributed to the food-aid package.

## Health and Nutritional Status

The anthropometric data available are weight-for-age (W/A) figures for the 21 children in Mbuvhenyi, 37 children from the Msidunyi subsample households, and 169 children from a 100-household Msidunyi sample recruited for a long-term study of socioeconomic factors and nutrition. A comparison of percent of median W/A figures, using the National Center for Health Statistics (NCHS) reference standard (WHO 1983), for these three groups follows.

|  | Percent | Number |
|---|---|---|
| Mbuvhenyi | 81.6 | 21 |
| Msidunyi subsample | 76.5 | 37 |
| Msidunyi main sample | 78.2 | 169 |

As can be seen, as a group the children in the feeding program have a better mean W/A achievement than do those in either group in the comparison community. Another contrast is in the percent of children in each group with a W/A greater than 80 percent of the NCHS median:

|  | Percent | Number |
|---|---|---|
| Mbuvhenyi | 57 | 12 |
| Msidunyi subsample | 38 | 14 |
| Msidunyi sample | 46 | 77 |

One interpretation of the above findings is to take them as evidence that the food-aid program has had a positive impact on the nutritional health of participating children. Examination of the children's clinic charts, however, suggests little program influence on their growth. Recipient children have either maintained the same pattern of growth consistently since the time of entry into the program, or have experienced a decline in their W/A as a percent of the NCHS median. Although duration of program membership varies from 2 months to 31 months, there is no relationship between the length of participation and the nutritional status of the child as measured by W/A as a percent of NCHS median. It is therefore difficult to credit the program with any improvement in nutritional status. The data rather imply, as has been suggested elsewhere (see Stevens 1979:142), that self-selection among program participants yields recipients who are more receptive and more affluent and whose children are better nourished than others in the community even prior to the intervention. Patterns of self-reported illness episodes in the two communities also do nothing to explain the differences in observed anthropometric results. Malaria accounted for two-thirds of all cases of illness reported. Only one episode of gastroenteritis was reported, and the victim was an adult. Even though there have been recent reports that febrile illness is closely associated with short-term weight loss in children (Brown et al. 1985), the distribution of such illness between the two samples does not explain the poorer W/A picture among Msidunyi children.

## Summary and Conclusions

I have addressed the problem of incomplete knowledge and understanding of the dynamics of household-level commodity utilization by PL 480 Title II food-aid recipients by collecting and analyzing a body of detailed data from both recipient and nonrecipient households in the Taita Hills of Kenya. These data reveal that rural Taita households are quite diverse in demographic and socioeconomic particulars, varying with respect to size, composition, income-generating strategies utilized, cash income, and investment capacity.

With respect to the expressed objectives of food assistance, and the utilization of Title II foods, the following points can be made.

1. Income value of the ration, Ksh 131.63, augments total household income (cash plus food production) by between 5 and 20 percent. This figure is misleadingly high, however, since the ration during the study period was atypically large. When adjusted to account for unused quantities remaining and those given or thrown away, the income effect declines to Ksh 97.04, or an increment to household income of 4 to 15 percent. More meaningful is the 1 to 5 percent increment of Ksh 25.28 now received, since the ration quantity has been reduced to its former

level. The income effect is minor, certainly insufficient to promote economic development.

2. In all recipient households the ration serves a primarily substitutive rather than supplementary role. The bulgur is used in lieu of less-expensive, home-produced tubers rather than in lieu of maize meal, even when maize must be purchased. Hence taste preference seems to be a more important determinant of use than reallocation or reduction effects on food expenditures, or supplementation for nutritional improvement. In terms of calorie and protein values, the diet is enhanced by the consumption of bulgur and oil; CSM provides a small protein increment. The additional calories from bulgur and oil do not reach children under the age of one year, but other household members benefit, although not sufficiently to have an unequivocal impact on nutritional status.

3. The effectiveness of targeting to reach the poorest and most malnourished can be treated on two levels. So far as geographical targeting is concerned, Mbuvhenyi is not the ideal site. The food-aid recipients are more affluent and their children better-nourished than nearby nonrecipients, and Mbuvhenyi and environs certainly are not the most deprived area of Taita.

So far as targeting of items in the ration is concerned, only the CSM is to some extent reserved for consumption by nutritionally vulnerable household members. Bulgur and oil are freely available to all householders over about one year of age. There is nothing to suggest that such intrahousehold allocation is an artifact of the very large amount of bulgur received during the study period. The foods provided do not possess qualities that make them especially suitable for the young children and adult women who are supposed to be the principal beneficiaries of the program.

4. No conclusions can be reached about the differential utilization of Title II foods in different sorts of recipient households. Comparisons between rich and poor and between male- and female-headed households revealed no profound differences between the categories in their meal patterns, consumption practices, or sources of foods consumed in the home. The following observations may be made: targeting of CSM to young children is more effective in well-to-do households than in poor; the well-to-do spend substantially more money on food than do the poor, principally for non-staple food items such as milk and meat. A significant difference in food consumption between recipient and non-recipient households is the fact that bulgur provided by the Title II program substitutes principally for cheaper, low-status tuberous foods in the meal pattern. This finding confirms the significance of culturally conditioned food preferences in commodity selection, and further dilutes the income effect of the Title II foods. Replacement of tubers with bulgur

does provide a substantial increment in calories and protein to food-aid recipients. Both recipient and nonrecipient households spend the same amount of money per week on food, differentially allocated; the income effect of the ration package may permit the purchase of more meat, dairy products, and vegetables, but apparently also creates an artificially high demand for fats and oils.

At the local level it is clearly difficult to assess the program's ability to satisfy certain objectives of food aid, such as foreign policy or the creation of agricultural markets, but the provision of CSM, equated in the minds of recipients with yellow maize unsuitable for human consumption, does nothing to generate satisfaction or positive program evaluation among those recipients. Insofar as serving the poorest of the poor is concerned, Mbuvhenyi is by no means a deprived area. Examination of public records shows that it rarely suffers from the drought and food-production shortfalls that routinely afflict other parts of the district, because its relatively high altitude, widespread use of traditional irrigation, and large number of well-employed labor migrants ensure both food production capacity and cash income to purchase food during times of stress. If poverty, need, and failures of food production capacity are taken as the principal criteria of geographic targeting, Mbuvhenyi is a poor choice. This is not to say that the area entirely lacks needy and deserving individuals to whom food aid makes a real difference. It is to say, however, that if an objective of the program is to serve the greatest number of needy individuals, there are many other localities in Taita and in Kenya where that objective could be better served.

In the context of development, this program does not have a great deal to offer either by augmenting total household income significantly, by actively promoting development activities, or by combating protein-energy malnutrition and thus contributing to human capital formation.

Recipients view the proposed income-generating activities with suspicion and hostility because so much time has elapsed without action or progress since compulsory membership contributions were collected. In any event, the groups created are much too large to serve as effective vehicles for the promotion of cooperation and to avoid fragmentation, declines in membership, and financial problems. The fact that many current recipients have never exhibited a W/A below 80 percent NCHS median, or have not shown an improvement in their nutritional status despite long-term participation, indicates that protein energy malnutrition is not being effectively dealt with.

While there is little to show that this Title II MCH program is meeting the differing objectives and expectations held for it by beneficiary, donor, and PVO, there is no evidence that the program has negative effects on the recipients. Despite food aid, the households studied continue to produce most of their own food, so the rations cannot be said to function as a disincentive to agriculture or to foster dependence. Although local food preferences are not a criterion of commodity selection, the bulgur, oil, and CSM all nonetheless fit into existing dietary niches with greater or lesser degrees of success. While the particular combinations of foods provided may have increased consumption of fats and oils, these are still minor components of Taita diet. Nor is there any evidence of mismanagement, malfeasance, or deliberate exclusion of malnourished or needy individuals from participation.

Previous attempts to determine patterns of utilization of food aid (see Sahn et al. 1981; Katona-Apte 1984) have been based on data collected at the delivery point or on program-level (and program-supplied) statistics. The household context in which consumption occurs is not explored. These other studies have consequently not been able to provide direct evidence concerning the actual uses to which the food is put by the recipients. Substitution effects are assumed, rather than demonstrated; income effects are thought to be direct, and the importance of culturally determined food preferences is dismissed or underemphasized; while the undifferentiated poverty of food-aid recipients is assumed. My household-based anthropological study, on the other hand, has demonstrated that in one area of rural Kenya, Title II food aid is used as a substitute rather than a supplement; that income value of the food should not necessarily be the principal criterion for determining the content of ration packages; and that food-aid recipients are drawn from the relatively well-to-do as well as from the poor. These data were gathered and analyzed in a timely and cost-effective way. Similar studies from other regions clearly can contribute data essential to the formulation of appropriate food-aid policies.

## Notes

1. "Food aid" is the in-kind transfer of food from excess to deficit nations or regions. Such aid may be delivered in a number of different ways: as emergency relief to disaster victims; as a donation in support of health facilities, schools, or rural development activities; in the form of concessional sales to governments, who usually deliver the food to recipients through commercial channels, often at subsidized prices; or, in the form of either a donation or a concessional sale, as an incentive for policy reform.

2. This chapter is based on a report originally prepared for the Program, Policy and Evaluation Office, Bureau of Food for Peace and Voluntary Assistance, U.S. Agency for International Development. Support for data collection in Mbuvhenyi, as well as for the preparation of the report, was provided by USAID; data collection in Msidunyi was part of a long-term study, "Ecological Assessment of Nutritional Status in Taita, Kenya," funded by the National Institutes of

Health (HD13575–01 and amendments) and the Social Science Research Council. Special thanks go to Sister H. Mbando, Chief M. Irenge, Kim Lucas, Deborah Vrabel, and data-gatherers Donart Mwakio, Fergus Mnyanya, Elizabeth Righa, and Deborah Mchegu. The analysis and interpretations presented herein are entirely my own responsibility and do not represent the views of USAID or any other agency.

3. The communities have been given pseudonyms in order to protect the identity and confidentiality of informants.

## Acronyms

| | |
|---|---|
| CRS | Catholic Relief Services |
| CSM | Corn-soy milk |
| FFW | Food for work |
| FY | Fiscal year |
| MCH | Maternal and child health |
| NCHS | National Center for Health Statistics |
| NFDM | Nonfat dry milk |
| PVO | Private voluntary organization |
| SFP | School feeding program |
| USAID | United States Agency for International Development |
| W/A | Weight for age |

## References

Austin, J.
  1981   Nutrition Programs in the Third World: Cases and Readings. Cambridge, MA: Oelgeschlager, Gunn and Hain.

Brown, K., R. Black, A. Robertson, and S. Becker
  1985   Effects of Season and Illness on the Dietary Intake of Weanlings during Longitudinal Studies in Rural Bangladesh. American Journal of Clinical Nutrition 41:343–355.

Cook, J., and J. Csete
  1983   An Ethnographic Investigation into the Validity of the Notion of Contractual Obligation to Participate in the Government of Rwanda-Catholic Relief Services Nutrition Center Program. Report prepared for USAID.

Field, J., and M. Wallerstein
  1977   Beyond Humanitarianism: A Developmental Perspective on American Food Aid. *In* Food Policy. P. Brown and H. Shue, eds. Pp. 234–258. New York, NY: Free Press.

Fleuret, A.
  1985   Indigenous Taita Responses to Drought. Paper presented at the Annual Meeting of the American Anthropological Association, Washington, DC.

Harris, A.
  1972   Some Aspects of Agriculture in Taita. *In* Population Growth: Anthro-
         pological Implications. B. Spooner, ed. Pp. 180–189. Cambridge, MA:
         Massachusetts Institute of Technology Press.
Katona-Apte, J.
  1984   Analysis of Commodity Appropriateness for Bangladesh 2226. Report
         prepared for the World Food Programme.
Reutlinger, S.
  1984   Project Food Aid and Equitable Growth: Income Transfer Efficiency
         First. Paper prepared for the Subcommittee on Nutrition, Administrative
         Committee on Coordination, United Nations.
Sahn, D., B. Rogers, and D. Nelson
  1981   Assessing the Uses of Food Aid: PL 480 Title II in India. Ecology of
         Food and Nutrition 10:153–161.
Schuh, G.
  1981   Food Aid as a Component of General Economic and Development
         Policy. *In* The Developmental Effectiveness of Food Aid in Africa. Pp.
         69–90. New York, NY: Agricultural Development Council.
Shepherd, J.
  1985   Ethiopia: The Use of Food as an Instrument of U.S. Foreign Policy.
         Issue 14:1–9.
Stevens, C.
  1979   Food Aid and the Developing World. New York, NY: St. Martin's
         Press.
Tarrant, J.
  1980   Food Policies. New York, NY: Wiley.
WHO (World Health Organisation)
  1983   Measuring Change in Nutritional Status. Geneva: WHO.

# 5

## Drought and Famine Management in Kitui District, Kenya

### Joshua Akong'a

*The history of famine is long and dreadful.*

Thorkil Kristensen (1975:25)

### Introduction

During the 1970s and 1980s the people of Africa south of the Sahara experienced acute shortages of food due to widespread and prolonged droughts (Cook 1978:2). This happened despite the fact that famine need not be a logical consequence of drought. People in this region "try to plan against hunger, but they are usually unable to prevent its occurrence." Thus, "arid and semiarid conditions do not permit long-range subsistence planning. These conditions include the ecological limitation on the amount of food that each family can grow (and harvest) at any given time" (Ogbu 1973:3). This is why Peckolm noted that "droughts are an unavoidable" aspect of the arid environment. Though they cannot be predicted with any precision, they should never come as a shock (Peckolm 1975:142).

Yet although much of the recorded history of the Kamba people living in Kitui District is about severe droughts and famines, each has been handled as if it were not expected (O'Leary 1979; Government of Kenya 1981a:DP4–37; Akong'a 1982a). The human suffering that has been taking place in Kitui District, and the recognition that the majority of the people in the district live from hand to mouth, stimulated my interest in studying their response to drought and famine. The aims of the study were:

1. To examine how the people in the district have in the past coped with drought and famine

2. To identify the impact of drought and famine on interpersonal relations and on relations between the people and such external agencies as the government—to count the costs and to identify some of the attempts that have been made to minimize the costs of drought and famine

3. To examine some of the practical alternative solutions to the problems, identified within the framework of existing national food policy (Government of Kenya 1981b).

*Background*

Kitui District is located in a semiarid region of Kenya in Eastern Province. It is one of the six districts in the province, the others being Meru, Embu, Machakos, Isiolo, and Marsabit. It has an area of 29,123 square kilometers of which 6,039 are uninhabited since they are part of Tsavo National Park to the southeast. The district is hot and dry most of the year, with minimum mean annual temperatures varying from 14°C and 18°C (57.2°F and 64.4°F) in the western parts to 18°C and 22°C (64.4°F and 71.6°F) in the eastern parts of the district. The maximum mean annual temperatures on the other hand vary from 26°C and 30°C (78.8°F and 86°F) in the west to 30°C and 34°C (86°F and 93.2°F) in the east (Government of Kenya 1980a:3). On average, there are 20 wet days in a year, over the two planting seasons. From 1974 to 1978, for example, the mean annual rainfall for 20 recording stations was 464.14 mm (Government of Kenya 1981a:DP4–13). The people have to depend on rainfed agriculture, and the rainfall is grossly inadequate. Since much of the little rainfall falls within a few days (and causes rill and gully erosion), it is not only inadequate but also unreliable, the amount varying from one year to another and from one recording station to another.

In terms of potential land use, therefore, only 2.2 percent of the district land mass, receiving between 762 and 1,270 mm (30–50 inches) can be classified as high potential. This includes Mulango, Kisasi, Miambani and Matinyani locations of Central Division, in which Kitui Town, the district headquarters, is located. While 36.6 percent of the land mass, receiving 500–762 mm of rain (20–30 in.), is medium potential, 61.2 percent of the district is rangeland, suited only for livestock keeping.

*Methodology*

The information presented here is based on research carried out in 1980 and 1985. Several data-collection methods were used. First, historical data were collected by scanning government records in Kitui District archives in Kitui, Embu, and Nairobi. Second, a standard questionnaire was administered in 1980 to 345 household heads, of whom 74.5 percent were male and 25.5 percent female. The majority of the questions were open-ended, designed to elicit the respondents' own categorization of their socioeconomic and environmental predicament. The respondents were as widely scattered as possible, so as to cover all the parts of the district, as follows: southern, 19.4 percent; central, 21.2 percent; eastern, 22 percent; western, 19.1 percent; Mwingi (northern), 11.6 percent, and Kyuso (far north), 6.7 percent. Holding thematic discussions with elderly people either singly or in groups for supportive information was the third method of data collection.

## Causes of Drought and Famine

According to Nyaga Mwaniki, the phenomenon of drought and one of its major consequences, famine, "has been blamed on many factors, the most frequently mentioned being climate, environmental degradation, outmoded and inefficient traditional agricultural methods, customary land tenure, systems which inhibit innovation by individual farmers, lack of incentives to farmers to increase food outputs, bad agricultural policies, high population growth rates, and agrarian dualism" (Mwaniki 1986:210). Although there is strong evidence that inadequate and unreliable rainfall has been the major cause of drought in Kitui District, it is not the only factor that is responsible for famines. Other natural and man-made circumstances that impede food production and distribution include destruction of crops by locusts and birds, armed conflicts, national pride leading to deliberate concealment of drought and famine, apathy or non-action in attempting to alleviate food and water deficit, environmental degradation, and overemphasis on cash crop production for export (Hancock 1985). A historical account of the most memorable famines in Kitui District from 1897 to 1985 reveals that famine is persistent in the district and that coping strategies vary from one famine to another.

## Famines in History

One remarkable cultural phenomenon of the Kitui Kamba is that each major famine is remembered by its name, which describes how the people responded to it. In 1897, for example, a famine called locally as *lwaya*, rinderpest, broke out. The famine became prolonged and widespread. It came to be known as *nzaa tene* or *nzaa kubwa*, the big famine, or *ngomanisye*, meaning worldwide or widespread, since it also affected neighboring societies like the Kikuyu. In 1898, when a colonial post was established in Kitui Town, famine relief was brought in. The famine therefore came to be known as *magunia*, sacks of *mvunga*, rice.

The drought and famine were so severe that some people had to set aside their moral principles in order to survive. For example, pawning wives and daughters in neighboring societies in exchange for food became common. Some people thus nicknamed the famine *maseng'eng'e*, cheap wives. Pawning women in exchange for food credits has been observed not only in Kitui District, but also among the Lugbara of Uganda (Middleton 1965:6). This is how Kamba satellite clans emerged among the neighboring Kikuyu, Meru, Embu, and Mbeere societies.

People's definition of what was edible also changed for purposes of basic survival. Ambler created vivid images of what the people ate when he wrote:

> Animals became a main source of food; goats were held in store to be exchanged for grain. Men turned avidly to hunting; large groups from both sides of the Tana even met at the river to organize the killing of hippos. All kinds of wild fruits and berries became dietary staples, and small children spent their days foraging for these and the roots called *ngatu* that were prepared and eaten. But such actions were only stop-gap measures; they could not possibly support people through famine lasting several years. Indeed, the traditions recall that people were soon reduced to eating the skins that they slept on, their quivers and . . . slings (Ambler 1977:7).

Noting how desperate the situation was, the first African District Commissioner (ADC) in the district led a caravan of 5,000 people into neighboring districts in search of food. Even though the Kamba were familiar with these areas, security was required in order to protect the hunters from food piracy by roaming bands of hungry people.

In 1901, the famine of *malakwe*, beans, or *kilovoo*, rupee, surfaced. This was the time when money, more specifically, the Indian rupee, had been introduced by Arab and Swahili traders. In exchange for their commodities, the Kamba received money with which they bought beans, which they had neither seen nor eaten before.

The administration dealt differently with the famine that came in 1908. Instead of distributing maize, which had been moved from other districts in western Kenya, to people as famine relief, the administration forced headmen to purchase it in bulk, using their own money, and to sell it to famine-stricken families in order to recover the money.

In 1915, 1917, 1918 and 1928, locust swarms and *quelea* (weaver) birds destroyed the crops before the onset of drought and famine. The 1918 famine is remembered as *mukuna kiongo*, that which beats the head, because during the famine many people were struck by severe headaches, most probably cerebral menengitis. Many died of the disease. The 1918 famine is also associated with *vita kuu*, the big (First World) war. In fact, it is said that the disease started among men returning from the war.

The 1928 drought, on the other hand, is associated with extensive destruction of vegetation by locust swarms and is viewed by some old informants to have been the origin of *mang'alata*, pieces of land completely denuded of vegetation. They point out that the vegetation cover never recovered after 1928, and that this has led to the drying up of wells, springs, and rivers. The colonial administration, however, attributed *mang'alata* to overstocking.

During that famine, an estimated 30,000 people crossed the Tana River into neighboring districts through northern Kitui in search of food. An additional 5,000 left through southern Kitui for coastal settlements. In order to help the remaining population cope with the immediate problem, tax collection was deferred and road construction, which would assist in the importation of food, was accelerated. Road construction workers were given food in lieu of their cash wages.

The droughts and famines of 1929, 1932, and 1934 were also preceded by locust swarms. To assist the people, the administration not only provided maize and pigeon peas as famine relief but also deferred tax collection. For the first time, the administration confessed that taxation in the form of livestock as an indirect destocking measure was partly to blame for the hardships experienced by some families in coping with the famine. It deprived them of their major source of livelihood (Colony and Protectorate of Kenya 1931–1945).

Famine resurfaced in 1935 with far-reaching implications in terms of response and cost. It is remembered as *mavindi*, bones. During this famine, people collected animal bones, sold them to Asian shopkeepers, and used the money to buy food. According to O'Leary, the administration not only stockpiled food for sale but also arranged for livestock auctions. Through publicly arranged auctions, 20,698 head of cattle and 63,718 head of small stock (goats and sheep) were exported on the hoof (O'Leary 1979:89). Famine relief food was also provided in schools, dispensaries, and other public centers. One consequence of the famine was that many people emigrated. It was estimated that "a quarter of the population were still refugees in other districts, more especially Machakos, Embu and Meru" by the end of 1935 (Colony and Protectorate of Kenya 1935).

Further, a significant number of able-bodied men left the district for towns and sisal farms at Ruiru, Thika and Taita Taveta. Tax exemption was considered for the first time, and the ban on hunting wild game was temporarily lifted. The severity of the famine led to the official recognition that "the problem of recurring famines is most prominent and difficult of solution [in Kitui]. It is obviously a policy of despair to accumulate local native Council balances merely to deplete them by famine relief. . ." (Colony and Protectorate of Kenya 1936).

That many livestock were sold, died for lack of pasture and water, or were slaughtered for food, was viewed by the colonial administration as a blessing in disguise. They saw it as nature's solution to the overstocking problem, which the administration had failed to alleviate through peaceful or forceful means.

In 1939 came the famine of the Italian war, when the Kamba men participated in the clash between the British and Italians over Kenya's boundary with Somalia. It was followed by other famines in 1942, 1943, 1944, 1945, and 1946. These famines found the administration better prepared for quick importation of food from other districts. The famine of 1946 is remembered as *mutulumbu Katune* because the maize flour provided as famine relief was red in color. It was also referred to as *ndovoi*, boreholes, for this was the time the idea of sinking boreholes and constructing earth dams and wells was introduced.

During the famine of *makonge*, sisal, between 1949 and 1950, people in the northern, central, and western parts of the district sold sisal in order to buy food (Colony and Protectorate of Kenya 1951). In 1951, due to the persistence of food shortages, 4,920 tons of maize costing Ksh 2.8 million were imported from other areas. In 1955, widespread food, water, and pasture shortages led to large-scale food imports. During that year 30,000 cattle were exported on the hoof (Colony and Protectorate of Kenya 1955). Other exports included 117,049 goat and sheep skins, 102,858 poultry, beeswax, castor oil seeds, and hides (O'Leary 1979:94).

The famine that came in 1960–1961 was unique. First, it was a national, not a regional, famine. Second, it was brought about by a combination of drought and floods. Drought preceded a prolonged rainfall, which destroyed what would have been a good harvest. In Kitui District, the famine is remembered as the famine of *mbua*, rain, or of *ndege*, aeroplane, because food relief was dropped from helicopters since floods made roads impassable. The third unique characteristic of the famine was that, for the first time, a massive quantity of yellow maize from outside the country was imported. Such large-scale maize imports have been repeated during the 1979–80 and 1984–85 national famines, which also affected Kitui District adversely.

The monetary cost of such movement and distribution of food relief can be staggering. During the 1960–1961 famine, for example, "Kenya spent 12.5 million shillings on internally purchased maize and transportation alone" (Mbithi and Wisner 1972:5). In response to the 1976 famine, when Kitui District was receiving food relief at the rate of 8,000 to 10,000 bags of maize and 1,000 to 1,500 bags of beans a month in addition to other aid from church groups, educational institutions, and

TABLE 5.1
Responses in the Kitui District Survey to the Question:
What Does the Government Do to Assist People in the District During Famines?

| Response | Number of Household Heads (N = 345) | Percent |
|---|---|---|
| Controls food prices | 8 | 2.3 |
| Gives food to be sold in shop | 104 | 30.1 |
| Provides relief food | 289 | 83.8 |
| Does nothing | 86 | 24.9 |
| Other responses | 5 | 1.4 |

individuals, the government spent Ksh 2,177,560.25 toward relief food in the district alone. In that year, it was resolved that people had to be assisted to recover from the ravages of famine through the provision of seeds for planting.

In 1980–1981 Kitui District was once more caught up in a famine that affected directly or indirectly nearly every Kenyan. While people in semiarid regions were starving, those in high-potential regions were responding to the government's appeal for voluntary contributions in the form of money and foodstuffs to be sent into affected areas. The famine was caused by the combined effects of prolonged drought, hoarding of essential foodstuffs by businessmen, and smuggling of these foodstuffs across international boundaries.

In Kitui District, there was no distribution of free famine-relief food. Overcharging on foodstuffs was quite common, making it difficult for the majority of the people to afford the food. This was confirmed by responses to the question, "What does the government do to assist the people of this district to cope with recurrent famines?"

From the responses, as recorded in Table 5.1, it is evident that the government is perceived as responsible for bringing in as famine relief the food that is sold in the shops during famine. On the other hand, the government is perceived as doing very little to control food prices. This is partly why the 1980–1981 famine was nicknamed *nikwa ngwete*, I die holding (money), implying that food was not readily available even to those who had money with which to buy it. In accordance with free market behavior, the food that was available was exorbitantly priced (Akong'a 1982a:27).

During the 1984–1985 national drought and famine the government demonstrated its ability to manage effectively a famine that otherwise would have had devastating consequences for the nation. Of Kenya's 41 districts, 25, including Kitui, were famine stricken. Massive importation

TABLE 5.2
Responses in the Kitui District Survey to the Question:
How Have Droughts and Famines Affected You?

| Response | Number of Household Heads (N = 345) | Percent |
|---|---|---|
| 1. Not much | 5 | 1.4 |
| 2. Poverty has increased | 139 | 40.3 |
| 3. Social disorder increased | 70 | 20.3 |
| 4. Temporary migration (in search of food or work) | 60 | 17.4 |
| 5. Permanent migration | 144 | 41.7 |
| 6. Children drop out of school | 33 | 9.6 |
| 7. Loss of livestock | 57 | 16.5 |
| 8. Loss of human life | 76 | 22.0 |

of yellow maize from friendly nations was undertaken. To assist the government to offset the external debt from these imports, and to establish tree nurseries for its afforestation program, an internal famine relief fund was set up, which received contributions from all quarters of Kenya and from people of all walks of life.

Thus, through government administrative and transportation machinery, and the efforts of the National Famine Monitoring Committee, Kenya averted a catastrophe that had befallen her neighbors to the north, more particularly the Sudan and Ethiopia, where thousands of people died. Kenya's response demonstrated that famine need not arise as a logical consequence of drought if coordinated efforts of the local residents, the government, and the international community are mobilized in time. If peace and security are allowed to reign, the people's efforts can be channeled to solving the pressing human and environmental problems facing them. This is, however, impossible in war-torn countries such as Sudan, Ethiopia, and Chad.

## The Impacts of Drought and Famine

This brief history of drought and famine in Kitui District indicates that much of the efforts of the local people and the government have been directed toward coping with drought and famine rather than making tangible progress in the area of socioeconomic development. The result is that the people in the district are generally poverty stricken. A sample of responses to the question, "How have droughts and famines affected you?" appears in Table 5.2.

The table summarizes the major costs or implications of drought and famine in Kitui District. The loss of both human and livestock lives as a result of starvation and thirst is common in all drought and famine-prone areas. Between 1968 and 1974, for example, the Sahelian drought and famine killed an estimated 10,000 people (Torry 1984:228). In Kenya in 1984–1985, drought killed up to 50 percent of the livestock in pastoral districts (which include Kitui). The pastoral districts, which are in arid and semiarid regions of the country, constitute 75 percent of Kenya's land mass and contain 80 percent of all the livestock in the country. In fact, meat has generally been in short supply since that time, especially in urban areas, because it takes longer to recover from stock than from crop losses.

The costs of drought and famine are not only social and economic but also physiological and psychological. While human deaths in Kenya arising directly from starvation have been eliminated, a "famine weakened population is far more susceptible to other diseases including pneumonia, dysentery, tuberculosis, cholera, worms, and when rains do eventually come, malaria" (Miller 1974:12). Calorie malnutrition, or marasmus, the inadequate supply of heat-producing substances such as carbohydrates and fats, can only be eliminated if the victim is well fed. Lack of protein causes kwashiorkor in children. The symptoms include body swelling, hair turning red, and skin peeling. It can cause death. Kwashiorkor is severe in children up to 8 years of age, a most critical period when one grows fast not only in body mass but also in intellect. A shortfall in protein-containing food such as eggs or meat will cause a deficit in growth, because these are the food substances responsible for body building.

Vitamin deficiency during a famine is also very common. One significant effect of lack of vitamins—substances responsible for metabolic processes in the body—is the drying and ulceration of the eyes. This may cause xerophthalmia, which is responsible for night blindness. Iron deficiency, together with vitamin deficiency, is caused by lack of fruits and vegetables in the diet. Its symptoms are anemia and a lack of vitality. In arid and semiarid areas in general, fruits and vegetables are lacking in the diet.

Psychological effects of famine include "depression, apathy, and loss of initiative, accompanied by obsession with the idea of food" (Aykroyd 1970:18). A recent study of malnourished children of school age revealed that malnutrition dulls the emotions and curtails sociability. It may even lead to peer rejection (Gachiri 1986).

The people of Kitui District do not always suffer the whole range of the physiological and psychological problems related to deficiency in general food supplies, but they do live in a situation of persistent drought and famine. In fact, malnutrition is one explanation that we can attribute to spirit possession so common among the women, especially in northern Kitui (Akong'a 1987). People who have suffered from spirit possession belong to the cult of Nzambi, the female spirit with one leg, breast, eye and hand. When the spirit wishes to win an extra vessel into her company of followers, she afflicts the person with prolonged, apparently incurable illness until she brings her revelation that she is the source of the affliction. To become healed, the patient is attached to two witchdoctors, a male and a female, both of whom must be members of the cult, having suffered themselves from similar afflictions.

The patient is then given a drum from her natal home, a rattle of gourds, and a bow. A bow with arrows suggests masculinity, but this bow is without arrows, meaning that it is blunt, feminine, and impotent. After the woman receives the bow, however, she acquires some masculine characteristics. After getting healed, she is permitted certain activities normally expected of men, such as drinking beer and participating in rituals in the company of men. Receiving information from the underworld of Nzambi and advising the community what crops should be planted relative to the amount of precipitation expected is one of the major functions of the cult members.

Psychological and nutritional research carried out among the Zulu and Nguni of South Africa by Lee (1969) and Gussler (1972), indicates that *ukuthwasa*, or the crying disease, could be brought about in women by the "convergence of biological, environmental, and cultural factors" (Gussler 1972:87). The symptoms of *ukuthwasa* resemble those of spirit possession in Kitui, and the folk diagnoses of both afflictions are similar. In both, the problem is not considered biological but psychological and the patient has to accept the calling to serve the afflicting spirit, a process that transforms the patient not only into a medium or diviner but also an herbalist through prolonged training. The channeling of the affliction into culturally acceptable and useful behavior helps the patient to acquire a new personality. The common occurrence of spirit possession in Kitui District may be due to recurrent famine, making for shortfalls of certain nutritional elements, such as calcium, and producing sociopsychological and biological states similar to those observed in the politically oppressive, male-dominated South African ethnic groups studied by Lee and Gussler.

Table 5.2 shows that from the respondents' point of view, migration, either temporary or permanent, is a basic survival technique. Famine triggers population movements that destroy systematic, culturally controlled behavior patterns (Aykroyd 1970:18; Jellife and Jellife 1970:57). Some of these traditional patterns of survival become outdated, increasing future vulnerability. In the words of Torry, famine stretches institutionalized behavior to its limits, "revealing the extent of receptivity of social organization to new ideas and exposing the strengths and weaknesses of moral and legal controls under a full range of conditions of risk and stress" (1984:229).

In the general absence of employment opportunities within the district, one significant outlet of the excess population is migrant labor in urban centers. During the 1979 census, for example, 15.3 percent of the total population of 464,283 people born in Kitui District was found residing outside the district (Government of Kenya 1980b). Approximately two-thirds of these people were male, as is typical of a migrant population (Kalule 1985:74). The majority were economically dependent, for 50.6 percent were children below the age of 15, and to them we must add the population that is above 55 (retirement age in the civil service in Kenya is 55). One of the major implications of rural-to-urban migration is that it gives rise to "compound obstacles besetting anticipated or on-going development projects by altering the demographic composition of a region" and thus it contributes to the lack of self-sufficiency in food production. The wage remittances from the labor migrants are therefore critical to recovery from the deleterious effects of drought for those in rural areas, who use the money to buy food and replace lost livestock (Torry 1984:228).

A population more than half of whose members are under the age of fifteen manifests high fertility. High fertility is due to the predominance of the values that support having and claiming the custody of children. This is a sociocultural obligation some people cannot avoid, for they are obliged to succumb to levirate, woman to woman, ghost, and old-age marriages, which partly account for the prominence of polygyny. In a study carried out in neighboring Machakos District, which is also inhabited by the Kamba people, Kabwegyere and Mbula found that the incidence of polygyny varies directly with the age of the male household head. Out of a sample of 224 household heads aged between 20 and 40 years, 84 percent had one wife each while 16 percent had two wives or more. On the other hand, out of 125 household heads aged between 41 and 60 years, 64 percent had one wife each while 36 percent had two or more wives. Lastly, they found that out of the sample of 18 household heads aged over 61 years, 44 percent of them were married to one wife each while 56 percent had two or more wives (Kabwegyere and Mbula 1979:34). The implication is that polygyny is a social phenomenon that will disappear with time. Apart from age, the Kenya Fertility Survey of 1977–1978 also revealed that there is correlation between the level of education and polygynous marriage. Few highly educated women would like to be married as second or subsequent wives, just as highly educated men avoid marrying several wives (Government of Kenya 1980c:80).

In terms of social disorder, what Elizabeth Colson referred to as negative survival techniques emerge during a severe drought and famine (Colson 1960:54). Urban and village prostitution in exchange for food and shelter increases, giving rise to venereal diseases and more premarital pregnancies among teenage girls. Begging in market centers, abandonment of families by men or women who refuse to see their families suffer helplessly, and petty crimes also increase. The hardships experienced in Kitui and other arid and semiarid districts of Kenya would be sufficient justification for massive contraceptive use to limit family size. Statistical evidence suggests, however, that in Kenya more than 80 percent of a large sample of women know of at least one modern form of contraception (Government of Kenya 1984:65), but only 29 percent of all women in the sample, and 33 percent of ever married women in the sample, have ever used any form of modern contraception (Government of Kenya 1984:77). In some families, bridewealth for underage girls is hastily arranged and demanded, causing the persistence of child marriage. Dirks (1980) would say that such is the time when the individual rather than the family becomes the unit of survival.

## Reciprocity

Through reciprocity networks, married women play a significant role in the survival of the family in Kitui District. Reciprocity is mutual exchange of food and services. According to Marvin Harris (1965), reciprocal exchange has three distinctive features. First, there is no immediate return of the goods and services rendered; second, there is no systematic calculation of the value of the goods and services exchanged; and third, there is overt denial that a balance is calculated or anticipated.

While Harris implies the existence of a pure gift, let us say, a coin thrown to a beggar in the street, Marcel Mauss contends that there is no such thing as a pure gift. What appears in theory to be voluntary, disinterested, and spontaneous is, in fact, interested. That is, "total prestation not only carries with it the obligation to repay gifts received, but it implies two others equally important: the obligation to give presents and the obligation to receive them" (Mauss 1965:168–169).

Reciprocity among the Kamba of Kitui is not a purely economic exchange. Of course, the gifts involved are utilitarian commodities such as sugar, maize, beans, flour, cowpeas, and pigeon peas, measured in calabashes, dishes, or cups in anticipation that an equal amount will be returned. Paraffin is measured in bottles or poured directly into the lamp brought by the debtor without getting its exact measure. Before manufactured commodities became essential for basic survival, only locally produced goods featured in the exchange. However, pumpkins and bananas have never featured significantly in the exchange, probably because they were rare and a loan of such a commodity would have been difficult to repay in kind. What is surprising to the author as an outsider is that although salt is a very basic and desirable commodity, it is never loaned. This is the converse of what happens in other ethnic groups such as the Luo and the Luyia in western Kenya, among whom salt, flour, cooked and green vegetables, and embers of fire or several match sticks are the only loanable commodities. People can beg and can be given other commodities as gifts, not on a loan basis.

In Kitui District, food is borrowed or loaned on behalf of children, who are viewed as innocent victims of circumstances. (During times of famine, children are given two meals in a day, while adults have only one.) Thus, reciprocity minimizes the deleterious effects of famine and, at the same time, engenders personal obligation, gratitude, and mutual trust among the givers and receivers (Blau 1964:94). In many Kenyan societies, however, debtors of such loans are never reminded of their loans, the use of the word "loan" is simply an idiom of reciprocity, and more often than not, the loan is never repaid. In fact, reminding a person of the loan or debt is very rude and is intended to remind the person of his or her family's poverty. It is therefore done only under exceptional circumstances of economic deprivation on the part of the creditor, as when the debtor is in a better economic condition than the creditor.

The most organized form of reciprocity is manifested in the predominantly female mutual work groups known as *mwethya*. Through mwethya, women help each other in performing farm and other work, such as thatching houses. Today, many of these groups are mobilized by the administration for cooperative construction of schools, dispensaries, and watering places. Other groups have become multipurpose, serving the traditional roles and generating income for members through bricklaying, cooperative sale of traditional baskets (*ciondo*), and performing as dance groups. The mwethya group therefore provides married women with a forum for identifying with each other's problems and doing something practical about them. It also provides emotional satisfaction through singing, dancing, eating, and talking in the course of performing their duties.

In the past, it was not simply internal reciprocity networks that helped some families survive through the exchange of essential commodities and information about where food was, but also long distance external trade (Cummings 1976; Jackson 1976). The Kamba exchanged arrow poisons, livestock, hides and skins, pottery, dyes, and iron implements for yams, beans, cereals, and sweet potatoes with their Kikuyu, Embu, and Meru neighbors. From the Swahili, they received cotton fabrics,

TABLE 5.3
Responses in the Kitui District Survey to the Question:
What Would You Do if You Were Warned of a Forthcoming Drought or Famine?

| Response | Number of Household Heads (N = 345) | Percent |
|---|---|---|
| 1. Save money to buy food | 254 | 73.6 |
| 2. Sell livestock to buy food | 46 | 13.3 |
| 3. Stay and see (persevere) | 45 | 13.0 |
| 4. Work for food | 17 | 4.9 |
| 5. Improve farming | 15 | 4.3 |
| 6. Migrate | 6 | 1.7 |
| 7. Stop wasting time on the farm | 5 | 1.4 |

beads, copper and brass wires, pepper, and salt in exchange for ivory. According to Cummings, "trading . . . served primarily to raise their living standards through increased trading commodities, and also to raise their socioeconomic prestige while supplementing their existing food supplies" (1976:87).

Through past experience the people in the district reckon that their problems stem mainly from natural causes that they or the government can do little to alleviate. Of the respondents to the Kitui survey, 69.9 percent said that crop failures are likely to occur in the future due to drought; 6.1 percent indicated that there are no possibilities of future crop failures; while 24.1 percent did not respond to the question.

Asked to name their sources of food whenever famine occurs, 92.8 percent said they obtain food by buying it. The validity of this response was tested by asking the respondents what they would do if they were warned of a forthcoming drought and famine. Nearly three-quarters said they would save money to buy food. See Table 5.3.

Buying food is therefore a basic survival strategy in Kitui District. The question is whether the majority of the people can do so with ease. Families that have some members on migrant labor elsewhere can benefit from small amounts of cash remittances. The rest rely on the sale and slaughter of livestock, if they have any. O'Leary came to the same conclusion when he observed that "overall the one most important means of surviving drought periods nowadays is the purchase of food by cash; and the cost of food purchase is primarily met from the sale of livestock and wage remittances" (O'Leary 1980:96).

Since livestock is central in the family economy as a source of income for food, school fees, clothes, and household equipment, it is unfortunate that livestock keeping will not persist for long in the district due to the diminishing size of pasture land, increasing population, and increasing cost of living. The people of the district are not likely to become self-sufficient in food production unless there is a breakthrough in semiarid agricultural or pastoral technology. Agricultural and pastoral development programs in the past have attempted to treat both the disease and its symptoms without much success in attaining self-sufficiency in food production.

## Food and Livestock Production

In the area of crop production, maize, a very risky crop, has almost replaced the traditional early maturing crops such as sorghum and millet. If manure were used in planting maize—it is not—the yield would be good in a good season. Otherwise, commercial fertilizers are too expensive for people to afford. The traditional crops suffer from disadvantages, too. They require extra labor, which is not always available, for chasing birds away from them. Bananas, yams, and sugarcane are grown only in the few wet river valleys, while cash crops, such as coffee, cotton, and tobacco, are limited in acreage because they require so much in the way of inputs and caretaking that they are not economically viable. Pigeon peas, suitable for the whole district, take two whole seasons to mature, although it is hoped that the pygmy variety developed by the University of Nairobi, which can mature in only one season, will soon be introduced to farmers. It would also be of significant economic benefit if farmers were encouraged to try sesame and groundnuts as cash and food crops.

Livestock keeping, on the other hand, has been an important economic activity. The survey that was carried out in 1980 revealed that of the 345 household heads interviewed, 75.1 percent owned livestock and 68 percent of those who owned livestock had sold some within eight months prior to the survey.[1] During the colonial era, steps were taken to prop up traditional pastoralism by closing Kitui District to white settlement and by introducing relevant development programs. Two rotational grazing schemes were initiated for the people of Kitui District in the Yatta plains, which had previously been set aside for white settlements. These were B2 Yatta and Athi-Tiva grazing schemes, in which fees were paid for every animal grazed and where watering facilities had been provided. Water was provided from Thika by the Yatta Furrow, which was constructed between 1956 and 1959 using Mau Mau detainees (Akong'a 1982b).

The purpose of these ambitious efforts was to relieve pressure in Central Kitui, which had become overgrazed due to higher population, and thus to upgrade the quality of livestock before sale so that they could fetch higher prices. The grazing schemes have since become individual, group, company, or cooperative ranching schemes, implying that there is no systematic policy as to which of the ranching schemes is suitable for Kitui District.

A good system of grazing must be able to prevent the spread of contagious livestock diseases through the use of dips, vaccination, and quarantines; minimize overgrazing through a system of rotation; guarantee regular offtake when livestock are in good health instead of receiving throw-away prices during drought and famine; and use ranches as security for obtaining investment loans. Today livestock keeping faces acute problems in the district. Water and pasture are insufficient and unevenly distributed. Veterinary services are sorely inadequate. On ranches, major constraints are bush encroachment, antagonism among the owners, misappropriation of funds, diminishing land size, and labor shortage. Labor is a constraint for both crop and livestock production because many men are away on migrant labor and children are at school. Women are therefore overloaded with work (O'Leary 1980:221).

## Water Harvesting

Large-scale irrigated agriculture has never been conceived since colonial days, because the two permanently flowing rivers, the Tana on the northern boundary and the Athi on the southern boundary, flow only peripherally to the district, and thus the district never has an abundance of water. Usually, when news of the occurrence of drought and famine are reported in the mass media, response for food relief is spontaneous in Kenya, but it is easily forgotten that areas experiencing acute shortages of food also lack water for human and livestock use. And yet a person can survive longer without food than without water (Wilson et al. 1959).

In Kitui District, sources of water are few. They include springs located close to hills, seasonal rivers, weirs, and rock and roof catchment storage tanks. Thus the Kenya government's objective of having an adequate water supply available to the entire population soon after the year 2000 may not be realized in such areas as Kitui district. In fact, "there will be little public health benefits from a water supply which does not provide water in adequate quantity and quality and in a way convenient to the population" (Wagner and Lanoix 1959:10).

Water-borne diseases, including diarrhea, worms, and dysentery, accounted for about 75 percent of all the diseases treated at hospitals in Kitui District. Diseases that arise from the general state of sanitation, such as leprosy, tuberculosis, and cholera, are also very common, implying that increasing the availability of clean water would greatly improve the general health of the people.

Paying attention to the quality of the water available to a population is important, partly because 65 percent of the body weight comes from water (Wilson et al. 1959:203). When the United Nations launched its world drinking water sanitation decade, it was revealed that "dirty water and lack of sanitation help cause 80 percent of the world's diseases" (Sunday Nation 1980:8). Because of the acute shortage of water of any kind in Kitui District, people do not seem to pay much attention to its state, yet improving its quality is not beyond the people's means. It can be filtered using a clean rag, boiled, and then stored in pots. Experience from western Kenya among the Luo and Luyia indicates that storing water in a pot not only makes it cold and therefore palatable, but also makes the remaining sediment settle.

It is possible that a definite increase in the amount of water available to the population would increase the people's concern for the quality of the water consumed. To this end, international aid agencies such as USAID and DANIDA (Danish International Development Agency) are reinforcing local efforts to increase water sources. In order to avoid environmental degradation by sinking too many wells, which in the long run may lower the water table, emphasis should be placed on harvesting rainwater through rock and roof catchment. Finding a solution to the water problem will affect the work regime in the district. For example, the labor and time spent walking long distances to watering places would be redeployed in other critical areas—herding, cultivating, cleaning, trading, and participating in cooperative and self-help activities.

## Environmental Degradation

The last impact of drought and famine to be mentioned in this chapter, environmental degradation, is caused partly by human activities and partly by natural factors. In Kitui District, former rangelands, marginal for agricultural purposes, have been exposed to wind and water erosion through settlement and cultivation that stem from population pressure and the desire to cultivate large plots of land in case the season turns out to be good. Marginal agriculture is in direct competition with pastoral practices. For example, with the individualization of land in central and southern parts of the district through land adjudication and registration, it has become impossible to continue the practice of taking livestock away to the dry-season common grazing grounds, *kyengo*. Instead, the trend has been reversed in some areas. During the rainy season livestock are grazed on public land such as roads and marketplaces, and during the dry season they are grazed on individual plots of land where trespass is carefully monitored and prosecuted.

In some African societies, environmental degradation is made worse by the lack of clear policies aimed at environmental restoration through afforestation and measures to conserve soil and water. During the 1950s, a program generally referred to as the Kitui Betterment Scheme was established by the then African Land Development Board for the purpose of conserving soil and reclaiming eroded areas (African Land Development Board 1962). The scheme involved the following:

1. the closure of overgrazed or severely eroded areas to agricultural or grazing purposes;
2. the deployment of traditional female work groups (mwethya) in plowing the closed land;
3. the scattering of seeds of wild grasses;
4. the use of oxen to pull branches of thorny trees to harrow in the seeds;
5. the fencing of ploughed areas to allow for regeneration; and
6. the imposition of fines on trespassers by local chiefs.

These efforts were continued within the national effort of afforestation led by the president of the country. In 1982, for example, President Daniel Toroitich Arap Moi led all the members of Parliament into Matinyani location of Central Kitui District to demonstrate to the local people and the nation how strongly committed the government is to soil and water conservation programs. According to one report,

> Soil degradation in cultivated areas could be greatly reduced by terracing, grass stripping, trash lining, vegetative edges, contour cultivation, strip cropping, the proper use of fertilizers, the incorporation of organic matter (including resting of cropped areas) and by minimizing clearing by fire. Studies have proved that practices that reduce soil degradation also increase crop yields. In cultivated areas, erosion could be minimized by maintaining vegetation cover (Government of Kenya 1981a:DP4–9).

## Practical Alternative Solutions

This study has revealed that there are direct and indirect causes of drought and famine. There are also direct and indirect costs or implications of these phenomena, implying that their eradication can be no easy task. It calls for direct methods that bring about short-term solutions, such as famine-relief food provision and purchase of food. The more long-term solutions have been attempted through indirect methods, such as agricultural, pastoral, and environmental-conservation development programs. The eradication of the problem of famine in Kitui District can therefore only be achieved within a national rather than regional framework. That is, if marginal agricultural practices were avoided in Kitui District in favor of commercial livestock keeping, the people in the district could obtain the required grains from agriculturally high-potential areas in exchange for livestock sales. Thus, the implementation of the national food policy of 1981 should encourage regional specialization in production and interregional commercial exchanges through such established government machinery as the Kenya Grain Growers Cooperative Union and the Kenya Meat Commission. There should also be local or district famine monitoring committees to report instances of famine, or its absence, to the national committee. As we have learned from the national famines in the 1980s, it would also be appropriate for Kenya to formulate a national famine-relief policy to be implemented whenever a local or national famine is reported. This will keep the nation on a state of alert so that famine-relief food can reach those affected before it is too late. Kenya's recent success in managing famines should be an encouragement toward even more preparedness for future calamities.

## Notes

1. Compare these figures with those presented by Mbithi and Wisner, who observed that "in our Kitui sample of 120 farmers only 53 percent owned cattle because, as many explained, they had just sold the last of their cattle this year to make ends meet. Fifty-nine percent owned goats and sheep" (Mbithi and Wisner 1972:23).

## References

African Land Development Board
　1962　African Land Development: 1946–1962. Nairobi: Government Printer.
Akong'a, Joshua
　1982a　Famine, Famine Relief and Public Policy in Kitui District. Working Paper No. 388, Institute of Development Studies, University of Nairobi.
　1982b　Persistence and Continuity in Traditional Pastoralism in Kitui District of Kenya. African Journal of Sociology 2(2).
　1987　Rainmaking Rituals: A Comparative Study of Two Kenyan Societies. In African Study Monographs, 8(2):71–85. Kyoto: The Centre for African Area Studies, Kyoto University.
Ambler, Charles H.
　1977　The Great Famine in East Central Kenya 1897–1900: A Regional View. Nairobi: The Historical Association of Kenya Annual Conference, 1977. Department of History, University of Nairobi.
Aykroyd, W. R.
　1970　Definition of Different Degrees of Starvation. In Famine: Dealing with Nutrition and Relief Operations in Times of Disaster. A Symposium of the Swedish Nutrition Foundation. Gunnar Blix, et al., eds.

Blau, Peter
    1964    Exchange and Power in Social Life. New York: Wiley.
Colony and Protectorate of Kenya.
    1931–1945   Kitui District Annual Report. Handwritten daily file, Kitui District
            Commissioner's Office Archives, Kitui Town.
    1935    Kitui District Annual Report. Handwritten daily file, Kitui District
            Commissioner's Office Archives, Kitui Town.
    1936    Kitui District Annual Report. Handwritten daily file, Kitui District
            Commissioner's Office Archives, Kitui Town.
    1951    Kitui District Annual Report. Handwritten daily file, Kitui District
            Commissioner's Office Archives, Kitui Town.
    1955    Kitui District Annual Report. Handwritten daily file, Kitui District
            Commissioner's Office Archives, Kitui Town.
Colson, Elizabeth
    1960    Social Organization of the Gwembe Tonga. London: Manchester University Press.
Cook, H. J.
    1978    The Problem of Drought in Botswana. Gaborone, Botswana: National
            Institute for Research in Development and African Studies Documentation Unit. Working Paper No. 17.
Cummings, Robert
    1976    The Development of Akamba Local Trade History, 1780–1920. Kenya
            Historical Review: The Journal of the Historical Association of Kenya
            4(1).
Dirks, Robert
    1980    Social Responses During Severe Food Shortages and Famine. Current
            Anthropology 21(1):21–44.
Gachiri, Joyce Wanjeri
    1986    Malnutrition and Later Life. B.A. Dissertation, Department of Sociology,
            University of Nairobi.
Government of Kenya
    1980a   Kitui District Development Plan 1979–1983. Nairobi: Ministry of Planning and Development.
    1980b   Kenya Population Census, 1979. Vol. 1. Central Bureau of Statistics,
            Ministry of Planning and National Development. Nairobi: Government
            Printer.
    1980c   Kenya Fertility Survey Report, 1977–1978, Central Bureau of Statistics,
            Ministry of Planning and National Development. Nairobi: Government
            Printer.
    1981a   Kitui District Environmental Assessment Report. Nairobi: National
            Environment Secretariat, Ministry of Environment and Natural Resources.
    1981b   Sessional Paper No. 4 of 1981 on National Food Policy. Nairobi:
            Government Printer.

1984    Kenya Contraceptive Prevalence Survey, 1984, First Report. Nairobi: Central Bureau of Statistics, Ministry of Planning and National Development.

Gussler, Judith
1972    Nutrition and Behaviour: Ecological Factors and Possession Illness in South Africa. Rural Africana: Current Research in Social Sciences, Rural Health in Africa. A Publication of the African Studies Center, Michigan State University. Simon and Messing, eds. Winter.

Hancock, Graham
1985    Ethiopia: The Challenge of Hunger. London: Victor Gollancz, Ltd.

Harris, Marvin
1965    Culture, Man and Nature. New York: Crowell.

Jackson, K.
1976    The Dimensions of Kamba Pre-Colonial History. *In* Kenya Before 1900: Eight Regional Studies. B. A. Ogot, ed. Nairobi: East African Publishing House.

Jellife, Derrik B., and Patrice E. F. Jellife
1970    The Effects of Starvation on the Function of the Family and Society. *In* Famine: Dealing with Nutrition and Relief Operations in Times of Disaster. A Symposium of the Swedish Nutrition Foundation.

Kabwegyere, Tarsis, and Judith Mbula
1979    Changing African Family Project Series: A Case of the Kamba. Monograph No. 5. Canberra: Australian National University.

Kalule, Henry
1985    Demographic Profile of Kitui District. *In* Kenya Socio-Cultural Profiles: Kitui District Draft Report. Joshua Akong'a, ed.

Kristensen, Thorkil
1975    An Assessment of the Assessment. *In* Hunger, Politics and Markets: Issues in the Food Crisis. Sartaj Aziz, ed. New York: New York University Press.

Lee, S. G.
1969    Spirit Possession among the Zulu. *In* Spirit-Mediumship and Society in Africa. John Middleton, ed. London: Routledge and Kegan Paul.

Mauss, Marcel
1965    Reciprocity. *In* Theories of Society. Talcott Parsons, et al., eds. New York: The Free Press.

Mbithi, P. M. and B. Wisner
1972    Drought and Famine in Kenya: Magnitude and Attempted Solutions. Discussion Paper No. 144, Institute of Development Studies, University of Nairobi.

Middleton, John
1965    The Lugbara of Uganda. New York: Holt, Rinehart and Winston.

Miller, Norman
1974    Food and Drought in Ethiopia-Kenya Borderlands. *In* North Eastern Africa Series, Vol. XIX, No. 4. New York: American Universities Field Staff, Incorporated.

Mwaniki, Nyaga
  1986    Against Many Odds: The Dilemmas of Women's Self-Help Groups in
          Mbeere, Kenya. Africa: 56(2):210–228.
Ogbu, John U.
  1973    Seasonal Hunger in Tropical Africa as a Cultural Phenomenon. The
          Onicha Ibo of Nigeria and Chakaka Poka of Malawi Example. Africa
          43(4):317–332.
O'Leary, Michael F.
  1979    Variation and Change Amongst the Kitui Kamba: A Comparative Study
          of Two Vicinages. Ph.D. thesis, University of Manchester.
  1980    The Growth and Decline of Household Herds in Eastern Kitui, Kenya.
          Ethnos 45(3–4).
Peckolm, Erick
  1975    Desertification: A World Problem. Ambio: A Journal of the Human
          Environment Research and Management 4(4). Royal Swedish Academy
          of Sciences, University of Laget.
Sunday Nation (newspaper)
  1980    Nairobi, Kenya. November 2, page 8.
Torry, William L.
  1984    Social Sciences Research in Famine: A Critical Evaluation. Human
          Ecology: An Interdisciplinary Journal 12(3).
Wagner, E. G., and J. N. Lanoix
  1959    Water Supply for Rural Communities. Geneva: World Health Orga-
          nization.
Wilson, Eva D., et al.
  1959    Principles of Nutrition. New Delhi: Wiley and Eastern.

# 6

## Insect and Weed Control in Subsistence Farming Systems: Western Kenya

*W. Thomas Conelly*

### Introduction

Agricultural pests, especially insects and weeds, play an important role in the chronic underproduction that characterizes many East African farming systems. Though research to control crop pests began soon after the establishment of colonial rule in East Africa, a practical and truly effective method of pest management for subsistence farmers has yet to emerge. Chemical controls, available since the 1940s and widely applied to export crops such as coffee and cotton, have never been an economically feasible option for small-scale farmers for protecting food crops such as maize or sorghum. Recognizing the economic and environmental shortcomings of insecticides and herbicides, various national and international research organizations have recently initiated programs in "integrated pest management" that target specific pest problems in the region, but much additional research is needed before these programs will provide tangible benefits to farmers.

This chapter focuses on Mbita Division, a low-rainfall farming region in South Nyanza District of western Kenya. The Mbita area illustrates the significant threat that pests can pose to basic food security and agricultural development, with particular reference to semiarid environments in East Africa. The chapter documents the severity of pest hazards in Mbita Division both now and during the colonial period when the first agricultural development programs were initiated in the area. Focusing on insect pests and the parasitic weed *Striga hermonthica*, it then discusses the traditional pest control practices of subsistence farmers and the difficulty of integrating into the local farming system the pest management recommendations developed by agricultural scientists that form the basis of current government policy. Finally, it examines the potential for introducing alternative "integrated pest management" techniques such as resistant crop varieties and intercropping.

The data discussed in this chapter are based on historical materials located in the Kenya National Archives, Nairobi, as well as anthropological and agronomic research conducted in South Nyanza District during 1984 and 1985 when I was affiliated with the International Centre of Insect Physiology and Ecology (ICIPE) in Kenya, an organization conducting research on integrated pest management techniques for the control of crop and livestock pests in the tropics (see Conelly 1985, 1987). Throughout, the chapter emphasizes the importance of understanding pest management strategies within the broader context of the overall farming system and the necessity of considering farmers' goals and priorities in order to develop appropriate and effective policies for pest control.

## Research Area

Mbita Division is a semiarid agricultural area located along the shores of Lake Victoria in South Nyanza District of western Kenya. As in many parts of the country, rainfall is bimodal in distribution, with a "long rains" from March through early June and a "short rains" from October to December. Though the average rainfall in Mbita ranges between 700 and 900 mm/yr, precipitation in most parts of the division is highly unreliable; and, especially along the lakeshore and on Rusinga Island, rainfall is sufficient for only a single cropping season during the long rains. The climate, vegetation, and agricultural productivity of Mbita contrast strongly with the higher elevation inland areas of the district and the adjacent Kisii highlands where rainfall and agricultural potential are noticeably greater.

The population density in Mbita ranges from less than 100 persons/ sq km in the hilly inland areas to well over 200 persons/sq km on Rusinga Island. Maize and sorghum are the main subsistence crops produced in the division. These crops are usually grown in intensively cultivated fields, prepared either by hoe or cattle-drawn plow, with little or no fallow period. Intercropped legumes, including cowpea and green gram in the drier lakeshore areas and beans and groundnuts in the wetter inland areas, are also major crops. Cassava and some sweet potato are produced as well, especially on sandy soils near the lake. Sugar cane, vegetables (kale, onions, tomatoes), bananas, and fruit trees (papaya, citrus, mango) are grown in a few areas with higher soil moisture, such as along swamp margins and streambeds and adjacent to the lake, especially in years with good rainfall. Cotton is the only export crop in the division, but its production is limited to the moister inland areas. Though there is some marketing of farm produce, in general Mbita is a food-deficit area in which farmers rely on imports of basic food commodities from outside the division.

## Pests as a Constraint to Production—The Colonial Period

Reports by district and agricultural officers early in the century commonly remarked on the poor agricultural performance of what is today called Mbita Division, particularly as it compared with the high productivity of the nearby Kisii highlands. Initially, government officials blamed the low yields on the laziness and conservatism of local farmers and their strong preference for raising livestock over farming (e.g., KNA 1912, 1914).[1] Between the two world wars, however, as the British gained more experience in the region, environmental factors, including recurrent drought and a variety of crop pests, were most often cited as the causes of underproduction in Mbita Division.

During the 1920s and 1930s, concern about serious pest problems was frequently expressed in government reports. Wild animals, including elephants and hippos, as well as smaller animals such as porcupines, monkeys, and baboons, were mentioned in nearly every report during this period as a serious menace to production. Game protection laws and restrictions on traditional hunting practices made it difficult to control animals destroying farmers' crops. A District Commissioner from South Kavirondo (now South Nyanza) reported that "at every turn I am faced with complaints with regard to destruction of crops by vermin and game, and I feel that if we are to be successful in our endeavours toward increased production, we must take steps to assist the people" (KNA 1935).

During the same period the first references to *Striga hermonthica*, a parasitic weed that attacks the roots of maize and sorghum, began to appear in government reports for the lakeshore areas of Nyanza Province. During the next two decades striga became a major cause for concern, and strict rules for its elimination by uprooting before seed dispersal were developed. Officers working in the area reported that "probably the worst pest in South Nyanza is Striga" (KNA n.d.a) and that "last year thousands of pounds of maize, . . . [sorghum], and . . . [finger millet] were lost owing to . . . [striga]. We cannot afford this, particularly in those areas . . . where it is possible to grow only one crop a year" (KNA 1935–1950a).

In subsequent years, agricultural officers repeatedly commented on the seriousness of striga in South Nyanza and complained of the unwillingness of farmers to uproot the weed before it set seed as was required by the Plant Protection regulations. The Nyanza Province Agricultural Officer commented that "so deep rooted is the belief that it is impossible to control the weed that even under the [Plant Protection] Rules [farmers accept] punishment in a fatalistic way. . . . Large numbers of offenders are fined up to Ksh 25 each during the crop ripening periods" (Watt 1936).

In addition to losses caused by wild animals and striga weed, a variety of insect pests further reduced agricultural production in Mbita. These insects fell into two categories: (1) those that were periodic in appearance, such as locusts and armyworm, with the potential of causing severe crop loss, and (2) those chronic in occurrence, such as stem borers, that generally resulted in yearly but slight-to-moderate damage.

The 1929–31 locust plague, which devastated farming throughout much of Kenya, had serious consequences for Mbita farmers. In April 1931 the District Officer for South Nyanza reported that:

> the situation appears far more serious than was at first supposed. Locusts appear to have laid in vast quantities in locations bordering the lakeshore and the hoppers are now moving inland in an easterly direction. . . . [S]hamba after shamba of . . . [finger millet] and young . . . [sorghum] have been wiped out (KNA 1931a).

Thousands of local inhabitants were mobilized by the government to oppose the advance of the locusts, but these efforts failed and crop losses were severe, especially in the lakeshore region. "Famine conditions began to be apparent during May and the situation became acute in June. . . . [Farmers] received 1,695 tons of maize during the year and paid only 47 percent of their tax. These facts indicate the serious nature of the famine" (KNA 1931b).

Though locust swarms were reported in South Nyanza intermittently during the following decades, the devastating losses of 1931 did not occur again. Other insect pests, however, continued to disrupt agricultural production. In roughly one or two years out of five, African armyworm larvae (*Spodoptera exempta*), which periodically swarm in tremendous numbers attacking the seedlings of maize, sorghum, and finger millet, were reported in the annual district agriculture report to be the cause of considerable crop loss, especially in the drier areas of Mbita Division.

Stem borers (primarily *Busseola fusca* and *Chilo partellus*), the larvae of moths that feed on the stalks of both sorghum and maize, also began to receive yearly mention in the late 1930s. Initial damage by stem borers occurs when the young larvae begin to feed on the leaves. More mature larvae bore into the developing stem, causing damage by extensive tunnelling. In severe cases of infestation, plant growth is stunted and grain production may be reduced significantly (Teetes et al. 1983).

Though serious outbreaks of stem borer were reported in European farming areas in the Rift Valley and western Kenya during this period (Anderson 1929; KNA 1937–1948), in South Nyanza during the 1930s and 1940s damage from stem borers was usually described as "slight" or "negligible" except for occasional more serious localized outbreaks (KNA 1935–1950b). In recent years, however, stem borers have developed into a major pest along the lakeshore and on the islands of Lake Victoria.

## Pests as a Constraint to Production—1985

Despite decades of research on pest management, the availability of chemical controls since the 1940s, and government policies to limit the spread of pest hazards, pests remain today a significant constraint to agricultural production in Mbita Division, especially in the drier lakeshore areas. A survey of farmers in 1984 revealed that wild animals, including hippos, monkeys, baboons, porcupine, and wild pig, continue to be a hazard that can result in serious crop losses in fields that are not carefully guarded. Likewise, birds are reported to be a persistent, though generally moderate, hazard to production, especially in areas where large colonies of weaver birds (*Ploceus* spp.) are found (Conelly 1985, 1987).

In addition to animal and bird hazards, farmers living in the drier lakeshore areas of the division, particularly on the islands of Rusinga and Mfangano, report insects and striga weed to be especially serious pest problems. Recent survey findings indicating exceptionally high population levels of stem borers on the islands confirm this assessment by farmers. Infestation by striga weed is also very heavy on both Rusinga and Mfangano Islands, where the plants dominate almost every field during the months of June and July. A survey of sample sorghum and maize fields on Rusinga Island during 1985 showed that virtually every plot was infested with the weed, with 63 percent of the sorghum hills having at least one striga plant, and many having five or more (Conelly 1985).

Similar high levels of striga infestation have been reported throughout semiarid Africa. Yield losses are reported to be as great as 60–70 percent in heavily infested areas. Striga thrives in environments with low soil fertility and unreliable rainfall, as on Rusinga Island, and thus most seriously affects poor farmers living on marginal agricultural land who can least afford to implement control measures (Ayensu et al. 1984).

## Recommended Management Practices
## for Control of Stem Borers

The existing package of recommendations for the control of stem borers is based on a combination of cultural and chemical controls. These recommendations have remained virtually unchanged since the colonial period despite their failure to provide effective control and their inappropriateness for the circumstances of the majority of small-scale, resource-poor farmers in East Africa.

The usual recommendations for the control of stem-borer infestation in maize and sorghum are:[2]

1. Cultural controls such as early and simultaneous planting by all farmers in an area. These practices help to prevent a buildup of high levels of stem-borer population that may occur when planting is delayed beyond the onset of the rains and when neighboring farmers widely stagger their planting dates, permitting a second generation of borers to mature.
2. Burning, after the harvest, of the crop residue, in which stem borers are able to survive the dry season.
3. Where cultural controls are inadequate, the use of an appropriate insecticide.

In the late 1920s a campaign mandating rigid control of planting dates, the burning of the crop residue, and a closed season was reportedly effective in controlling a major stem-borer outbreak in European areas of the Rift Valley and western Kenya (Anderson 1929). Soon after, however, government officers were frustrated by the "apathy" of European farmers who complained that the labor and cash costs resulting from the regulations were excessive. During the 1940s, the recommendation to burn the crop residue, rather than working it back into the soil, was criticized as running counter to efforts to prevent soil erosion, a paramount concern among agricultural officers at the time. A similar set of compulsory regulations was developed for African farming areas, but enforcement appears to have been erratic and the response of African farmers less than enthusiatic (KNA n.d.b).

Early and simultaneous planting, and destruction of the crop residue remain today the most commonly recommended methods for controlling infestation by stem borers for small-scale farmers. As in the past, however, most farmers continue to ignore the recommendations.

Many Mbita farmers would agree in theory that early planting is beneficial because of the very short duration of the rainy season in the area (usually mid-March to late May). Late-planted crops run the risk of inadequate precipitation at the end of the cropping season, when the plants are maturing and very vulnerable to water stress. Simultaneous planting by neighboring farmers is also seen as advantageous because it reduces the risk of heavy damage by birds—especially serious for sorghum—that is common in crops that mature out of sequence with those in nearby fields. In fact, however, numerous environmental and socioeconomic constraints make early and simultaneous planting difficult for farmers to achieve. These constraints include:

1. *Advantages of staggered planting.* Many farmers intentionally stagger their planting dates to avoid labor bottlenecks (at planting and weeding) and, because of the unpredictability of the rains, to increase the chances that at least some of their crop will mature during a period of reliable precipitation.
2. *Availability of seed.* Because of Mbita's isolation, farmers are sometimes unable to obtain seeds for planting early in the season. It is especially difficult following years of drought when harvests are very poor or failed altogether and all planting material has been consumed by the household.
3. *Difficulty of access to a plow and plow animals.* Only 40 percent of a sample of farmers using a plow for land preparation (n = 34) owned their own implements and animals. The remaining 60 percent were required to borrow or rent a plow and/or plow team from relatives or neighbors, which often resulted in a considerable delay in land preparation.
4. *Competing demands on the farmers' time.* As in many areas of East Africa, farming is only a part-time occupation for most Mbita residents. Wage labor, fishing, marketing, and charcoal production, to name a few, are all important sources of income, often more profitable than farming, that may compete for labor time at peak periods of the agricultural cycle.

Burning the crop residue after the harvest also remains an unpopular recommendation because of the many important ways in which farmers use the maize and sorghum stubble. Seventy-five percent of the sample farmers in the 1984 survey (n = 48), for example, reported that they leave stalks in the field as fodder for their livestock during the dry season. Many others collect the stalks as a substitute for fuelwood (48 percent), or use them in the construction of granaries (56 percent). Given these considerations, alternative ways of controlling the carryover of stem borers will need to be identified. Partial burning of the stalks (Adesiyun and Ajayi 1980) or delaying the destruction of the stalks until the end of the dry season, when the remaining residue will have little value as fodder or fuelwood to the farmer, are two possible solutions. Further research is needed, however, to verify that these alternatives are compatible with the existing farming system.

A third alternative, the use of insecticides, has great appeal for many Mbita farmers, who believe that chemicals are the most effective means of controlling insect pests. Few farmers in the area, however, report ever having used insecticides to protect their food crops, explaining that the chemicals are usually not available, that they lack the knowledge of how to apply them, and/or that they are too expensive. A few farmers nevertheless reported applying insecticide on vegetable crops destined for the market, and chemicals are also widely used to protect cotton (cf. Goldman 1987).

Several indigenous methods of insect pest control are practiced by Mbita farmers, but they appear to be of limited effectiveness. A traditional herbal "insecticide" produced from local plant materials is remembered by some farmers but has virtually disappeared from use and, based on farmers' reports, was apparently never very successful. Another local method of control is to uproot maize or sorghum plants that have been heavily damaged by insects and then to kill the insects with a stone or hoe. The resulting gap is filled by transplanting healthy plants from elsewhere in the field. This technique is possible because Mbita farmers plant cereal crops in very high densities, which permits the thinning and transfer of surplus plants from undamaged portions of the field. The fact that this method does little actually to limit insect pest populations and requires a significant expenditure of labor restricts its usefulness as an effective means of pest control.

Recognizing the excessive cost of chemical controls and the inappropriateness or ineffectiveness of many of the standard agronomic recommendations, an alternative "integrated pest management" (IPM) approach to the control of insect pests has emerged in the last decade (Matteson 1984). For the management of stem borers, as well as certain other insect pests, these integrated techniques fall primarily into three broad categories (e.g., ICIPE 1984):

1. The development of resistant crop varieties
2. Cultural practices, including intercropping
3. Biological control.

The three techniques are usually proposed as a "package" of pest management recommendations that will be most effective when introduced in combination rather than individually. Here I briefly discuss the potential of resistant cereal varieties and intercropping as methods of insect pest control for small-scale farmers in East Africa.

The development of a resistant maize or sorghum variety is an attractive strategy because its adoption could make a significant contribution to cereal production without requiring major or expensive modifications in existing farming practices. Many Mbita farmers are keen to try new crop varieties, sometimes setting aside a small portion of their field as an experimental plot to test new seeds. In developing improved varieties, however, care must be taken that research does not focus too narrowly on insect resistance per se, ignoring other important characteristics that farmers look for in cereal varieties.

Some of these other characteristics are: yield performance, tolerance to low rainfall conditions, taste and cooking characteristics, and response to such non-insect pests as weeds, birds, animals, and diseases. A new cereal variety that is resistant to insect pests but susceptible to striga weed, or one that is lower yielding or less palatable than local varieties, is unlikely to be acceptable to farmers who view insect pests as only one constraint in their farming system.

A second approach emphasizes the potential of intercropping as a means of limiting insect pests. There is growing experimental evidence that the intercropping of maize and sorghum with legumes helps to limit population levels of certain insect pests such as stem borers. The greater plant diversity in crop mixtures may provide physical or biological barriers to the buildup of insect pests and may also promote the survival of predators and parasites that can reduce the number of harmful insects in a field (e.g., Altieri 1985; Amoako-Atta and Omolo 1983; Litsinger and Moody 1976). The approach has the added advantage of building on traditional farming practices in Africa where intercropping is a common subsistence strategy (Okigbo and Greenland 1976; Steiner 1982).

Mbita farmers often intermix their maize and sorghum with legumes such as cowpea, beans, and green gram, but it does not appear that this intercropping strategy was adopted because of any perceived benefit for insect-pest control. In a sample of farmers (n = 48) asked to explain the reasons behind their intercropping practices, only one claimed that he utilized mixed cropping because he thought it helped control insects. Many of the respondents (41 percent) indicated that they used inter-cropping because it helped alleviate labor and land shortages. A few (8 percent) mentioned that intercropping helped to prevent weeds. Others said that certain crop combinations give an "adequate" or "good" yield (27 percent), without specifying a reason, or simply stated that inter-cropping was a traditional practice (11 percent).

In fact, preliminary agronomic data indicate that farmers' sorghum/ legume intercropping on Rusinga Island does not provide any significant advantage over monocropping in terms of insect pest damage as measured by leaf damage or the number of stem borers found inside the stalks of sorghum immediately after the harvest. This appears to be caused, at least in part, by the fact that most Mbita farmers give priority to cereal production and intermix only low populations of legume with their sorghum, thus minimizing the amount of plant diversity present in their intercropped fields (Conelly 1985).

Similarly, the spatial or temporal arrangement of crops in farmers' fields may influence the effectiveness of traditional intercrop systems as a means of insect pest control (Altieri 1985; Steiner 1982). For example, the common practice of relay cropping, in which a legume is planted several weeks after the cereal, may significantly reduce the advantages of intercropping as a means of pest control by postponing interaction between the crops until after the cereal insect pests have already become established. Thus, although traditional intercropping offers considerable potential for the control of insect pests, we need to gain a better understanding of indigenous practices and how these practices can be best modified to improve crop performance.

## Recommended Management Practices
## for Control of Striga Weed

As with the control of stem borers, many of the current recommendations for the management of striga weed have been around for decades, but have failed to provide effective control for small-scale farmers in Africa. In a 1936 article, Watt, the senior agricultural officer for Nyanza Province in western Kenya, recommended the following control measures:

1. Hand weeding and burning of striga before it sheds seed
2. The use of early maturing varieties and research to identify resistant varieties of maize and sorghum
3. Rotation of nonsusceptible crops such as cassava in heavily infested fields
4. The use of farm manure to maintain higher levels of soil fertility as striga was observed to flourish in poor soils.

Mbita farmers are apt to claim that they are "helpless" in the face of heavy striga infestation, yet several of these recommendations are part of the indigenous weed management system and, as far as can be determined, predate the intervention of colonial agricultural research.

Many farmers, for example, make at least a halfhearted effort to weed out striga plants when they begin to emerge, and some conscientiously eliminate the weed repeatedly throughout the season. But like their predecessors during the 1930s, farmers today claim that weeding is largely ineffective as the striga inevitably grows up again: "As a man shaves his chin today, so must he shave it again tomorrow" (Watt 1936). In fact, recent agronomic research indicates that thorough hand weeding often requires an uneconomic level of labor and, in any case, is effective only in fields where striga populations are relatively low (Ayensu et al. 1984).

Though it may not be a deliberate strategy, Rusinga farmers appear to have selected over the years varieties of sorghum that are tolerant to striga infestation. Local varieties such as *ochuti* and *andiwo* continue to produce adequate yields despite heavy striga infestation, especially in years of good rainfall (Conelly 1985). In India, too, indigenous cereal varieties are noticeably less susceptible to striga infestation than the high yielding "green revolution" varieties that have been introduced in recent years (Ayensu et al. 1984).

In cases of very serious striga infestation of cereal crops, some Rusinga farmers practice a rotation in which they substitute crops, such as cassava, that are not susceptible to striga and that also are able to tolerate low soil fertility. This strategy, however, is often not effective since striga seeds can remain dormant for up to 20 years under dry soil conditions. It is also an unpopular alternative since, with small landholdings, it often leaves too little land to produce sufficient grain for the basic subsistence requirements of the household (cf. Ayensu et al. 1984; Tarr 1962).

Farmers also report that they use cattle manure to increase the fertility of soils heavily infested with striga weed. This strategy is based on the belief that manure not only increases the nutrient content of soils but also actually reduces striga infestation. Agronomic evidence indicates that manuring (or the application of nitrogen) is in fact beneficial in some circumstances, apparently because it enables the parasitized plant better to withstand attack by striga (Ayensu et al. 1984; Tarr 1962). On Rusinga, farmers tether their cattle in the fields so that they can graze on recently harvested maize and sorghum stubble, which results in the accumulation of manure in the soil. In addition, some farmers intentionally select areas of their fields with low fertility and high striga infestation as the place to tether their animals during the dry season.

Unfortunately, the amount of manure available to most island farmers is sufficient to fertilize only a small portion of the cropped land. Some farmers have no cattle at all, and the average herd size on Rusinga is only about seven animals per household. In addition, because of severe deforestation in the region, manure also serves as a substitute fuel for cooking and for smoking fish caught in Lake Victoria. It is also used, seasonally, mixed with mud, to smear the walls and floors of houses and to line the inside of granaries.

Though each of these indigenous techniques of weed management may contribute to the control of striga infestation, most farmers feel that they are waging a losing battle. Clearly, there is need for new strategies of striga management that build on local farmers' practices yet offer more effective control.

Recent research has identified two other possible strategies for striga control (Ayensu et al. 1984; Nour et al. 1986; Tarr 1962):

1. The use of herbicides to kill the striga plant after it has emerged
2. The use of synthetic stimulators to induce "suicide germination" that causes the striga seedlings, which can survive only a few days without a host plant, to germinate and die.

Unfortunately, because of their expense neither of these methods offers a practical solution for resource-poor farmers in East Africa.

## Conclusion

The consensus of recent research suggests that the best strategy for the control of striga, as with stem borers, is an integrated approach combining the development of resistant sorghum and maize varieties with appropriate and low-cost agronomic techniques that both reduce the amount of striga seeds in the soil (e.g., by using suitable crop rotations) and increase the fertility of the soil. For the management of both insect and weed pests, however, much work is still needed before farmers receive tangible benefits. To be successful, pest management research must build on the existing knowledge and practices of farmers and provide solutions that are both technically feasible and appropriate to the circumstances of small-scale farmers.

## Notes

The research was supported by a generous Social Science Research Fellowship from the Rockefeller Foundation while the author was at the International Centre of Insect Physiology and Ecology (ICIPE), Kenya. The opinions expressed in this chapter, however, are those of the author and do not necessarily reflect the opinions of the Rockefeller Foundation or ICIPE. A. Dissemond (University of Bonn, West Germany) collected and helped to analyze much of the agronomic data presented in this chapter. My thanks to E. Omolo, J. K. O. Ampofo, M. Botchey, A. Alghali, K. Ogada, and S. Ambogo of ICIPE for their support during the course of the research. I would also like to thank the officers and staff of the Kenya National Archives, Nairobi, for their always efficient and friendly assistance.

1. Materials in the Kenya National Archives (KNA) relevant to pest management in Nyanza Province are scattered in many different files, including the District and Provincial Annual Reports and the correspondence and reports of the Agricultural Department. Citations refer to the specific deposits where the material cited was located, including the abbreviated reference number used to identify each file.

2. For information on recommended practices for stem-borer control see Acland 1971; Anderson 1929; Gahukar and Jotwani 1980; Lawani 1982; Ministry of Agriculture 1980; Seshu-Reddy 1982; Wheatley and Crowe 1967; Young and Teetes 1977).

# References

Acland, J. D.
1971    East African Crops. London: Longman.

Adesiyun, A. A., and O. Ajayi
1980    Control of the Sorghum Stemborer, *Busseola fusca*, by Partial Burning of the Stalks. Tropical Pest Management 26(2):113–117.

Altieri, M.
1985    Developing Pest Management Strategies for Small Farmers Based on Traditional Knowledge. Development Anthropology Network, Bulletin of the Institute for Development Anthropology 3(1):13–18.

Amoako-Atta, B., and E. O. Omolo
1983    Yield Losses Caused by the Stem-Pod Borer Complex within Maize-Cowpea-Sorghum Intercropping Systems in Kenya. Insect Science and Its Application 4(1/2):39–46.

Anderson, T. J.
1929    Control of Maize Stalk Borers. Department of Agriculture, Colony and Protectorate of Kenya, Bulletin No. 7F.

Ayensu, E. S., H. Doggett, et al.
1984    Striga: Biology and Control. Papers presented at a workshop on the biology and control of Striga. Dakar, Senegal, 14–17 November 1983. ICSU Press and the International Development Research Centre (IDRC), Canada.

Conelly, W. T.
1985    On-Farm Evaluation of Traditional Intercropping Systems in Relation to Pest Control, Mbita Division, South Nyanza District, Kenya. Manuscript Report, International Centre of Insect Physiology and Ecology (ICIPE), Nairobi, Kenya.
1987    Perception and Management of Crop Pests among Subsistence Farmers in South Nyanza, Kenya. *In* Management of Pests and Pesticides: Farmers' Perceptions and Practices. J. Tait and B. Napompeth, eds. Boulder, CO: Westview Press.

Gahukar, R. T., and M. G. Jotwani
1980    Present Status of Field Pests of Sorghum and Millet in India. Tropical Pest Management 26:138–151.

Goldman, A.
   1987    Agricultural Pests and the Farming System: A Study of Pest Hazards
           and Pest Management by Small Scale Farmers in Kenya. *In* Management
           of Pests and Pesticides: Farmers' Perceptions and Practices. J. Tait and
           B. Napompeth, eds. Boulder, CO: Westview Press.

ICIPE (International Centre of Insect Physiology and Ecology)
   1984    Annual Report, 1983. Nairobi, Kenya.

KNA (Kenya National Archives)
   n.d.a   AGRI KISUMU/1/803.
   n.d.b   Ministry of Agriculture. Deposit #1/787.
   1912    DC/KSI/I.
   1914    DC/KSI/I.
   1931a   PC/NZA/3/2/114.
   1931b   DC/KSI/1/3.
   1935    PC/NZA/3/12/3.
   1935–1950a   PC/NZA/3/2/212.
   1935–1950b   AGRI/KISUMU/ 1/803.
   1937–1948   Ministry of Agriculture. Deposit 1/787.

Lawani, S. M.
   1982    A Review of the Effects of Various Agronomic Practices on Cereal
           Stem Borer Populations. Tropical Pest Management 28:266–276.

Litsinger, J. A., and K. Moody
   1976    Integrated Pest Management in Multiple Cropping Systems. *In* Multiple
           Cropping. American Society of Agronomy, Special Publication No. 27.

Matteson, P. C.
   1984    Modification of Small Farmer Practices for Better Pest Control. Annual
           Review of Entomology 29:383–402.

Ministry of Agriculture
   1980    Field Crops Technical Handbook. Nairobi, Kenya: Agricultural Infor-
           mation Centre.

Nour, J., M. Press, G. Stewart, and J. Tuohy
   1986    Africa in the Grip of Witchweed. New Scientist No. 1490, 9th January.

Okigbo, B. N., and D. J. Greenland
   1976    Intercropping Systems in Tropical Africa. *In* Multiple Cropping. Amer-
           ican Society of Agronomy, Special Publication No. 27.

Seshu-Reddy, K. V.
   1982    Pest Management in Sorghum II. *In* Sorghum in the Eighties: Pro-
           ceedings of the International Symposium on Sorghum, 2–7 November
           1981. Patancheru P.O., Andhra Pradesh, India: International Crops
           Research Institute for the Semi-Arid Tropics (ICRISAT).

Steiner, K. G.
   1982    Intercropping in Tropical Smallholder Agriculture with Special Ref-
           erence to West Africa. German Agency for Technical Development
           (GTZ), No. 137.

Tarr, S. A. J.
  1962  Diseases of Sorghum, Sudan Grass, and Broom Corn. Kew, Surrey: The Commonwealth Mycological Institute.

Teetes, G. L., K. V. Seshu-Reddy, K. Leuschner, and L. R. House
  1983  Sorghum Insect Identification Handbook. Information Bulletin No. 12. Patancheru P.O., Andhra Pradesh, India: International Crops Research Institute for the Semi-Arid Tropics (ICRISAT).

Watt, W. L.
  1936  Control of Striga Weed in Nyanza Province, Kenya. The East Africa Agricultural Journal, January.

Wheatley, P. E., and T. J. Crowe
  1967  Pest Handbook: The Recognition and Control of the More Important Pests of Agriculture in Kenya. Nairobi: Republic of Kenya.

Young, W. R., and G. L. Teetes
  1977  Sorghum Shootfly Entomology. Annual Review of Entomology 22:193–218.

# 7

## Anthropology and Interdisciplinary Agricultural Research in Rwanda

*Angelique Haugerud*

### Introduction

The president of an African nation, after flying in his helicopter over the experimental fields of his country's largest agricultural research station, asked why the researchers' fields bore so little resemblance to those of farmers immediately beyond the station perimeter. A discrepancy between research conditions and reality is not unusual in Africa. African agricultural researchers too often are taught to dismiss the farming techniques and special knowledge with which they grew up, in favor of unadapted foreign techniques and practices. Peer evaluation standards depend more on application of textbook experimental design than on the local applicability of results.

A number of social scientists have made a good case for tapping indigenous agricultural knowledge (see, for instance, Richards 1985 and Brokensha et al. 1980). Many development programs now share a "farmer first" rhetoric, but they differ widely in the degree to which they actually focus explicitly on farmers' knowledge, constraints, and practices, and in the extent to which they carry out research in farmers' fields as well as on research stations. Much agricultural research is still station centered, technical and biological in orientation, and relatively uninfluenced by local farmers' practices.

Biological and technical research in agriculture have of course produced enormous benefits. One of the areas of heaviest investment, for example, has been plant breeding, which accounts for about 50 percent of the research effort of the International Agricultural Research Centers (IARCs) (Simmonds 1984:43). Plant breeding research led to the improved strains of wheat and rice that substantially increased food production during the 1960s and 1970s "green revolution" in Asia. The agricultural challenges of the post–green-revolution era, however, are enormous. In Asia, researchers now consider how to extend the benefits of technological improvements beyond the 25 percent of the continent's farmers who live in areas suitable to high-input, high-yielding irrigated rice varieties (Murphy 1985:10). More research effort is going to areas poor in resources, and to the development of crop varieties suitable to a wider range of agronomic and environmental conditions (e.g., nonirrigated rice cultivars).

In Africa, staple food crops are different, and environmental, economic, and sociopolitical conditions contrast markedly with those under which the improved rice and wheat cultivars flourished in Asia. Research must focus on crops such as cassava, maize, sorghum, millet, cowpeas, beans, sweet potatoes, and potatoes, some of which were neglected until recently. Communications, food transport costs, methods of distributing agricultural inputs on time, water availability, soils, and climate are all less favorable than in Asia. Foreign exchange for importing chemicals and fertilizers is scarce. Markets are less well-developed, and many small farmers continue to produce crops for home consumption, and to minimize their dependence on uncertain markets and government services (see Hyden 1980). To meet the needs of African agriculture, plant breeding research must focus on disease-resistant crop varieties that are productive on poorer soils, that do not require chemical inputs, and that tolerate rainfall extremes.

Breeders of new food-crop varieties for Africa must also address a number of special characteristics of small-scale agriculture that were once widespread in Europe, but that have disappeared there with the spread of highly organized, specialized markets and of large-scale commercial farming. In managing their limited resources in the face of the hazards of the natural environment, African farmers have developed complex strategies to guarantee their food security. These include carefully managed crop species and cultivar diversity, staggered planting and harvesting dates, mixed cropping, relay cropping, cultivar mixtures within plots, and the planting of scattered plots in a variety of microenvironments. Such practices are necessary considerations when defining plant breeding and germ-plasm screening objectives.

Plant breeding is a long-term investment, with payoffs expected only after ten to fifteen years. Germ-plasm screening programs that only test rather than breed new genotypes are likely to require at least five years to screen locally and to select promising new cultivars. Given the time and other resources involved, it is particularly important that plant scientists not define cultivar selection criteria intuitively and informally, but rather that they carefully identify and rank them through systematic prior assessment of farmers' practices, needs, and constraints.

The following case study from Rwanda in eastern Africa illustrates how interdisciplinary farm surveys affected germ-plasm screening criteria in a research program focused on potatoes (*Solanum tuberosum*). The Rwandan program had already had notable successes with some of its new potato varieties. Other varieties introduced more recently, however, were beginning to be considerably less acceptable to farmers. Overproduction of the less appreciated varieties in the national seed program could threaten the program's excellent reputation. A reduction in the capacity of the local market to absorb some of the newer varieties, together with an expansion of large-scale potato production, helped to bring the issue to a head. Proposed program changes involved unexpected information picked up in farm surveys, as well as confirmation through the surveys of prior guesses by various team members. In both cases, survey data are helpful, since it is easier to justify program changes proposed on the basis of observations of over 350 potato fields and responses from 200 farmers in several ecological zones than it is to do so with information gathered through informal conversations with a few farmers near a research station.

## Potato Research in Rwanda

This case study concerns a Rwandan potato research program (hereafter referred to by its French acronym–PNAP) that had attracted national and international praise before the research discussed here began.[1] Reasons for the program's acclaim are as follows. First, it screened and introduced during its first five years six improved cultivars whose yields under farm conditions are two to five times the national average (without fertilizers, chemicals, or purchased inputs other than the seed itself, which farmers can multiply without subsequent purchase for up to ten years in that environment). Second, although PNAP receives technical support from an IARC (the International Potato Center), it is well-integrated into and supported by national political and administrative institutions,[2] and its foreign-financed expatriate minority is integrated into a team of national scientists. Third, since its inception the program has given explicit attention to farmers' needs and constraints, conducting about 100 on-farm trials each year (see Devaux and Tegera 1981). Fourth, although it is part of a larger national agricultural research institute, it is based in northern Rwanda in its commodity's major production zone, four hours by road from the national institute's headquarters, and was granted relative autonomy and flexibility in its day-to-day administration and management. Fifth, it is a small team that operates by consensus and holds frequent formal and informal meetings. Sixth, the crop upon which it focuses is highly valued locally as both a prestigious consumption item and as one of the country's few cash crops. Seventh, the program is a cell of the national political party, and like all such cells, writes songs that on special occasions (e.g., visits by such notables as the president and cabinet ministers) are performed by its own colorful troupe of traditional singers and dancers. The program's songs have publicized its new cultivars through performances at local political competitions and on the radio.

## Potato Development in Rwanda

Substantial increases in Rwanda's potato production in recent decades have been associated with population growth, extreme land scarcity, and expansion of cultivation in higher altitude zones. Although the degree of land scarcity is unusual (with an average of less than one hectare of land per household and over 600 persons per square kilometer in some agricultural areas) (Government of Rwanda 1985), Rwandan agricultural conditions resemble those elsewhere in Africa's highland tropics. Households use fragmented parcels of land across different ecological zones, across local administrative units, and occasionally even across national boundaries. There is a low degree of economic specialization, so that each family produces a range of essential foods for the household and minimizes reliance on markets and exchange. Cropping systems are complex, and a wide diversity of crops and cultivars are grown. Farm households have multiple production objectives, including nonfarm investments and production of food, cash, and gifts as investments in sociopolitical relations. They can afford few cash inputs and have a low capacity for risk because they operate close to food subsistence margins. Seasonal agricultural labor migration, especially among young, unmarried men who lack land, is important. Opportunities for formal-sector salaried employment are limited, and more than 90 percent of the population resides in rural areas and practices agriculture.

Potatoes are a relatively recent introduction in Rwanda. They arrived early this century with explorers, traders, soldiers, and missionaries, but local food taboos at first limited their adoption (Poats 1981). Although it took Europeans two centuries to accept potatoes as human food (Salamon 1970), in Rwanda potatoes were widely produced and consumed within a few decades of their introduction. Their relatively high output of energy and protein per unit of area and time (see CIP 1984) and their relatively short growth cycle eased their incorporation into existing cropping systems.

When the Rwandan potato research program was established in 1979, potato varieties then cultivated in the country had low yields (about six or seven tons per hectare), and were very susceptible to late blight and bacterial wilt (the two most common potato diseases in Rwanda and in much of the tropics). Since the 1930s, the Belgian colonial government had introduced dozens of European varieties into the country, but these were adapted to temperate zone conditions (longer day length, lower temperatures, different diseases and soils) and performed less well in Africa. Temperate zone potato cultivars, however, represent only a small fraction of the crop's available genetic diversity.

The wider diversity of the genus *Solanum* has been systematically exploited in the last 15 years by the International Potato Center (CIP), whose headquarters are in Lima, Peru, near the crop's Andean center of origin. The center's scientists cross both wild and cultivated species, in order to profit from tolerance of varying day lengths and from a wide array of available resistances to pathogens, pests, and other environmental stresses (see CIP 1984, 1985). CIP distributes its germ plasm to dozens of nations in Africa, Asia, and Latin America, and provides the technical support necessary for them to set up their own germplasm screening and evaluation programs so that they can produce locally adapted, improved varieties. Rwanda is one such program (see Nganga 1983 and Bicamumpaka and Haverkort 1983).

Plant breeding and selection are the foundation of PNAP's work. Given the resource constraints of Rwandan farmers (scarce land and little cash), a program emphasis on improved cultivars that require no complementary inputs is one of the most immediately effective ways to increase agricultural production. PNAP selects and multiplies seed of new disease-resistant cultivars after a number of seasons of testing (under the same low-input conditions that farmers face) on the research station, in multilocal trials, and in farmers' fields (see PNAP 1984, 1985).

In cultivated areas, potatoes are the sixth most important crop in Rwanda; they follow bananas, sweet potatoes, cassava, beans, and sorghum (Government of Rwanda 1985). A substantial increase in potato production over the last two decades has accompanied expansion of area under the crop (from about 18,000 to over 42,000 hectares), especially as population pressure has led to clearing and cultivation of new lands in the higher altitude zones. In areas above 2,000 meters in altitude, particularly in the northern volcanic soils zone, potatoes have become both a primary food staple and a cash crop.

Expansion of the crop is likely to have a positive nutritional impact, as it is an excellent source of vitamin C, the B vitamins (niacin, riboflavin, and thiamine), and protein (see Woolfe 1986). Farmers also find it a better source of cash than most alternative crops, including nonedible export crops such as pyrethrum and tea.

## Farm Surveys

What could interdisciplinary research involving anthropology contribute to a program that had become a success within its first five
years? Given PNAP's emphasis on locally screening and releasing new
disease-resistant, high-yielding potato cultivars, anthropological research
first addressed the appropriateness of its germ-plasm selection criteria
and priorities. Are the new potato varieties acceptable? If so, why, to
what kinds of farmers, and in what types of environment? If not, to
whom are they unacceptable, and why? To answer these questions, field
interviews addressed farmers' strategies in selecting and using both old
and new potato cultivars already in circulation.[3]

Five themes illustrate implications of the farm survey findings for
germ-plasm screening and other potato research in Rwanda:[4]

1. farmers' preference for cultivar diversity and field mixtures,
2. intercropping,
3. varied production goals and changing markets,
4. seed selection and the division of labor, and
5. local preferences concerning such traits as tuber skin color, length
   of growth cycle, and length of dormancy.

This chapter addresses the implications of these findings for PNAP's
future agronomic research and for its germ-plasm screening criteria.
Finally, it considers the impact and distribution of the new cultivars,
and possible means to expand farmers' access to improved seed.

### Farmers' Preference for Cultivar Diversity and Field Mixtures

A potato field that contains five different cultivars with different
maturity and harvest dates, and different phenotypic traits such as tuber
color and shape, would be a nightmare for a Western, commercial,
mechanized farmer. In Africa's tropical highlands, however, maintenance
of such diversity is an important means of managing risk, environmental
hazards, and resource limitations; and a means of meeting varied
production goals (e.g., home consumption, sale in different types of
markets). In Africa, yield stability depends on "a patchwork quilt of
many different varieties planted on the same farm," whereas in Western
commercial agriculture, yield stability "depends on a continuous supply
of new cultivars" (CIMMYT 1986:1).

In the West itself, trends toward homogeneity in farmers' fields ("one
clone, one pure line, one hybrid"), and toward a narrowing of the genetic

base of breeding as well as producing populations, are now belatedly questioned (Simmonds 1979:12–13; MacFadyen 1985). Extreme uniformity is known to pose biological hazards (especially from disease). Plant scientists themselves acknowledge that insufficient research has been done on possible positive interactions of species and cultivars planted in mixtures (Thresh 1982; Altieri 1985; Willey 1979). Possibly complementary effects involving the uptake of soil nutrients or water, for example, are poorly understood (Willey 1979). When farmers grow a number of varieties of each crop (as well as many different crops), the spread of pathogens and pests may be slowed. The degree to which this slowing depends on the presence of some resistant cultivars or on genotype heterogeneity itself is not known.

While agriculture in developed countries is made vulnerable by increasing genetic uniformity in the form of varietal specialization, the cultivar mixtures and intercropping already practiced by so many African farmers are an excellent first line of defense against biological and climatic hazards to crops. Given the probable long-term absence of field mechanization in Africa's mountainous highland tropics, mixtures of cultivars with different growth cycles and other traits are not the disadvantage they are in Western commercial agriculture.

Rwandan farmers surveyed usually grow three to eight different potato cultivars at once, mix cultivars within fields, and find advantageous the mixtures' variability in such traits as length of growth cycle and dormancy, disease resistances, tolerances of rainfall excesses and deficits, dry-matter content (which affects taste and storability), and marketability. (They also cultivate many varieties of other crops such as bananas, beans, and sweet potatoes.)

Over 65 different names of potato cultivars were elicited from farmers surveyed in Rwanda. Possibly 20 percent of them are synonyms. Potatoes are locally known as *ibirayi*, a word denoting something of European origin. Farmers distinguish among cultivars according to plant and tuber traits, and can describe varietal differences in agronomic and culinary characteristics. Cultivar names refer to presumed regional or national centers of diffusion, to plant and tuber characteristics, to extension agents associated with their introduction in a particular locality, and sometimes to historical events that occurred at the time of their introduction. Electrophoresis protein band analysis shows that names are not necessarily consistent across localities or regions (as Brush et al. [1981] also found in Peru).

Table 7.1 shows how 186 Rwandan farmers assess a number of characteristics of the four most frequently grown potato cultivars in the country. The variety Gashara, for example, introduced a number of decades ago, is degenerated, and farmers would have abandoned it long

TABLE 7.1

Farmers' Assessments of the Four Most Frequently Grown Potato Cultivars in Rwanda (percentages of farmers citing each characteristic of each cultivar)[a]

| Characteristic | Cultivar | | | |
|---|---|---|---|---|
| | Montsama[b] | Sangema[b] | Gashara | Muhabura[b] |
| **Growth Cycle** | | | | |
| Long | 1 | 59 | 0 | 55 |
| Medium | 22 | 25 | 0 | 28 |
| Short | 77 | 16 | 100 | 17 |
| **Dormancy** | | | | |
| Long | 8 | 86 | 13 | 14 |
| Medium | 23 | 7 | 4 | 42 |
| Short | 69 | 7 | 83 | 44 |
| **Taste** | | | | |
| Good | 93 | 84 | 100 | 14 |
| Medium | 6 | 15 | 0 | 39 |
| Poor | 1 | 1 | 0 | 46 |
| **Starch Content** | | | | |
| High | 88 | 60 | 97 | 4 |
| Medium | 12 | 28 | 3 | 25 |
| Low | 0 | 12 | 0 | 71 |
| **Cooking Time** | | | | |
| Long | 0 | 9 | 0 | 48 |
| Medium | 18 | 18 | 2 | 26 |
| Short | 82 | 73 | 98 | 26 |
| **Storability** | | | | |
| Good | 38 | 58 | 67 | 22 |
| Medium | 22 | 23 | 17 | 36 |
| Poor | 40 | 19 | 15 | 42 |
| **Yield under good rainfall** | | | | |
| Good | 57 | 84 | 41 | 63 |
| Medium | 34 | 12 | 43 | 12 |
| Poor | 9 | 4 | 16 | 25 |
| **Yield under poor rainfall** | | | | |
| Good | 44 | 49 | 35 | 30 |
| Medium | 31 | 34 | 33 | 42 |
| Poor | 25 | 17 | 32 | 28 |
| **Late blight resistance** | | | | |
| Good | 38 | 50 | 14 | 27 |
| Medium | 26 | 32 | 26 | 22 |
| Poor | 36 | 18 | 60 | 51 |
| **Bacterial wilt tolerance** | | | | |
| Good | 47 | 56 | 53 | 40 |
| Medium | 19 | 20 | 26 | 30 |
| Poor | 34 | 24 | 21 | 30 |
| **Market acceptability** | | | | |
| Good | 89 | 88 | 33 | 9 |
| Medium | 11 | 11 | 14 | 30 |
| Poor | 0 | 1 | 52 | 61 |
| **Suitability for intercropping** | | | | |
| Good | 64 | 33 | 55 | 12 |
| Medium | 32 | 32 | 28 | 45 |
| Poor | 4 | 35 | 17 | 43 |

[a]Each of these four cultivars is grown by at least 30 percent of the farmers interviewed (N = 186) in four production zones.
[b]Improved cultivars distributed by the Rwandan National Potato Improvement Program (PNAP).

ago if yield and disease resistance were their sole criteria of choice. Gashara is still among the most frequently grown varieties, however, because of its short growth cycle, short cooking time, short dormancy, good taste, and high starch content. The variety Muhabura, though not appreciated for its taste or storability, is valued for its relatively short dormancy. Farmers appreciate the variety Sangema for its taste, market acceptability, yields under good rainfall, and late-blight resistance (which Rwandan farmers equate with good performance in heavy rain), though they do not appreciate Sangema's long dormancy and long growth cycle.

Rwandan farmers explicitly relate their preference for growing mixtures of cultivars to food security. They find that by maintaining field variation in such traits as tolerance of rainfall excesses and deficits, they reduce the risk of total crop loss in any given season. Some plants are likely to survive whatever environmental stresses occur in a particular season. Mixtures also allow the use of staggered harvests and varied growth cycles, which permit farmers to extend the period of food and cash availability (and to even out periods of peak labor demand).

A recommendation based on these findings was that PNAP should begin on-station research with cultivar mixtures to test their comparative performance under late blight and other environmental pressures. Trial comparisons could include (a) a mixture of nonresistant cultivars, (b) a mixture of resistant cultivars, (c) a mixture of nonresistant and resistant cultivars, (d) a pure stand of a nonresistant cultivar, and (e) a pure stand of a resistant cultivar.

## Intercropping

Intercropping, or crop association, is a widespread practice in eastern Africa for some of the same reasons that cultivar mixtures are. Farmers recognize the yield stability advantages of crop associations, but some also practice it because they believe it is a better use of scarce land. In Rwanda, there is evidence that far from being a dying "traditional" practice, intercropping is increasing over time as population density increases (Janssens et al. 1985).

Over half of Rwanda's total cultivated area is intercropped, according to national agricultural survey data (Government of Rwanda 1985:71). According to the same national survey, 48 percent of the area under potatoes is intercropped (ibid. 1985:72). Nearly half (47 percent) of the 360 potato fields observed in the author's survey were intercropped. The most common crops associated with potatoes are maize, beans, sorghum, colocasia, and sweet potatoes (see Table 7.2). Nearly half of the fields are two-crop associations, 31 percent include three crops, and 21 percent four or more crops (see Table 7.3). Most farmers in Rwanda

TABLE 7.2
Most Common Crops Observed in Association with
Potatoes in Four Production Zones in Rwanda[a]

| Associated Crop | Percent of Intercropped Potato Fields in Which Observed[b] |
|---|---|
| Maize | 41 |
| Beans | 40 |
| Sorghum | 26 |
| Colocasia | 13 |
| Sweet potatoes | 13 |

[a]Based on observations of 360 potato fields between July and September 1985 in all of Rwanda's potato-production zones—the volcanic soils zone, the Buberuka highlands (lateritic soils), the Zaire-Nile Crest, and the Central Plateau.
[b]We observed 168 intercropped fields; percentages do not total 100 because some fields contained more than one crop associated with potatoes.


TABLE 7.3
Number of Crops Associated with Potatoes in 168 Intercropped Fields
in Four Production Zones in Rwanda[a]

| Number of crops in Association | Percent of Intercropped Fields[b] |
|---|---|
| 2 | 48 |
| 3 | 31 |
| 4+ | 21 |

[a]Based on observations of 360 potato fields between July and September 1985 in all of Rwanda's potato-production zones—the volcanic soils zone, the Buberuka highlands (lateritic soils), the Zaire-Nile Crest, and the Central Plateau.
[b]We observed 168 intercropped fields.


(79 percent of 186 farmers surveyed) prefer potato varieties that have short stolons because they are a better use of scarce land, are easier to harvest, and are better for crop associations.

Recommendations based on these findings were as follows. First, given scarcity of land, increasing population pressure, and likely increases in intercropping, it would be useful to conduct agronomic trials testing common crop associations to determine land equivalent ratios, possible positive effects of intercropping on disease and pest vulnerability, and the performance of different potato cultivars in crop associations. Second, germ-plasm selection criteria for some material should include short stolons and vertically rather than horizontally extensive leaf coverage (i.e., height rather than breadth of foliage could be emphasized) in order to decrease competition of potatoes with associated field crops.

## Varied Production Goals and Changing Markets

Farmers produce potatoes both for home consumption and for sale, and many use different cultivars for the two purposes. Rwandan farmers prefer to keep for home consumption those cultivars that have high dry matter or starch content and to sell those that have high water content, which weigh more and fetch more cash, but store poorly and do not taste as good.[5] When there are production deficits, large tubers with high water content remain marketable. When production increases and more new cultivars become available, however, markets become more specialized and consumers more selective. As occurred in Asia after the International Rice Research Institute (IRRI) introduced new rice varieties (see Murphy 1985:5), so too in Rwanda, there is now greater demand for cultivars with better consumption and storage qualities (i.e., higher dry-matter content).

In 1986, good rainfall and expanded acreage in Rwanda created market gluts of potatoes, particularly of a high-yielding but watery PNAP cultivar called Gahinga.[6] Some traders then consciously selected for sale the smaller-sized tubers of Gahinga so that buyers would mistake it for a more popular cultivar (Sangema) that has lower water content and better taste. These trends suggest that PNAP must monitor market factors (specialization, demand) so that its germ-plasm screening strikes a suitable balance between yields and dry-matter content in new cultivars. Maximization of yield per se becomes less desirable once yield increases entail raising water content to locally unacceptable levels. (Cultivars that contain at least 22 percent dry matter are preferred locally.) Since buyers have become more selective as production has increased both domestically and in neighboring countries, PNAP should decrease the proportion of seed allotted to cultivars—such as Gahinga—whose lower dry-matter content reduces their market acceptability.

PNAP scientists at first opposed the recommendation to de-emphasize seed production of its highest yielding cultivars in favor of others available. For the seed program to shift from higher- to lower-yielding cultivars contradicts agronomists' and breeders' professional emphasis on yield maximization—even if higher yields entail loss in consumer acceptability as tuber water content increases. By mid-1986, when rising potato production and falling prices made the high-yielding but watery variety Gahinga virtually unsalable, PNAP had no choice but to shift the emphasis of its seed program to more acceptable (even if slightly lower-yielding) varieties. PNAP needs to be able to respond quickly to changes in demand for any particular cultivar. To do so, it must maintain diversity in its seed stock.

TABLE 7.4
Sex of Household Member Who Usually Selects Potato Seed
(in percent of households sampled)[a]

| Female | Male | Both |
|--------|------|------|
| 71 | 20 | 9 |

[a]Based on interviews in 186 households in Rwanda's four potato-production zones between July and September 1985.

## Seed Selection and Division of Labor

How farmers select and store seed tubers has a substantial effect on the crop's health and productivity.[7] Most Rwandan farmers select seed from their own crop at harvest or immediately after. Their main seed selection criterion is tuber size, with the smallest tubers used as seed and the larger ones consumed or sold. Few farmers report selection according to plant characteristics, which means their seed selection practices can increase the rate of degeneration if small tubers are diseased and come from the least hardy plants.

Planting the smallest tubers is a widespread practice in developing countries. Rhoades (1985:14) notes that small farmers in Nepal, for example, also use small tubers as seed, and plant small seed at higher density than Western agronomy usually recommends, in order to have denser emergence and to reduce production inputs and risks. Similar considerations apply in Rwanda.

It is usually women who select seed in Rwanda, as Table 7.4 shows. Women participate more often than men in all potato production tasks— land preparation, planting, applying manure or compost, weeding, and harvesting. The tasks in which men are most likely to take part are land preparation and planting.

The Rwanda survey findings suggest that rural extension efforts to teach farmers to select potato seed according to plant characteristics have had little impact. Because women play a substantial role in seed selection and in productive labor tasks, they should be the specific recipients of such extension efforts. (At present male extension agents teach male farmers improved seed selection practices.)

## Tuber Skin Color

Potato markets and consumer preferences in Rwanda are unspecialized with respect to skin color. Tuber color preferences arise by association with a particularly successful cultivar, but skin color itself is not genetically linked to consumer quality. In Kenya, for example, a preference for red-skinned cultivars has arisen by association with the very successful

Kerr's Pink cultivar introduced there about 60 years ago. In that country, potatoes are often separated by color when marketed, and red-skinned tubers are likely to fetch higher prices than white. In Rwanda, on the other hand, potatoes are usually marketed as color-variegated mixtures, without price distinctions among cultivars or skin colors.

When 186 Rwandan farmers were asked to rank the importance of cultivar traits, tuber skin color was last in importance in a list of seven traits. Red, purple, and white tubers are all locally acceptable. The only negative reaction with respect to tuber skin color is associated with russets, which Rwandan farmers believe to be diseased.

All of the improved cultivars released by PNAP since 1980, however, have red skins. Some are quite popular, and there is a weak emerging preference for red skins in the north (and occasional price differences favoring red skins and the improved PNAP cultivars). In the south, where PNAP varieties are less widespread, some farmers express a preference for white-skinned tubers. Tuber color preferences are not strong in Rwanda, however, and are likely to continue to change as individual cultivars become more or less popular and enter and leave particular regions.

The absence of a strong farmer preference for red-skinned tubers was a surprise to some PNAP scientists, who had favored red tubers in the germ-plasm screening. If such a screening bias is strong, it can lead to unnecessary elimination of potentially useful genetic material.

Selection of red skins initially might have been a convenient means for producers, traders, and consumers to distinguish PNAP's new high-yielding varieties from others available. Since both regional preferences and the popularity of specific PNAP cultivars vary over time, however, red skins are not necessarily a universal advantage. Diversity of skin color in PNAP's new cultivars is a safer strategy than specialization. Tuber skin color at present need not be a basis for elimination of genetic material during germ-plasm screening. Periodic reevaluation of the local importance of tuber skin color is necessary, however, since Kenya's experience indicates that under some circumstances color preferences become fixed and affect profits.

## Length of Growth Cycle and Dormancy

One of the more controversial research issues at PNAP concerns the appropriate cultivar maturity period to emphasize in germ-plasm screening. Since yields are generally higher in longer-cycle cultivars (because of the longer duration of photosynthetic intake), this issue, like that concerning tuber water content, creates conflict between plant scientists'

TABLE 7.5
Farmer's Preferences for Length of Growth Cycle and Dormancy in Potatoes (in percent)[a]

| Growth Cycle | | | | | Dormancy | | |
|------|--------|-------|-----|---|------|-------|------|
| Long | Medium | Short | All | | Long | Short | Both |
| 2 | 2 | 52 | 44 | | 3 | 43 | 54 |

[a]Based on interviews in 186 households in Rwanda's four potato-production zones between July and September 1985.

professional emphasis on high yields, and social scientists' emphasis on farmers' preferences and constraints.

It is sometimes tempting to assume that since developing countries need more food, breeding and germ-plasm screening should emphasize maximization of yield and intercepted light radiation. In reality, the appropriate length of a crop's growth cycle is determined by characteristics of local farming systems.

In Burundi, for example, agronomists found that farmers' concern with food security led them to reject a new late-maturing, high-yielding maize variety (Ziegler and Kayibigi 1984). Although the new maize cultivar yielded 20 to 40 percent more than previously released varieties, farmers cited the important disadvantage that its later maturity (which required a harvest delay of six weeks) precluded the possibility of a good second pea crop. That is, the longer-cycle maize cultivar did not fit into the complex system of intercropping maize and beans and relay-cropping maize with peas. Trials testing the new late-maturing maize cultivar in the local cropping system showed it to have neither an economic nor a protein yield advantage, since yield gains in the late-maturing maize were at the expense of the second season legume crop.

In such a situation, selecting a new cultivar on the basis of single-crop yield trials rather than mixed cropping and relay-crop trials would tell us nothing about the cultivar's suitability to local farmers' circumstances. Plant scientists attempting to maximize yields of one crop must take into account other local crops that place demands on farmers' land and labor resources and that make essential economic and nutritional contributions to farm families. The Rwanda farm surveys indicate that farmers prefer potato cultivars that have either short maturity and short dormancy,[8] or a mixture of cultivars with long and short dormancy and growth cycles. As Table 7.5 shows, almost none prefer only long-cycle cultivars.

Because land is scarce and rainfall distribution permits multiple cropping of potatoes, cultivars that have short growth cycles are the most frequently stated preference.[9] The next most common preference is for diversity—that is, for a combination of cultivars with varying maturity periods. Many farmers grow both long- and short-cycle cultivars in order to increase the number of months when fresh potatoes are available for sale and consumption, to reduce the risks of rainfall uncertainty, and to exploit different ecological zones. If a farmer grows a short-cycle cultivar that she can harvest early, she is then more likely to be able to afford (if she has adequate land) to wait for the later harvest (and higher yield) of a longer cycle cultivar as well.

Agricultural scientists and Rwandan farmers define maturity periods differently. To local farmers, a potato cultivar in the 110- to 120-day range is "late"; to breeders and agronomists it is "medium" to "early." In Rwanda, the acceptable range of days to maturity is strikingly skewed toward the short end of the international breeder's theoretical range (which extends to over 150 days). Rwandan farmers' preference for a mixture of long- and short-duration cultivars then translates into short and medium maturity on a plant breeder's scale.

One constraint on reducing potato cultivars' maturity period in germplasm screening in Rwanda is that late maturity and late-blight resistance tend to be associated traits (though current research addresses late blight screening in earlier-maturing cultivars). Some PNAP scientists believe that later maturity is not a local disadvantage if it is associated with better resistance to late blight. Rwandan farmers' traditional means of controlling blight is to plant late in the rainy season. Although they do not necessarily recognize late blight as a disease in the Western sense, they know that blight symptoms increase during heavy rain. Indeed the word for late blight in the Rwandan language is the same as that for rain (*imvura*). (Heavy rain increases the spread of fungal spores that transmit blight.)

Some PNAP scientists assume that if they introduce blight-resistant cultivars, farmers can plant earlier in the rainy season and obtain higher yields. In theory this is sensible. In practice, earlier planting is difficult for many farmers, which contributes to the high frequency (52 percent) of stated preferences for short duration cultivars (Table 7.5).

Short dormancy (to minimize the time between harvest and adequate sprouting of seed for replanting) is an advantage where rainfall distribution allows double and sometimes multiple cropping. Many farmers surveyed, however, again prefer diversity in this trait. Having cultivars with both long and short dormancy allows farmers greater flexibility in managing seed stocks and harvest and planting dates.

One PNAP cultivar with short dormancy (four to eight weeks) is Cruza 148 (not yet locally named). A purple ring in the flesh of this variety initially made some international scientists skeptical of its acceptability to producers and consumers. On-farm trials in Rwanda and Burundi, however, showed that its short dormancy and bacterial-wilt tolerance outweighed any possible disadvantages of tuber flesh color. Rwanda farm surveys showed that an older local cultivar (Magayane) has long been widely accepted in spite of purple spots in the flesh of the tuber.

PNAP scientists agree that short dormancy is a desirable screening criterion that deserves greater emphasis (without excluding long dormancy). Dormancy data should then begin to be recorded during the multiseason germ-plasm screening process so that this trait can be taken into account formally.

In sum, survey findings concerning farmers' preferences about length of growth cycle and dormancy suggested that PNAP's germ-plasm screening program should include an emphasis on cultivars with short dormancy (four to eight weeks) and short to medium growth cycles (75–90 and 100–110 days). Longer-cycle cultivars should not be excluded, but neither should they dominate PNAP's seed production.

### Suitability of PNAP's Improved Cultivars

Table 7.6 summarizes characteristics of the eight improved cultivars PNAP had introduced in Rwanda by mid-1986. The acceptability of some of these cultivars in such traits as dry-matter content, maturity period, dormancy, and cooking time has already been discussed. The type of cultivar recently emphasized in the germ-plasm screening and seed-production programs has large tubers, high yields, relatively late maturity, long dormancies, and good late-blight resistance (as in the varieties Gahinga, Kinigi, and Sangema). Farmers who can benefit most from this type of potato cultivar have above-average land and capital assets. They can afford to keep plots of land occupied with longer-maturing varieties, and they have adequate cash to purchase food while awaiting the potato harvest.

A central recommendation from the farm surveys, however, was that PNAP's germ-plasm screening and seed programs give less emphasis to the type of cultivar just described and more emphasis to those with early maturity, short dormancy, or both (as in the cultivars Montsama, Gasore, and Cruza 148). Given Rwanda's very small farms and high population density, many farmers can benefit from this type of cultivar. They cannot necessarily afford to keep scarce land occupied under longer-maturing varieties, and they do not have adequate cash to purchase food while waiting for the potato harvest. PNAP has released a diverse set of improved cultivars. The program's future success depends on such diversity, so that it can shift the proportion of seed of any of a number of cultivars in its repertoire in response, for example, to loss of disease

TABLE 7.6
Potato Cultivars Selected and Distributed by PNAP[a] in Rwanda

| Cultivar and Date of Introduction | Germ-plasm Source | Length of Vegetative Cycle (days) | Skin Color | Starch Content (%) | Late Blight Resistance | Bacterial Wilt Tolerance | Length of Dormancy (days) | Approx. On-Farm Yields[b] (t/ha) | Observations |
|---|---|---|---|---|---|---|---|---|---|
| Montsama (1972–ISAR[c]) (1980–PNAP) | Mexico/CIP 720049 | 90–100 | red | 14–19 | intermed. | poor | 80–90 | 18 | Taste and short cycle appreciated by farmers. |
| Sangema (1972–ISAR) (1980–PNAP) | Mexico/CIP 800948 | 110–120 | pink with red eyes | 12–16 | intermed. (declining) | good | 90–105 | 15 | Taste much appreciated by farmers; very marketable. |
| Gasore (1982–PNAP) | Belgium (Graso-28; Gracilia x Soraia) | 75–90 | red | 15–18 | poor | intermed. | 30–45 | 12 | Earliness and short dormancy appreciated by farmers. |
| Gahinga (a.k.a. Uganda II, Murca) (1982–PNAP) | Mexico/CIP 720097 (Greta x Alpha) | 110–130 | red | 12–13 | good | poor | 100–120 | 35 | Farmers do not appreciate its taste/high water content, poor storability, and large tubers. Markets declining. |
| Kinigi (1982–PNAP) | CIP 378699-2 | 110–120 | red | 13–16 | intermed. (declining) | good/intermed. | 100–120 | 15 | Deep eyes—difficult to peel. |
| Nseko (1982–PNAP) | Mexico (65-ZA-5)/CIP 720055 | 110–130 | red | 13–17 | good | poor | 100–120 | 35 | |
| Petero (1985–PNAP) | CIP 380083-2 | 110–120 | red | ? | good | ? | 90–105 | 22 | Large tubers, deep eyes. |
| Cruza 148 (1985–PNAP) | CIP 720118 | 110–130 | white with purple eyes | ? | intermed. | good | 30–60 | 22 | Purple spots in flesh acceptable to Rwandan farmers. Very short dormancy much appreciated. |

(Other clones in advanced stages of screening: 380083-3, 380083-4, 380505-5, and 800935.)
[a]PNAP = Programme National d'Amelioration de la Pomme de Terre (National Potato Improvement Program)
[b]Mean yields based on 8 to 15 on-farm trials for each cultivar. (PNAP Annual Reports 1980–1986)
[c]ISAR = Institut des Sciences Agronomiques du Rwanda (Rwandan Institute of Agronomic Sciences)

resistance or to change in demand. Appropriate responses of course require accurate monitoring of producers, consumers, and markets.

## Impact and Distribution of New Cultivars

With a small research team and modest resources, the Rwandan potato-research program quickly achieved a remarkable impact. Two improved cultivars PNAP released in 1980 (Montsama and Sangema) are found in all of the country's major potato-production zones and are among the four most frequently encountered potato cultivars in the country (see again Table 7.1). In 40 percent of the potato fields observed in four production zones, Sangema is the cultivar occupying the largest area. In nearly another quarter of the observed fields, the largest area is allocated to the variety Montsama. Later cultivar releases have yet to achieve a comparable distribution for two reasons.

First, the time elapsed simply has been shorter. The four cultivars PNAP released subsequent to Sangema and Montsama had been available for three years rather than five at the time of the farm surveys. Second, the seed distribution system itself allows farmers limited and slow access to new cultivars.

PNAP provides each year over 600 tons of seed of improved cultivars to a government seed multiplication service and to up to two dozen rural development projects, which in turn multiply the seed and sell it to farmers. PNAP itself is not responsible for selling seed directly to individual farmers. As the high yields and profitability of improved potato cultivars became known, however, both PNAP and the seed multiplication projects experienced increasing unofficial private demand for seed from prominent individuals. Such demands, politically difficult to refuse, diminish the stock of seed available for multiplication and subsequent distribution to farmers.

Poor roads and communications also limit the distribution of improved seed. The rural development projects that receive seed to multiply are well distributed throughout the country, but inadequate transport limits access for farmers who live more than a few kilometers beyond a project. Only 11 percent of the farm households surveyed report they obtained seed from rural development projects.

PNAP has considered at least two means of widening the distribution of improved seed to farmers. One possibility is to authorize private traders to sell certified seed in rural market centers. A second option is for PNAP itself to obtain permission to sell some of its seed directly to farmers in individually restricted small quantities (e.g., 5- to 10-kilogram sacks). PNAP could, for example, once or twice a year put announcements on the radio saying where its truck would pass on a particular day to sell seed in 5- or 10-kilogram units directly to individual small farmers on a cash-only basis. Even if PNAP were to sell only a small proportion of its seed in restricted units directly to individual farmers, the impact could be substantial, given the way small farmers themselves acquire, test, and manage new cultivars.

For farmers, cultivar adoption is a gradual process when production and food security risks are high. Some farmers, in first trying a new potato variety, begin with as few as five or ten tubers planted near home for observation. They can obtain such quantities through informal networks of exchange (and theft) from neighbors, research stations, and seed farms. Small farmers conduct their own informal experiments with small quantities of any new cultivar, and gradually incorporate it into their existing stocks if pleased with its performance over a number of seasons (Johnson 1971; Richards 1985).

In short, given the informal rural seed-distribution networks, PNAP could increase the impact of its new potato cultivars by selling some of its seed directly to farmers, by allowing private traders to sell certified seed, or both. The seed would have to be sold in small enough units to be an affordable risk for small farmers.

Increasing cultivation of the two most popular PNAP cultivars, San-gema and Montsama, carries biological risks that could be diminished if a number of other improved cultivars could be effectively distributed. Expansion of the area under just one or two varieties speeds the loss of genetic resistance to late blight (if the resistance is of the common type controlled by a single gene). For biological reasons, it is now especially important that cultivar diversity be encouraged among farmers, that PNAP's seed program itself avoid specialization in one or two cultivars, and that farmers' channels of access to new cultivars be improved.

## Conclusions

This chapter has focused on one of the best financed sectors of international agricultural research—plant breeding and germ-plasm screening. While such biological sciences dominate the International Agricultural Research Centers, social science involvement has grown in the last 10 to 15 years. This increase is linked to agricultural researchers' and donors' concern with the impact and suitability of new agricultural technologies, with constraints on the adoption of these technologies, and with the need to adapt them better to farmers' circumstances and to distribute them more rapidly.

The Rwandan field research discussed here drew attention to potato cultivar characteristics important to farmers, assessed the impact and distribution of PNAP's new cultivars, and suggested new agronomic research directions based on farmers' current practices (including trials testing cultivar mixtures and intercropping).

This approach does not suggest that nothing in existing farming systems can change. Farmers' varied resources confer different capacities to adopt innovations, however, and these capacities must be assessed in field interviews and tested in on-farm trials before investing substantial resources in a particular new cultivar or technique. Farmers' cultivar adoption decisions, for example, are affected by the seasonal availability of land, labor, and cash; by the competing demands that production of other crops places on these resources; and by the role of each crop in the household economy (as sources of food and cash controlled by different household members).

If interdisciplinary agricultural research begins and ends with the perspective of farmers (Rhoades and Booth 1982), technological improvements are more likely to be locally usable. Presidents viewing research stations from helicopters then will not glimpse a world alien to farmers. These observations are not new, and many readers will take them as common sense. Their influence on technical agricultural research, however, often has been negligible.

## Notes

The research upon which this chapter is based was supported by a 1984–86 postdoctoral fellowship from the Rockefeller Foundation. I am grateful for additional scientific and financial support from the Rwandan Institute of Agronomic Sciences (ISAR), the Rwandan National Potato Research Program (PNAP), and the International Potato Center (CIP). Eighteen students from the National University of Rwanda and the Women's Agricultural College at Nyagahanga ably and patiently conducted farmer interviews.

Views expressed here are those of the author alone and do not necessarily represent the official views of any of these institutions.

I thank the following individuals for comments on an earlier version of this paper: Primo Accatino, Martin Bicamumpaka, Kenneth Brown, Mike Dessert, Krista Dessert, Anton Haverkort, Douglas Horton, Juan Landeo, Sylvester Nganga, Robert E. Rhoades, Richard L. Sawyer, and Gregory Scott.

1. The program (PNAP–Programme National d'Amélioration de la Pomme de Terre) was, for example, nominated for the 1985 UNESCO prize for scientific achievement; the International Service for National Agricultural Research (ISNAR) at the Hague uses it as a case-study training document; the President of Rwanda awarded it a national prize for its role in helping to alleviate famine during the 1984 drought; it is widely praised by national officials and foreign-aid donors as one of Rwanda's most successful agricultural projects; and it is used as a model for new projects in Rwanda and neighboring countries.

2. PNAP was established by the government of Rwanda, with technical and financial support from the International Potato Center. PNAP is part of the Rwandan Institute of Agronomic Sciences (ISAR).

3. Similar studies on farmers' use of potato varieties have been done in Peru (Brush et al. 1981) and Nepal (Rhoades 1985). Previous social science research at PNAP in Rwanda had concentrated on the economics of production and marketing (Durr 1980; Monares 1984; and Scott 1985), and on consumption (Poats 1981).

4. Field research methods and procedures included formal and informal surveys of farmers in Rwanda's three major potato-production zones, as well as in the more marginal mid-elevation zones. Informal interviews were conducted with farmers, agricultural researchers, and technicians affiliated with rural development projects and with various programs of the National Agricultural Research Institute (ISAR) throughout the country.

In the formal surveys, data were collected both through interviews and through direct observation of farmers' potato fields. Fields were sketched and measured, and observations recorded on their distance from the family compound, intercropping, crop varieties, plant density, hilling and weeding practices, use or not of raised seedbeds, fertilizer, compost, manure, and crop diseases. Before beginning the surveys, all interviewers were trained at PNAP by Rwandan scientists on potato agronomy, storage, physiology, genetics, and pathology. The author trained interviewers in social science interview techniques, sampling procedures, and problems of data reliability.

Since there was not an adequate framework for systematic random sampling, survey farmers were purposely chosen to reflect important differences in wealth and in distance from primary and secondary roads, trading and administrative centers, and agricultural project services. Specific survey localities within regions were chosen so as to capture important differences in soils, rainfall, altitude, commercial opportunities, and infrastructure development.

In each survey household, both men and women were interviewed whenever possible, with interviewers instructed to rely most heavily on the individual with the best knowledge of potato varieties and of the household's cultivation activities. With two exceptions, all of the interviewers were female—an advantage, given the active role of Rwandan women in agriculture and the local unacceptability of having males interview female farmers.

5. Rwandan farmers use the same criterion of dry matter or starchiness (*gufufuka* in the Rwandan language) to define taste quality of sweet potatoes and cassava. While they rate some sweet-potato cultivars as being too starchy and having too little water, they do not rate any potato cultivars as having insufficient water.

6. In the first half of 1986, potato prices in northern Rwanda's major potato-production zone declined sharply—from 10 to 15 Rwandan francs per kilogram down to 2 or 3 francs per kilogram. The price decline was associated with production increases that followed the 1984 drought, and with the opening of previously forested land in the north. Influential individuals who acquired large landholdings in recently cleared areas planted new high-yielding varieties and

contributed substantially to production increases that led to the price declines of 1986.

7. In the high altitudes at which most potatoes are grown in Rwanda, the rate of seed degeneration from accumulation of viruses is low, so that farmers can multiply and plant their own seed of a new variety for up to a decade before having to purchase clean seed again.

8. Dormancy in a potato is the time elapsed between harvest of the tuber and optimal sprouting for planting. This trait varies by cultivar from a few weeks to several months.

9. Rwandan farmers can produce two to three potato crops per year—two rainy-season crops on the hills and one dry-season crop in the marshy valleys. In the higher altitudes where rainfall is well distributed all year, potatoes are continuously cropped.

# References

Altieri, Miguel A.
   1985    Developing Pest Management Strategies for Small Farmers Based on Traditional Knowledge. Development Anthropology Network, Bulletin of the Institute for Development Anthropology 3(1):13–18.

Bicamumpaka, Martin, and Anton Haverkort
   1983    The PNAP Approach to Potato Development in Rwanda. *In* Agricultural Research in Rwanda: Assessment and Perspectives. The Hague: ISNAR.

Brokensha, David, et al.
   1980    Indigenous Knowledge Systems. Lanham, MD: University Press of America.

Brush, Stephen, H. J. Carney, and Z. Huaman
   1981    Dynamics of Andean Potato Agriculture. Economic Botany 35:70–88.

CIP (International Potato Center)
   1984    Potatoes for the Developing World. Lima: International Potato Center.
   1985    Present and Future Strategies for Potato Breeding and Improvement. Lima: International Potato Center.

CIMMYT (International Maize and Wheat Improvement Center)
   1986    Sustaining Agricultural Yields, Part II. [Excerpts from publication by that title by D. L. Plucknett and N. J. H. Smith in Biological Science 36(1), January 1986.] CIMMYT Newsletter, No. 751. CIP (International Potato Center).

Devaux, André, and Pierre Tegera
   1981    Les parcelles d'évaluation: une solution au problème de transfert des technologies? Bulletin Agricole du Rwanda, No. 14:165–167.

Durr, George
   1980    Potato Production and Utilization in Rwanda. Social Science Department Working Paper 1983–1. Lima: International Potato Center.

Government of Rwanda
1985    Résultats de l'Enquête Nationale Agricole, 1984, Vol. I. Kigali, Rwanda: Ministry of Agriculture.

Hyden, Goran
1980    Beyond Ujamaa in Tanzania: Underdevelopment and an Uncaptured Peasantry. London: Heinemann.

Janssens, Mark, et al.
1985    Les cultures associées au Rwanda. Butare, Rwanda: Institut des Sciences Agronomiques du Rwanda.

Johnson, Allan
1971    Individuality and Experimentation in Traditional Agriculture. Human Ecology 1(2):149–159.

MacFadyen, J. T.
1985    United Nations: A Battle over Seeds. The Atlantic Monthly 256:36–39. November.

Monares, A.
1984    Building an Effective Country Program: The Case of Rwanda. Social Science Department Working Paper 1984-3. Lima: International Potato Center.

Murphy, Josette
1985    User-Oriented Research: A Synthesis of the IARC's Experience. Paper prepared for the Inter-Center Seminar on Women and Agricultural Technology. Bellagio, Italy.

Nganga, Sylvester
1983    The PNAP (Programme Nationale d'Amélioration de la Pomme de Terre) in Rwanda: Institutional Development, Organization and Achievements. *In* Agricultural Research in Rwanda: Assessment and Perspectives. The Hague: ISNAR.

PNAP (Programme Nationale d'Amélioration de la Pomme de Terre)
1980–1986    Rapports Annuels. Ruhengeri, Rwanda: PNAP/ISAR.

1984    Rapport Annuel. Ruhengeri, Rwanda: PNAP/ISAR.

1985    Rapport Annuel. Ruhengeri, Rwanda: PNAP/ISAR.

Poats, Susan
1981    La pomme de terre au Rwanda: résultats préliminaires d'une enquête de consommation. Bulletin Agricole du Rwanda, No. 14:82–91.

Rhoades, Robert
1985    Traditional Potato Production and Farmers' Selection of Varieties in Eastern Nepal. Potatoes in Food Systems Research Series, Report No. 2. Lima: International Potato Center.

Rhoades, Robert, and Robert Booth
1982    Farmer-Back-to-Farmer: A Model for Generating Acceptable Agricultural Technology. Agricultural Administration 11:127–137.

Richards, Paul
1985    Indigenous Agricultural Evolution: Ecology and Food Production in West Africa. London: Hutchison.

Salamon, R. N.
   1970   The History and Social Influence of the Potato. Cambridge: Cambridge University Press.
Scott, Gregory
   1985   Potato Marketing in Rwanda. Lima: International Potato Center.
Simmonds, Norman
   1979   Principles of Crop Improvement. London: Longman.
   1984   The State of the Art of Farming Systems Research. Report to the World Bank.
Thresh, J. M.
   1982   Cropping Practices and Virus Spread. Annual Review of Phytopathology 20:193–218.
Willey, R. W.
   1979   Intercropping—Its Importance and Research Needs. Field Crop Abstracts 31(1).
Woolfe, J. A.
   1986   The Potato in the Human Diet. Cambridge: Cambridge University Press.
Ziegler, Robert S., and M. Kayibigi
   1984   Quantifying Burundi Farmer Rejection of Late-Maturing High-Yielding Maize. Bujumbura, Burundi: Institut des Sciences Agronomiques du Burundi (ISABU).

# 8

# Issues in Agricultural Change: Case Study from Ismani, Iringa Region, Tanzania

*Benson C. Nindi*

This chapter examines agricultural change through the use of state coercion and ill-informed agrarian policies. Tanzanian party ideology accepts the desirability of an egalitarian society, with public control of productive resources and also with a national program of education and community service. Compulsory villagization (*ujamaa*) has been developed in haste, directed by bureaucratic authorities unresponsive to adverse economic effects, and unimaginative in regard to local conditions. This chapter analyzes the direction of change and the costs of administrative error and its consequence in a specific area—Iringa District, historically a "breadbasket" of Tanzania.

In order to clarify the implications of coercion and violence discussed in this chapter, I will give brief descriptions of the recent agricultural and social history of Iringa Region, including the farming system, sources of migrant labor, economic and political barriers to agricultural innovation, and the ujamaa policy.

## Recent Agricultural and Social History of Iringa Region

Iringa Region's first cooperative society, the Ismani Native Maize Growers' Cooperative Society, Limited, was established when Ismani became the most important maize-growing area in Tanzania in the early 1950s (Nindi 1977–1978:64). Its potential attracted the colonial state, which responded by focusing greater attention on the region. In 1957 the Ministry of Agriculture (Kilimo) seconded a full-time agricultural field officer to deal with development problems in Ismani (Bailey 1973:280).

After independence, in 1964, 19,700 tons of maize from Ismani were marketed through the official channels by five cooperative societies (Nindi 1977–1978:65). That was the zenith of its development. Since then yields have fallen and production has stagnated, so that now in years of normal rainfall approximately 2,000 tons of maize are marketed annually.

The development of Iringa District is closely related to the changing attitude of the largest ethnic group within the area, the Hehe. Although not united until the 1950s, this group had achieved sufficient military coordination to repel the first European incursion into its territory, but the strong adherence to tradition that has always been exhibited by the Hehe also kept them aloof from the economic changes taking place in East Africa. Rather than cooperate or work for someone else, the individual Hehe preferred to obtain cash from the sale of a few cows or surplus maize (Silberfein 1974:8).

Plans were initiated for a more rapid modernization of Iringa District in the early 1950s when Adam Sapi became the Hehe leader. Local Hehe subsistence cultivators were encouraged to engage in wage employment on a more sustained basis and to cultivate larger acreages of maize (Nindi 1985:3). They were also advised to emulate the more mobile migrant workers, (i.e., Kinga, Bena, and Gogo) who were more willing to respond to wage labor opportunities, and whom they had always held in low regard (Silberfein 1974:8). It is questionable, however, whether engagement in wage labor was beneficial for these groups, as well as for the Hehe.

Agricultural development was hindered at this point by the limited number of known cash crops available to African growers. The only way of earning income directly from agriculture was by increasing production of the basic food crop, maize. After World War II, as the demand for maize within Tanzania rose steadily, a market was created in Iringa with the establishment of a major mill in Iringa town. An expansion of maize production occurred in all parts of the district that had access to markets, resulting in land shortage in some parts, and a decline in soil fertility (Oxaal et al. 1975:156). It was at this time that Ismani was "discovered" by African entrepreneurs seeking to create new farms and expand existing maize production.

As Ismani was only sparsely settled by Hehe tribesmen who cultivated millet and maize for subsistence, early immigrants had no difficulty in obtaining areas of bush from the *jumbe* (headman) of Ismani.[1] The empty land was distributed freely until no more was available. This early settlement of Ismani saw a number of innovations in farm management and cultivation methods, including oxen traction and new tillage techniques. These same techniques are still being used, but they have proved unable to maintain output at its former high levels.

The immigration to Ismani was rapid. News of the success of the Ismani farmers spread quickly. Drivers passing along the road north of Iringa would observe the activity and then report on it after reaching their destination. Many farmers were attracted by the possibility of obtaining land and of acquiring an immediate cash return within just one growing season. Some even moved back and forth regularly between their home areas and their maize holdings to supervise the hired laborers who did most of the field work. While farmers gained free access to land in the first years of settlement, after a while there was no longer any empty bush available for allocation in this way, and land changed hands by private arrangement, either through sale or through rental agreements. By 1965, 4,000 cultivators of maize were occupying 80,000 to 100,000 acres (Nindi 1985:4). Ismani was transformed by African capitalist farmers into the single most important source of marketed maize in the country. It was the maize granary of Tanzania, producing in 1969 approximately one-fifth of the national maize supply.

This meant that some farmers were now in a position to accumulate increasingly large acreages—by 1969 a few farmers owned over 600 acres—while many others were landless, holding land only through annual tenancy agreements (Oxaal et al. 1975:157). The ownership of land had become increasingly monopolized by wealthier farmers.

In the 1970s Ismani experienced a decline in maize production, and most farmers have had little hope of advancing their living standard from the cultivation of maize. What are the reasons for this decline and why were not innovations introduced to compensate for declining production?

## Farming Systems

During the past forty years Ismani Division has experienced no fewer than three different systems of maize production (see Table 8.1). The first system emerged in the late 1940s, when rapid migration into the area, coupled with large-scale bush clearing and burning, resulted in an extensive but profitable system. Farmers who did not live in the area hired local migrant labor to burn the bush and broadcast maize seed on the land, without any attempts at cultivation. The method of farming was relatively simple, as may be appreciated from the description of the Agricultural Assistant, Mr. E. Edward:

Let us first examine the farmer's method of cultivation. In the first place he cuts the existing forest to within 4 to 5 feet of the ground, clears and

TABLE 8.1
Evolution of Maize Production in Ismani Division, Iringa District

| Features | Period 1 1950–1962 | Period 2 1962–1970 | Period 3 1970–1980 |
|---|---|---|---|
| Tillage techniques | Manual, clear and burn | Oxen plow | Full mechanization |
| Nonfarm inputs | None | Implements, tractors | Seed, insecticide, fertilizer |
| Sources of labor | Own plus local hired labor | | Group labor |
| Sources of capital | Trade and salary | Farming | Government |
| Principal factor limiting productivity | | Decline in soil fertility; shortage of labor | Soil fertility declining |
| Population | Rapid settlement | Peak | |
| Yield | High (ca. 3,400 kg/ha) | Declining (2,200 kg/ha) | Low (ca. 1,200 kg/ha) |

*Source:* Adapted from Tanzania Rural Development Bank (1976).

burns all undergrowth leaving a layer of ash on the surface of the soil. No further preparation of soil is made. When he is ready to sow his seed he merely chops a hole with his *jembe* (hoe), sows from 4 to 6 seeds per hole in the case of maize, and so the whole *shamba* (farm) is sown in usual native fashion. In the two remaining seasons no proper cultivation preparatory to sowing is done, other than to clean the *shamba* of any weed growth that might have appeared (Tanzania National Archives [TNA] File No. 24/A/3/36v).

Germination was good, however, as the land had benefited from many years of growth and decay of grass and leaves, and potash from wood helped to improve further the fertility of the topsoil (Nindi 1985:6). The same practice was carried out in the following agricultural cycle: maize stalks were burned and seeds again broadcast without any pretense at cultivation. In the fourth year in most cases, as the topsoil began to harden, it became more difficult to broadcast seeds without any cultivation. At this point, as tree stumps and roots that had been left began to make cultivation difficult, the land was usually abandoned and new areas were cleared for farming (Feldman 1971).

Since those who moved to new areas considered such new land to be theirs, while it was accepted that nobody could claim the areas that had been temporarily abandoned, land became scarce. Shifting cultivation was preferred, however, because it yielded the best results; for example, one acre produced about 15 bags of maize (Tanzania Rural Development Bank 1976:46). This was profitable because the expenditure on cultivation was negligible, and farmers weeded only once, not twice or three times as became necessary in later years.

The second farming system developed in a less dramatic fashion than the first as a consequence of the closing of the Ismani "frontiers." When most of the available land had been claimed, mechanized production using oxen and tractors began to expand rapidly, causing the distinction between a landed and a laboring class to become more obvious (Nindi 1985:7). The use of mechanization allowed wealthier farmers to cultivate increasingly larger holdings, often expanding their farm size through purchases or rental agreements.

Soil fertility declined during this period because the maize monoculture did not replace soil nutrients, but the crop production season in Ismani was complementary to that in the colder highlands of the region, so that it was possible to produce two maize crops per year by moving capital and labor between the two areas. This system was still practical even when yields were falling due to an inadequate fallow period and no use of manuring or fertilizer (Nindi 1985:8).

The labor utilized by the large farmers was generally migrant labor (a point to which we shall return), and the accumulation of land and wealth was exclusively in the hands of Africans (Lwoga 1985:23–24). The labor force came primarily from some distance, on a seasonal basis, which was unusual in the Tanzanian context. It consisted of impoverished agropastoralists from the Gogo area and poor farmers from the overcrowded highlands forced to look for cash income elsewhere while continuing the cultivation of their own land, on which they harvested their crops two months after the maize was harvested in Ismani. The farmers who cultivated the Ismani area in the first instance opened large tracts of land that they were able to work by using this migrant labor (Nindi 1984:67). The technique applied was labor and land intensive, with few technological improvements such as chemical fertilizers and insecticides. A peculiar relationship thus began to develop between the migrant workers and the landowners. The landowners had made the transition from smallholder agriculture to rural capitalism, utilizing a labor force that was not landless (Nindi 1984:70). Rather, these were laborers who were ready and willing to work both for others and on their own land, and were provided with opportunities by either the availability of more land or technological improvements.

An African "yeoman farmer" class was emerging. Many farmers expanded their farms, using ox-drawn or tractor-drawn equipment, enclosing their fields, and generally moving away from the traditional cultivation of a smallholding sufficient only for subsistence. In rural areas progressive innovators owned lorries and small transport companies. Individual farmers used mechanized equipment and employed labor (Nindi 1975:23). Privilege was a major consequence of the differentiation that had arisen, because in some cases rich farmers were able to use government cooperative tractors without paying for them, or to obtain their services at optimal times (Fortmann 1979).

Mr. Griffiths, Provincial Commissioner (P.C.) for the region, described the process:

> General indications throughout the province show a tendency among Africans towards a steady, slow increase in crop production and the departure from subsistence agriculture. The use of mechanical and other agricultural implements is becoming more popular and in one or two areas Africans are buying their own tractors. . . . There are over 11,000 ox-drawn ploughs in the province. The emergence of a yeoman farmer class is being encouraged and there are several farmers, both in Ismani-Iringa, and Njombe, who cultivate between 200 and 300 acres each. It is interesting to note that one or two of these are interested in taking out rights of occupancy (Tanzania 1958:140–141).

The third system, which came into operation in 1971, was the most dramatic of all. Private ownership of large holdings was prohibited, and much of the land that had been farmed privately was turned over to ujamaa villages. The complementary double maize-crop system based on seasonal migrations was abolished. Though the total area under maize in Ismani declined, there was a pronounced rise in the use of improved inputs, particularly seed, fertilizer, and insecticide, and a corresponding increase in multiple tractor operations on large communal plots. All inputs were government supplied, but their provision failed to have any significant impact on productivity, and marketed output dropped sharply, accounting for the low marketing of 1971–1972 (Nindi 1978:225–290).

## Sources of Migrant Labor

Migrant laborers, particularly the Gogo from Dodoma, came to work in Ismani. In Dodoma, drought constitutes the region's single biggest environmental problem. Partly in response to this environmental factor, the Gogo used to move their cattle temporarily in search of pasture and wage employment. As Rigby has pointed out, "a history of Dodoma Region is a history of famine among the Gogo cultivating pastoralists" (1969:21). For example, in the 1947–48 season Dodoma and Manyoni Districts had only 12 inches and 14 inches of rain respectively. In the following season, 1948–49, during eight months of drought and general famine, 12,363 tons of food had to be imported for sale, and a famine officer was appointed in Dodoma District.

The situation improved in the following two seasons, but again in the 1952–53 season there was a severe famine, and food reserves were rapidly exhausted. The estimated crop was only 25 percent of a normal harvest, with many farmers harvesting virtually nothing, and 100,000 cattle died during the drought. Prices of staple foodstuffs in the villages rose precipitously (Potton 1971:3–6).

By the end of 1954, some 10,000 people in Mpwapwa District, Dodoma Region, were working on famine-relief projects to obtain money with which to buy food. Drought had reduced cattle production by 60 percent since 1952. In the three Gogo districts, 1955 started with famine at its worst and ended with floods unprecedented in 30 years. Between these two major disasters, there was an invasion of desert locusts. In 1956 rains were good, but invasions of quelea birds caused great damage in many areas. In the mid-1950s, as a consequence, 5,000–7,000 Gogo searched for food and work in Iringa District (Nindi 1975:27).

While some Gogo people migrated to other areas in search of work, some took cattle and goats to Ismani and exchanged them for grain. This type of transaction was one of the ways in which the emerging yeoman class in Ismani started to accumulate wealth. Some migrants from Njombe District also came in search of work. These Bena and Kinga migrants from Njombe usually insisted on being paid in cash, as most of them had some experience as migrant laborers on the sisal or tea plantations (Nindi 1984:66–78), whereas Gogo migrants were sometimes paid wages, but most of the time they were given only food. The migrants from Njombe District usually stayed in Ismani for short periods before returning home, e.g., six months (Lwoga 1985:41–65), whereas the migrants from Dodoma are known to have stayed in Ismani and worked for longer periods, e.g., five years.

There are peaks and slack periods of labor activity. Feldman and Fournier (1976:453) have suggested, with regard to a comparable situation, that the seasonality of labor demand has caused agricultural production to depend on the utilization of a substantial casual labor force. The combination of a demand for surplus production in agriculture, with substantial seasonal variation in labor demand, in an economy with limited opportunities outside the surplus agricultural sector, must lead to the existence of a special kind of labor force. This is a labor force that can maintain itself in those periods when the surplus production system does not require it. The development of the agricultural surplus is therefore associated with two phenomena: seasonal migration and the existence of small, subsistence holdings alongside the large, surplus-producing enterprises (Nindi 1975:24). Accumulation through surplus agricultural production is a consequence of these social relations in production.

## Technical, Economic, and Political Barriers to Agricultural Innovation

Not all settlers in Ismani came with the same resources. A few who were already traders, large-scale cattle owners, or even commercial farmers at home, started maize cultivation in Ismani with considerably more capital than the majority. It was they who were able to clear and cultivate large acreages, employ labor, and adopt the new techniques of large-scale cultivation. Most farmers, by contrast, came with little or no capital. Over 60 percent of farmers surveyed by the Department of Agriculture in 1957 had less than 10 acres, and this was still the case in 1969 (Bailey 1973:282). Since their main implement for cultivation was the hoe, the majority of farmers could not be highly innovative even while yields per acre in the early years of settlement were still high. They were constrained by scarce resources into following conventional patterns of agriculture, while the bigger farmers could afford to carry out innovations. The failure of Ismani farmers (both large and small) to make further innovations is partly due to technical and economic factors, partly to a lack of access to new ideas or to the resources to implement them, but mainly to governmental policy mistakes (Nindi 1986:19).

The Ministry of Agriculture has recommended improvements in techniques of husbandry, soil conservation, and the maintenance of soil nutrients. Most of the advice, however, fails to take into account the risk and uncertainty that the innovation involves, the costs that it may incur not only in terms of purchased inputs but also of balances in the whole farm economy, and the differences in farming scale that make advice relevant or feasible for some farmers while not for others (De Vries 1978:76–90).

For example, farmers are advised to plant their seeds before the outset of the rains, some time during September (Bailey 1973:285), but this is impossible for farmers with more than a few acres unless tractors are used to plow up the hard-baked soil. Very few farmers own tractors, and those who do, recognizing the advantages of early planting, give themselves priority, so the others have no option but to plant later. Other difficulties are associated with very early planting. The first rainfall of the season is so erratic that the early planted seed may die, having germinated after a first rain and then been left dry for two or more weeks. Early planting also means that there is more weed growth with consequent increased labor costs for weeding (Nindi 1985:3–4). The earliest planted crops are also susceptible to a higher concentration of insect pests. Only the rich farmers have the means to deal with these factors.

Maize plants in Ismani are usually placed unevenly and planted at unequal and suboptimal depths, and peasants are constantly urged to improve these features of their cultivation. But this "bad" cultivation practice has its reasons, and a change would have important implications for the farmers. The level of mechanization is limited. Plowing and planting are carried out simultaneously, the seed being broadcast in the furrow by one person on foot who follows the plow in its path. The seed is then covered by the soil thrown up from the adjacent furrow. This system enables more land to be cultivated per unit input of labor and machinery, but it also leads to bad spacing and planting. This deficiency could only be corrected by reducing the acreage planted and spending more time on plowing and planting or by an investment in additional machinery, prohibitive for most farmers (De Vries 1976:91–94).

Advice to farmers to weed more thoroughly also takes little account of the labor problem that most families face (Nindi 1984:54). For weeding to be more effective without involving additional labor, the planting operations would need to be improved in the manner described above.

Ismani's erratic rainfall makes farmers reluctant to use chemical fertilizer. They experienced crop failure when fertilizer burned the plants in low rainfall years in the late 1960s and early 1970s, and again in 1984. The cost of fertilizer, which in the past has been generally met by cooperative society loans, augments the risk to the farmer by leaving him not only with less output, but also in debt (Nindi 1977–1978:73).

Other recommendations for longer-term maintenance of soil nutrients and structure involve planting trees, building contour banks, and rotating crops. In Ismani, my data show that there have usually been obstacles to the adoption of rotations. For example, for some the crops may not be suitable because of the conditions of the areas; for others they might be unsuitable because they have little usefulness. An interesting example here is that fodder crops have been recommended for rotations in Ismani, but at present rough common pasture is used for cattle (Bailey 1973:286). Fodder crops would simply divert scarce labor and land away from more valuable cash and food crops.

Negative responses to Ministry of Agriculture advice are thus far from irrational, given the way in which improvements are suggested. Nevertheless, the combination of a number of the recommendations suggested above with the provision of improved seed varieties might totally transform the pattern of response that now occurs (Nindi 1986:2–4).

From the position of the farmer, the opportunity to adopt an innovation differs according to his scale of farming and the relative importance of agriculture in his total economic activities. Most small farmers are also petty traders, casual workers, or artisans (Bailey 1973:287), for their income from agriculture does not satisfy their household wants and needs throughout the year. The income from trade or wage labor is not generally sufficient to provide capital for investment in agricultural innovations (Nindi 1986:10), and the shortage of family labor is another important barrier to innovation. Since small farmers derive their main income outside agriculture, their agricultural objective is to meet a target of staple needs rather than to maximize output. Many of the small farmers without regular sources of income rent their *shambas* (farms) and depend greatly on hired labor. Those with less than fifty acres do not usually own farm machinery and yet depend upon it for cultivation. They must hire machinery from other farmers who inevitably give themselves priority (Nindi 1986:14).

There is another kind of larger farmer, one who has some reserve capital and who can always finance a planned amount of cultivation, except perhaps after an exceptionally bad harvest or an unsuccessful nonagricultural investment (Bailey 1973:288). Farmers in such a position can afford the costs of at least some of the recommended innovations, yet most are not innovators. To explain this a distinction must be drawn between farmers at this level who confine their economic activity to agriculture, and those who combine agriculture with other enterprises (Coulson 1977:74).

Among the larger farmers who have regular work or who are engaged in trade are shopkeepers and transporters. The bus services to Ismani from Iringa and even as far as Njombe, Mbeya, or Itungi port are virtually monopolized by the Kwacha transport company, owned by a group of Ismani farmers and Iringa businessmen. This company has more than 30 vehicles. Small farmers may own lorries and retail shops in Ismani and Iringa town. Their affluence should not be overrated, but in rural Tanzania it places most of them significantly above the majority of the population. In some cases their enterprises are financed initially by agricultural profits from Ismani, and in others Ismani agriculture grew concurrently with the other businesses. People invest more in transport and other economic activities because they are safer and more profitable than agriculture, given the recent trends in policy that discourage large-scale farming (Nindi 1975:61).

There is in Ismani no institutional framework for the development and practice of new ideas for agriculture, and consequently farmers depend on outside agencies for innovations (Bailey 1973:292). There is a curious contradiction in the technology being indigenously generated in Ismani: agricultural inventions are occasionally made in Ismani, but other farmers do not adapt them (Nindi 1977–1978:74).

An example of this was a new method of threshing maize before packing it for sale. Most farmers placed cobs in sacks that were then beaten with sticks. This ruined the sacks, but it was easy to collect the seeds after separation. Another method was to beat loose cobs in a pile. This saved the sacks but was a messier process. A new manual process, which we observed, was to build a platform of sunflower stalks surrounded by walls on three sides, and to stake the poles supporting the platform into ground that had been prepared by having clean mud spread on it. The platform was latticed, and the maize cobs were beaten on it so that the seed fell through the gaps onto the clean floor, and was then packed into sacks. This manual operation seemed to combine the advantages of both the other methods, while avoiding each of their disadvantages (Bailey 1973:295). The platform, incidentally, could also be used for separating sunflower seed, which was the second main cash crop of Ismani.

Only a few farmers tried this quick, cheap, and clean method. The rest, presumably, did not think of experimenting and did not accept innovation unless it came from a legitimized source. In fact, the more well-to-do farmers had bought manually operated threshing machines that were costly and hard to use. There is some status involved in the ownership of a machine rather than a hand-made platform, but we do not think that this was the explanation. Rather, the machine was presented as an innovation, in a context where farmers expected to be able to relate what they saw to their own needs and aspirations. Such machines were on view in agricultural stores and in use on experimental farms in Ismani. In short, machines are invested with a quality that connects them immediately with a farmer's needs, while homemade adaptations are not (Bailey 1973:296).

Farmers are extremely dependent on external institutions for new ideas that might improve the presently stagnating agricultural system.

The most viable source of new ideas and goods from outside are the rural retail shops. The shops, *dukas*, are symbols of modernity to attract customers—transistor radios always blare from shop counters—and they make goods accessible to farmers in a context where novelty is acceptable. Although hoes, axes, and other small agricultural implements are sold in dukas, no innovative agricultural inputs are to be found in them because of the two following reasons (Nindi 1977–1978:75).

First, the Tanzanian government has declared the private retailing of all Tanzanian maize, including improved seed, illegal. This was intended to protect farmers from commercial exploitation by middlemen, in line with the government's socialist objectives (Bailey 1973:297). In practice, the result was that improved seed was effectively kept away from the bulk of the rural farmers by making them dependent on an inefficient distribution system through Kilimo (The Ministry of Agriculture). Second, credit for any capital inputs such as fertilizer was extended to farmers only if they purchased through cooperative societies. Hence one finds on the shelves of the well-stocked rural duka no improved seed varieties, insecticides, or fertilizer, but only such conventionally essential farm implements as hoes and axes, for which credit is not provided (Coulson 1977:86–90).

Exclusion of the dukas from any role in the dissemination of agricultural innovation keeps most currently available innovations inaccessible to most people in Ismani. The paradoxical effect of the government's policy of limiting profit for private retailers is to maintain existing economic differences in the countryside: richer and more educated farmers can seek alternative channels both for information about new inputs, and for obtaining them.

## Ujamaa Policy

Development of ujamaa villages in Iringa Region prior to 1975 varied a great deal from area to area. The ujamaa system was established in part to overcome the weaknesses in the agricultural system inherited from the colonial era, some of which had been accentuated in the early years of independence. These included dualism, growing economic differentiation among smallholders and among regions, low productivity and low level of labor utilization in the smallholder sector, and the pattern of rural settlement with isolated homesteads spread over a vast country (Nindi 1975:40). In addition to surmounting economic problems, the ujamaa system was designed to create the institutional framework for political democracy and for a socialist, self-reliant pattern of rural development. Thus the main objectives of Tanzania's rural development policies and programs may be summarized as follows:

- The creation of a framework that would facilitate both the mobilization of the rural population and the diffusion of technological and organizational innovations to diversify and increase agricultural and nonagricultural production
- The encouragement of collective and cooperative forms of production
- The distribution of goods and marketing—with a view towards transforming the rural sector into a socialist structure capable of promoting rural development without excessive differentiation in wealth, income, and power
- An improvement of the basic social and economic infrastructure, with particular emphasis on meeting the basic needs of the masses and the promotion of interregional equity (Ghai et al. 1979:52).

The guiding ideology stressed that responsibility for achieving these rural development objectives must lie primarily with the peasants who would be supported morally, organizationally, and materially by the party and the government, working mainly through district and other rural institutions.

According to the country's first president, Julius Nyerere, socialism in Tanzania will be achieved step by step, depending on how people understand it for their own development (Nyerere 1967:337–366). For example, Mkungugu ujamaa village in Ismani division was officially inaugurated on November 1, 1971. Accounts of how the program was introduced to Mkungugu village have varied, however. According to Martin Kalolo, who later became chairman of the village, the Iringa Regional Commissioner, Dr. Wilbert Klerruu, came to Mkungugu. Klerruu was a Chagga (from the most progressive farming area of the country, Mount Kilimanjaro); he also possessed a Ph.D. in political science from the University of California, Los Angeles (Coulson 1982:248–249), an unusual qualification for a politician; and he was probably the most able organizer in the party. In 1969 he was the Deputy Secretary General of the Tanganyika African National Union (TANU) and a member of the Central Committee as well as being publicity secretary of TANU,[2] and he was instrumental in the formation of the ten-cell system in the country.[3] He wrote a shorter version of *Democracy and the Party System*, which he called *One Party System of Government* (Bienen 1970:356–357), and he was certainly the most effective in creating ujamaa villages. As a regional commissioner of Mtwara in 1970, he claimed 750 ujamaa villages out of less than 2,000 in the whole country. After Klerruu was transferred to Iringa Region, the number of ujamaa villages in the area suddenly increased to 650 by the end of 1971.

Klerruu told the inhabitants of Mkungugu at a meeting that there would no longer be individual farming, but people should work on the communal farm together. On the first occasion, Kalolo denounced the proposal. In October 1971 Klerruu called the inhabitants together again, and at this meeting, after detailed discussions, villagers were told that any person who refused to be a member of an ujamaa village had to leave the village, and all those who remained must become members of the ujamaa village. Some people, most of the rich peasants, left, and others remained. Martin Kalolo had no choice. He decided to remain and to be a member of the ujamaa village (Tanzania High Court 1972:4).

Robert Nyenze, who became the vice-chairman of the village, said that a division secretary named Mduda, who worked for the party in promoting ideological work at the village level, had visited Mkungugu village and informed the people there about the ujamaa philosophy. The villagers rejected the idea. When land was officially expropriated in May 1971, nearby Igula village was among the first to accept the policy and become an ujamaa village. Senior government officials visited Mkungugu village again, and addressed the peasants at great length about the policy. Nyenze, who had experience in a cooperative society, took the initiative and held talks with the ten-cell leaders, who agreed to summon another meeting. Forty-four agreed to form an ujamaa village and requested the Divisional Staff to pass their ideas on to the government officials in Iringa town. The Divisional Staff asked the villagers why they had rejected the idea at the first meeting. They told the official that they had changed their position, and now accepted the policy's demands (Nindi 1985:15, Coulson 1977:94). What made the villagers change their minds? A lot of pressure from the government.

According to Nyenze, Klerruu had instructed that if the Mkungugu people were not ready to form an ujamaa village, he was prepared to split the village and merge one-half with Kisinga ujamaa village and the other half with Ndolela ujamaa village. Those who did not agree to these policy instructions would lose their shambas and would have to leave the area.[4]

The divisional secretary then suggested to the Mkungugu villagers that they form a committee, and when this was done Martin Kalolo was elected Chairman and Robert Nyenze became the Vice-Chairman. Mkungugu ujamaa village was officially opened. The Iringa Area Commissioner sent them axes, hoes, and a tractor, and the villagers proceeded to work (Awiti 1973:233).

After the ujamaa policy was implemented in Ismani, toward the end of 1970, the mobilization of the larger farmers hostile to the program grew rapidly. It culminated in the arrest of over 20 large-scale Ismani farmers after the assassination of Iringa Regional Commissioner Dr. Wilbert Klerruu by Abdallah Mwamwindi at Mkungugu village. These influential farmers had raised Tsh 30,000 (US $2,500) for the defense fund of the assassin (Oxaal 1975:157).

Abdallah Mwamwindi had been the owner of a 160-acre shamba, which included his residential premises consisting of two main houses and his family graveyard. He had started with three acres in 1955 when he was a lorry driver. Later he had given up the driving job and started farming, expanding the farm to about 160 acres before the ujamaa program started. Mwamwindi and others had hoped that it would be possible to implement a project for opening up virgin lands and using them for the communal farms, rather than expropriating private farms. It turned out, however, that individual holdings were required to be included in the program, and partly because of this, according to Mwamwindi, the project had been rejected. He felt his shamba had been stolen (Nindi 1985:15).

The Mkungugu ujamaa plan dealt with the big areas that had become ujamaa land. The program did not forbid individual holdings as such. The Iringa-Dodoma road runs through Mkungugu village, and the villagers chose to reserve the land on the south side of this road for their collective farms. Allotments of three acres of land for each were reserved on the other side for individual farming (Tanzania High Court 1972:7).

A member could own two pieces of land, one on each side of the road. Mwamwindi had been one such person. Mwamwindi, his brother, his sister, and his wives had been allotted about 20 acres as individual plots. How did Mwamwindi's former holding stand in relation to the ujamaa program and in relation to his new holdings? The fresh allocations of individual shambas on the north side of the road were cut out of his former holding in the area. The rest of his land was allotted to other members (Tanzania High Court 1972:8). The temporary individual plots allotted to Mwamwindi in the area reserved for communal activities were again taken out of his former holding. This area was some 350 feet from his premises and about 180 feet from his family graveyard.[5] It was on this shamba that Mwamwindi was plowing with his tractor when Klerruu met him on the afternoon of December 25, 1971.

The events of the previous day, December 24, 1971, as recorded in the transcript of Mwamwindi's trial, enable us to see how the policy of villagization was put into practice. To avoid the problems of pests and weeds mentioned earlier, the best period for maize planting is between early November and late December; maize planted after this period is unlikely to yield a good harvest. Klerruu was keen to help the ujamaa villagers plow their communal farms and plant their maize seeds before the end of the planting season. He spared no effort, but went from one village to another encouraging the people and personally helping peasants in different activities on their communal plots (Nindi 1985:17; Coulson 1977:92; Bienen 1970:356–357).

Klerruu arrived at the ujamaa village, Tarafani, on the morning of December 24, 1971, to supervise the tractors plowing the communal plots. From there he left for Igula village to check on the progress of communal activities. From Igula he proceeded to Ndolela ujamaa village. Work on the communal farm at Ndolela was interrupted by rain when he arrived there at about 5 p.m. Klerruu called a meeting of the villagers and asked if the members were prepared to work the following day. The ujamaa members agreed and Klerruu promised to return to help them in their work (Nindi 1985:17).

The following day Klerruu turned up as he had promised. There were two tractors on the farm and a team of 90 members of the Ndolela ujamaa village. The villagers and Klerruu spent their Christmas Day plowing and planting maize seed. They had no lunch on that day; by around 5:30 p.m. the villagers were exhausted and hungry, so they stopped for the day with Klerruu. By that time 60 acres had been plowed and planted with maize. The tired Regional Commissioner then left the village and drove alone and unescorted in his government car toward Iringa town.

Klerruu stopped at Mkungugu village and parked his car close to Mwamwindi's house. According to the evidence of the accused himself, Dr. Klerruu said to Mwamwindi:

> What are you doing? To this Mwamwindi said: Sir . . . I am cultivating this place which has been given to me by my fellow villagers! I do not know what annoyed him (the accused's testimony continues) he started to abuse me. . . . Then Mwamwindi said to Klerruu: Sir, why and what did I do? Mwamwindi goes on: He replied to me, Be quiet, shut your mouth, what hii, hii, hii? And he was abusing [me] in English (Tanzania High Court 1972:10).

According to the evidence produced in court, Klerruu asked Mwamwindi to climb down from the tractor. According to Mwamwindi's story Klerruu held a stick in his hand with which he was pushing him. Mwamwindi said: "I thought to snatch the stick from him, but I thought that he might have a pistol." Mwamwindi insists that Klerruu also abused him in English but he was only able to catch the phrase "Bloody fool." When Mwamwindi asked Klerruu why he was abusing him, Klerruu retorted: *"Tazama ninawaambia lakini hamsikii"* (Look, I tell you but you would not listen).

Mwamwindi then went into his house, collected a gun, and returned. Klerruu was shot and fell down dead. Mwamwindi called a boy to help him to put Klerruu's dead body in the R.C.'s car. Then Mwamwindi drove to Iringa town. Later, a jury found him guilty of the murder of Klerruu, and on October 2, 1972, he was sentenced to death (Nindi 1985:18).

The following points need to be considered. First, immediately after the incident 20 rich farmers, including some leaders of Mkungugu village, were arrested for having contributed money for the defense of Mwamwindi (Oxaal 1975:157). Second, there was a split among the jury assessors in court as to whether Mwamwindi was guilty. Third, there were rumors that earlier there had been plans to eliminate the Regional Commissioner at the Welfare Center in Iringa town. Klerruu had been tipped off about this, so he never turned up. Fourth, after Klerruu's death, Iringa town attracted national attention. The Party held a meeting in Iringa in 1972 and published *Siasa ni Kilimo* (Politics in Agriculture). This was a policy statement notable for its lack of emphasis on ujamaa as a means of raising production. Instead it emphasized technocratic methods, like applications of manure, the use of oxen, and so forth, that implied softening the policy (Nindi 1985:19; Coulson 1977:96).

The compulsory resettlement of most of the rural population in villages between 1970 and 1976 had both short- and long-term negative effects. The original document proposing *ujamaa vijijini* as Tanzania's means to achieve rural socialism and transformation categorically stressed persuasion, gradualism, and cooperation, rather than settlement and compulsion.

The most important reason for the change of ujamaa from voluntary cooperation to compulsory villagization seems to have been its definition as *policy*. Once defined as a government policy, ujamaa became the responsibility of government and party leaders to implement and to demonstrate that they had been doing so. Promotion of these officials was sometimes based on how effective they had been in advocating the policy. This led directly to a concern with the number of villages and villagers involved, since these were easier to implement and to demonstrate than the degree of cooperative production. This, in turn, introduced a competitive dynamic. One regional commissioner would announce that (say) three ujamaa villages had been formed in his region, another that five or ten had been formed, and so on. Within a couple of months, there were "campaigns" for whole districts and even regions (Raikes 1986:127).

"Persuasion" initially took the form of offering services to those willing to move. But this became increasingly difficult to afford as the number of villages increased. Thus it began to be replaced by direct compulsion. More important, in late 1973 Nyerere reversed his former position, stating that all the rural population should be in villages within three years and that, since voluntary persuasion had "failed," compulsion could be used to move people into villages. This set off a further burst of "campaigns," known as *sogeza* (which means to move) in Ismani, in which state force was used to move people and often to smash their previous houses to ensure that they did not return when things had quieted down. While three years is a very short time to move most of the rural population, true to the spirit of competition that had built up, many authorities found it still better to villagize within one or two years (Raikes 1986:128).

Villagization had seriously contributed to the food shortage. Movement to new and often unknown areas with different soils, rainfall, water availability, and disease patterns, together with the necessity to build new huts and get the rhythm of life and production going again, could not fail to have a serious negative effect. The long-term negative effects included increased traveling time to and from fields, overcultivation of fields close to the village, and greater distances to collect firewood and drinking water, all of which have both increased labor requirements and decreased soil fertility.

## Conclusion

Ever since the government started intervening directly in agricultural production, it has made both policy and technical mistakes that have led to failures and a waste of resources. The cost is not only financial: the social cost is an uncooperative peasantry. In the last few decades in certain conditions producers could innovate and increase agricultural production. The motivation then was of course the possibility of accumulating wealth and securing a better future. It seems unlikely that Tanzania's problems of agricultural production will go away while bureaucrats think that they understand what peasant producers ought to do, and while they see the solution to those problems in terms of enforcing their policies, in a top-down fashion, on the local peasantry.

Tanzania now faces the dual challenge of restructuring its economy while maintaining its fundamental commitment to freedom, equality, and growth for all its citizens. In contrast to the 1970s, macroeconomic concerns have moved to the center of the development dialogue in the 1980s. The state sets its goals as nothing less than the elaboration of effective policies firmly rooted in democratic and ethical norms. In this paper it has been shown that the villagization program was developed in haste, directed by bureaucratic authoritarians unresponsive to adverse socioeconomic effects, and unimaginative in regard to local historical and social conditions and problems.

Since it was clear that self-motivation of villages in Ismani and elsewhere could be a slow process, and since the chosen mode of implementation was administrative, there had to be specific kinds of incentives to co-opt peasants to join the ujamaa movement. One incentive could have been careful planning from below and political preparation to show peasants how they could improve themselves through cooperation. This strategy, however, would require genuine participation from below, knowledge, and patience, which were not forthcoming; and interestingly enough, quite a number of bureaucrats were themselves doubtful whether it could work. The latter might explain the hasty and uncreative nature by which ujamaa policies were initiated. The tragic case described above and other problems might have been avoided if peasant producers had been consulted and involved right from the beginning of this program, if the style of implementation had been less dogmatic, and if greater flexibility had been built into the program to allow a period of adjustment for large, private farmers.

Implementation measures should not, however, be regarded as being merely administrative or technical. Like ideologies and policies, they must be understood in the context of the different economic and political forces operating in the society. The facts of policy implementation also reflect the existing pattern of social forces—their relative power, their interests, their conflict, and their alliances.

Finally, this rush for villagization short-circuited technical planning that might have avoided the serious problems faced now in the form of overcrowding, great distances from water sources, and, most serious, lack of motivation. Even to build a common understanding about what villagization can produce takes considerable time. This is what ujamaa has failed to do, while it deprived farmers of status, property, and dignity.

## Notes

1. The village jumbe was a traditional administrator at the village level, answerable to the chief in the hierarchy (Adam Sapi, Chief of the Hehe) through ward, division, and sub-chief.

2. TANU was the only political party in mainland Tanganyika until 1977. After 1977 TANU and the Afroshirazi Party from Zanzibar were united and formed CCM (Chama Cha Mapinduzi).

3. The party reaches people at the grass-roots level through the ten-cell system. Every ten houses elects its leader, who handles household disputes, etc. Above the ten-cell leader is the ward, division, etc.

4. President Nyerere once welcomed the principle of compensation, in his essay on National Property: "When I use my energy and talent to clear a piece

of ground for my use it is clear that I am trying to transform this basic gift of God, so that it can satisfy a human need. . . . By clearing that ground, I have actually added to its value and have enabled it to be used to satisfy a human need. Whoever then takes this piece of ground must pay me for adding value to it through clearing it by my own labour" (Daily News 1973:1). The same source, on the other hand, quotes the Chief Justice as also saying that: "Since Tanzania believes in *Ujamaa*, the interests of many people in land cases should override those of some individuals. The Judiciary cannot be used as a tool to oppose *ujamaa*" (Daily News 1973:4). The contradictory views above created a dilemma for the people who were supposed to implement the policy and resolve disputes according to the law, especially since Nyerere also said: "The Rule of Law is part of Socialism. Until this prevails socialism does not prevail" (Daily News 1984:1).

5. The Hehe maintain a close connection with their ancestors and spirits; they bury their hereditary chiefs and care for their graves with great care and reverence. Rituals attached to the grave of a chief play an important part in their ancestor worship. When any pressing difficulty, such as the severe illness of a child or some complex internal conflict, had seemingly no solution with natural aid, the members of the family concerned would go and place a container of local beer at the graveyard in the hope that the spirit of their ancestor would succor them in their troubles (Nindi 1982:34). The next morning after sunrise, the container would be inspected, and if the level of the beer had dropped there was much rejoicing, for the spirit of their ancestor was deemed to have heard their prayers and, by drinking, expressed his willingness to help them solve their difficulties.

# References

Awiti, A.
  1973    Economic Differentiation in Ismani, Iringa Region. The African Review
          3(2). June.
Bailey, F. G., ed.
  1973    Ismani. *In* Debate and Compromise. Oxford: Basil Blackwell.
Bienen, H.
  1970    Tanzanian Party Transformation and Economic Development. Princeton,
          NJ: Princeton University Press.
Coulson, A.
  1977    Tanzanian Agriculture. Review of African Political Economy 10. Sep-
          tember–December.
  1982    Tanzania: A Political Economy. Oxford: Clarendon Press.
Daily News
  1973    Criminal Case No. 31 of 1972. Dar Es Salaam, Tanzania. May 25.
  1984    Dar Es Salaam, Tanzania. March 16.

De Vries, J.
   1976   On the Effectiveness of Agricultural Extension: A Case Study of Maize Growing Practices in Iringa, Tanzania. East African Journal of Rural Development 9.

   1978   Agricultural Extension and the Development of Ujamaa Villages in Tanzania: Toward a Dialogical Agricultural Extension Model. Ph.D. dissertation. University of Wisconsin, Madison.

Feldman, D., and A. Fournier
   1976   Social Relations and Agricultural Production in Nepal's Terai. Journal of Peasant Studies 3(4).

Feldman, R.
   1971   Custom and Capitalism: A Study of Land Tenure in Ismani, Tanzania. E. R. B. Paper 71.3, University of Dar es Salaam, Tanzania.

Fortmann, L.
   1979   Ujamaa Villages. Tanzania's Experience with Agrarian Socialism. Manuscript prepared for the World Conference on Agrarian Reform, Food and Agriculture Organization, Rome.

Ghai, D., E. Lee, J. Maeda, S. Radwan, eds.
   1979   Overcoming Rural Underdevelopment. Proceedings of a Workshop on Alternative Agrarian Systems and Rural Development. Arusha, Tanzania, 4–14 April. Geneva: International Labor Organization.

Lwoga, C. M. L.
   1985   Labour Migration and Rural Development. Ph.D. dissertation. Churchill College, Cambridge.

Nindi, B. C.
   1975   The Articulation of Ismani Social Economic Structure and Its Implications for Ujamaa Vijijini Policy. M.A. dissertation. Sociology Department, University of Dar es Salaam.

   1977–1978   A Historical Study of the Cooperative Movement in Tanzania. Transafrican Journal of History 6 and 7.

   1978   Agricultural Change and Rural Class Formation in Iringa District, Tanzania. Ph.D. dissertation. Department of Sociology and Social Anthropology, University of Hull.

   1982   Uhehe: 1850 to 1906. Tanzania Notes and Records. Nos. 88 and 89.

   1984   Impact of Migratory Labour on Health. Mawazo 5(4).

   1985   Compulsion in the Implementation of Agricultural Policies: A Case Study from Iringa District, Tanzania. Discussion Paper. The Scandinavian Institute of African Studies.

   1986   Traditional Agricultural Extension System in Tanzania: A Critical Analysis. Workshop on Economic Policies and Strategies, February 19–21.

Nyerere, J. K.
   1967   Social and Rural Development. New York: Oxford University Press.

Oxaal, I., T. Barnett, and D. Booth, eds.
   1975    Beyond the Sociology of Development. London: Routledge and Kegan
           Paul.
Potton, M.
   1971    Dodoma 1929–1959: A History of Famine. BRALUP Research Paper
           No. 44. University of Dar es Salaam.
Raikes, Philip
   1986    Eating the Carrot and Wielding the Stick: The Agricultural Sector in
           Tanzania. *In* Tanzania Crisis and Struggle for Survival. Jannik Boesen,
           Kjell J. Havnevik, Juliani Koponen, and Rie Odgaard, eds. Uppsala:
           Scandinavian Institute of African Studies.
Rigby, P.
   1969    Cattle and Kinship Among the Gogo. Ithaca, NY: Cornell University
           Press.
Silberfein, M.
   1974    Constraints on the Expansion of Commercial Agriculture: Iringa District.
           Athens, OH: Ohio University Center for International Studies. Africa
           Program.
Tanzania
   1958    Provincial Commissioner Annual Report. Government Printer. Dar es
           Salaam.
Tanzania High Court
   1972    Criminal Case No. 37. Iringa: The High Court of Tanzania.
Tanzania National Archives (TNA) No. 24/A/3/36v
   n.d.
Tanzania Rural Development Bank
   1976    Project URT/71/004, Iringa Region, Tanzania. Integrated Rural De-
           velopment Proposals. Vol.1, Part 1. Food and Agriculture Organization
           of the United Nations. East Anglia, Britain.

# 9

# Changing Perceptions of Pastoral Development: A Case Study from Turkana District, Kenya

*Richard Hogg*

## Introduction

Several recent books and articles have described the failure of pastoral development projects in Africa (see Horowitz 1979; Helland 1980; Galaty 1980; Raikes 1981; Swift 1982; Jahnke 1982; Sandford 1983). According to Sandford:

> Sensible pastoral development does not involve the wholesale adoption of stereotyped models; nor is it just a matter of devising a locally acceptable social framework within which to impose universal technical solutions. Neither the institutional framework nor the technical changes to be adopted are uniquely right. In pastoral development there are a number of choices to be made (1983:6).

Hitherto, one of the main assumptions of pastoral development has been the need to change traditional range management practices (see Allan 1965; L. Brown 1963, 1973; Pratt and Gwynne 1977). According to Brown, for example, "The problem posed by the semiarid areas is basically one of bad land use, through the keeping of very large numbers of poor quality livestock" (1963:2), and the only way to attack the problem was to increase control over the numbers and movement of livestock (see also Pratt and Gwynne 1977:190–192). Sandford has labeled this view "the Mainstream view" of pastoralism, and writes:

> A . . . consequence of the Mainstream view is the tendency for pastoral development programmes to assign a key role to firm intervention by government and to management of resources by government officials. There

is much talk of need for *control* and *discipline*. This follows from distrust of existing pastoral institutions and from the belief that modern science has discovered the technical solutions to the problems of the pastoral areas (1983:17–18).

In this chapter I describe the history and changing government and donor perceptions of pastoral development in Turkana District, Kenya (see Figure 9.1).

## Pastoral Development

Prior to World War II the British administration of Turkana was mainly concerned with keeping the peace and putting a stop to intertribal raiding; it had neither the manpower nor the resources to become directly involved in pastoral development. The lifting of the threat of an Italian invasion from Ethiopia in the early 1940s, however, as well as a growing concern over the effects of drought and famine, spurred district officials into taking a more active interest in the pastoral economy.[1] For example, according to Turnbull, the District Commissioner in 1943, "The Turkana are a pastoral people and every need and problem of the district is bound up with questions of stock management and the control of water and grazing" (Colony and Protectorate of Kenya 1943:2). Turnbull firmly believed that the chief problem in the district was to wean the Turkana "from unsuccessful ranching on land which is rapidly becoming fit for nothing but a desert stock economy" (Colony and Protectorate of Kenya 1943:15).

Turnbull's views reflected a growing concern in the colonial administration over land degradation in the African reserve areas. This concern had been greatly stimulated by the widespread publicity given in Kenya to the crisis in the American "dust bowl" states in the 1930s, and by Maher's reports on ecological degradation in Kitui and Baringo Districts in 1937 (see Anderson 1984).

By the 1940s, therefore, both district administrators and technical staff in Turkana had become firmly convinced that overstocking and overgrazing were widespread and increasing, and that the only possible remedies were: (1) to improve grazing controls (with a limited development of water supplies to open up new areas),[2] and (2) to encourage the development of alternatives to pastoralism, such as fishing in the lake and irrigation agriculture. Anything else was only likely to encourage the buildup of livestock herds.[3]

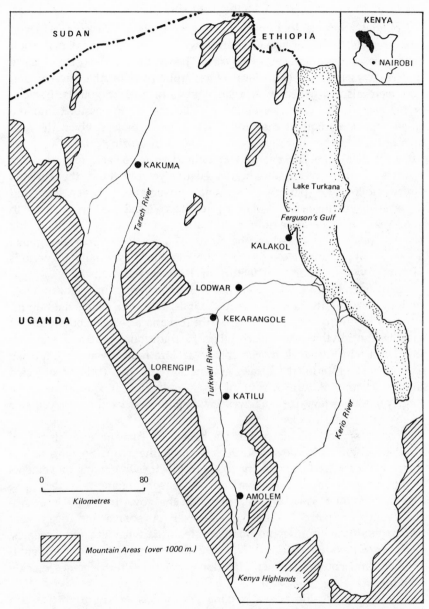

Figure 9.1 Turkana District. *Source:* Adapted from Gulliver, *The Family Herds* (London: Routledge and Kegan Paul, 1955), p. 25.

## Grazing Controls

Colonial attempts to impose grazing controls in Turkana achieved mixed results. In the early years controls were restricted to the demarcation of dry-season grazing reserves (*epaka*).[4] The opening and closing of these reserves was left largely to local chiefs appointed by the government, who were also provided with a small force of grazing guards. Because of the size of the reserves, effective policing was impossible, and the chiefs reported frequent cases of trespass. Nevertheless, given the vast area of the reserves and the small contingent of grazing guards assigned to patrol them, the Turkana appear by and large to have respected the reserves. Two major reasons motivated this respect. First, the Turkana already followed a pattern of seasonal movements between wet- and dry-season grazing areas. Adapting to the colonial system, at least in good years, was therefore not too difficult for them. Second, local grazing reserves (*amaire*), declared by the elders of a particular area to regulate access to important riverine and hilltop grazing, especially in periods of stress, were a traditional feature of Turkana pastoralism.[5]

Apart from their very large area, therefore, government epaka signified nothing particularly new. In the mid-1950s, however, when the administration began to introduce into North Turkana a formalized system of grazing control that was clearly alien to traditional practices and that interfered with livestock movements in a more radical way by imposing a four-block, rotational "Texas" grazing system, the Turkana objected to the scheme. Within a year of its introduction it was abandoned, largely because few Turkana were willing to restrict their movements to the prescribed blocks.

The history of colonial grazing schemes in Turkana is a history of good intentions with few resources to back them up. So long as the government allowed the Turkana to control their own grazing movements within a rather vague framework of dry-season grazing reserves, there was little conflict. The Turkana knew that the government did not have the resources to patrol the reserves effectively. As soon as the government attempted to institute more sophisticated rotational grazing schemes, however, which the Turkana regarded as inappropriate to their environment and counter to their traditional practices, the schemes quickly collapsed.

While colonial officers saw grazing schemes as an important weapon in their battle against drought and famine, the major thrust of colonial and post-colonial policy was to encourage the development of economic alternatives to pastoralism.[6]

## Economic Diversification

*Fishing*

Although a few Turkana had always fished in the lake, the development of a fishing industry started as a famine-relief measure. In 1937 the District Annual Report records 26 paupers at Ferguson's Gulf on Lake Turkana. This number slowly increased over the years as other Turkana were settled at the lake. In 1958 there were 200 destitute people at the Gulf, but the main expansion to the fishing industry came after the 1960–61 drought, when large numbers of destitute Turkana were settled along the lake shore. In 1967 the Turkana Fishermen's Cooperative Society was registered. At its height the Cooperative had more than 4,000 members and contributed substantially to the district economy. In 1978 the total value of fish bought was Ksh 6.2 million (Government of Kenya 1980), but in recent years fish catches and fishermen's incomes have plummeted, and Ferguson's Gulf, the original source of most of the fish, has dried up. According to a recent report in the *Kenyan Daily Nation* (September 26, 1986): "Today the Turkana whose living standards the project was supposed to uplift remain as miserable as ever. . . . Worse, the society [Cooperative] is today faced with liquidation." The large fish-freezing plant built at the lake with Norwegian finances in the early 1980s at a cost of approximately Ksh 25 million (US $1.6 million), has never been used.

Even in its heyday, the fishing industry never contributed to any permanent shift away from livestock keeping. What it did was to allow poor Turkana the opportunity to diversify economically while continuing to invest in livestock. As Henriksen, who studied the fishing industry in the early 1970s, writes, "A crucial point in connection with these new economic opportunities (irrigation and fishing) is that those who pursue them with some success invest as much as possible of their earnings in stock" (1974:54).

*Irrigation Agriculture*

The first government irrigation scheme to be established was in the Omo Delta in the 1940s, but due to international boundary changes the area was later incorporated within Ethiopia. Two further schemes were established in 1951–1952 on the Turkwel River near Lodwar, the district headquarters. Both were intended to increase local food production substantially by diverting unpredictable spate floods into leveled basins for crop production. The crop was intended to grow to maturity on a single flooding. Both schemes suffered from severe flooding, however, and were later abandoned when the river shifted its course.

These initial attempts at irrigation development were relatively modest, but in the early 1960s, after the 1960–61 drought, two influential reports (L. Brown 1963; FAO 1964) recommended a rapid expansion of irrigation in the district. According to Brown, only 2,430 families could exist off the products of the existing stock population in Turkana District, and "About 16,000 families should therefore be absorbed into other occupations" (1963:25). This assertion was later repeated in the 1964 Food and Agriculture Organization (FAO) report:

> Although a population of 125,000 in an area of 24,000 sq. miles may not seem much, agronomists agree that, in a purely pastoral economy, the district can only support a small fraction of this number . . . consequently, overgrazing has been going on for a long time causing a severe deterioration of the vegetation and a decrease in stock carrying capacity (1964:7).

The first FAO/UNDP[7] scheme to be established was in 1966 at Kekarongole, some 30km south of Lodwar; it was followed by Katilu and Amolem in the early 1970s (see Figure 9.1). The cost of these schemes was extravagant. The 1984 Ministry of Agriculture evaluation estimated total expenditure in 1983/4 at US $61,240 per hectare or $21,800 per tenant household, and the operating costs alone amounted to over three times the gross margin any farmer could expect from his plot (Government of Kenya 1984a).

Due to low and variable annual yields, irrigation farming in Turkana has never offered an even marginally secure economic existence, let alone a profitable alternative to pastoralism. Even in good years few farmers could support themselves from their plots alone. Talks (1983:34) calculates that after subtracting labor costs, the average net income from an irrigated plot in 1982 was only Ksh 1,545 (US $96). Broche-Due and Storås, two Norwegian anthropologists who studied the Katilu scheme in 1983, calculate that the net income from a typical irrigated plot was likely to be less than Ksh 1,000 (1983:78), or the equivalent of the price of one large cow.

Irrigation development has therefore done little to provide a viable alternative to pastoralism; farmers at the schemes continue to invest in livestock. Indeed, if anything, the process of desertification has been exacerbated rather than alleviated by the schemes. Along the Turkwel, for instance, the population of Katilu scheme increased from almost nothing in 1970 to over 10,000 by 1980. As a result there has been massive destruction of forest along the banks of the Turkwel for buildings, stock enclosures, fuelwood, and farm plots, and localized heavy overgrazing by settlement herds and flocks (see Broche-Due and Storäs 1983).[8]

The history of pastoral development in Turkana has been dominated by a widespread concern over the effects of overstocking and overgrazing. Almost every intervention in the pastoral sector has been justified in terms of these twin evils. As a result, not only has the lion's share of development resources gone into the development of alternatives to pastoralism, while the pastoral sector itself has been relatively neglected— in 1978–1979, for example, Ksh 104,000 (US $13,000) was allocated by the Ministry of Agriculture to irrigation development and only Ksh 9,500 (US $1,187) to range development and marketing together (see Government of Kenya 1980:27)—but when interventions have taken place, they have been imposed from above with little effort to involve the pastoralists themselves. Yet there has never been any serious investigation of "carrying capacity" nor of ecological trends in the district. As Horowitz writes of pastoral projects in West Africa,

> So many documents, officials, and even scientists repeat the assertion of pastoral responsibility for environmental degradation that the accusation has achieved the status of a fundamental truth, so self-evident a case that marshalling evidence on its behalf is superfluous if not in fact absurd . . . (1979:27).

## New Directions

In the last five years or so, largely as a result of the poor performance of past development projects and several critical studies by anthropologists (see Henriksen 1974; Hogg 1982, 1983; Broche-Due and Storäs 1983), there has been a rethinking of development priorities. The FAO and UNDP have withdrawn from the irrigation schemes, and the Norwegian government, the largest single bilateral donor in the district, is committed to a phased withdrawal not only from the agricultural schemes, but from its support of the Turkana Fishermen's Cooperative. The Norwegians no longer view either irrigation or fishing as an answer to the problems of pastoral destitution. Even among district officials there is a growing awareness of the need to emphasize livestock development; there is little point in spending large sums on a search for alternatives to pastoralism in a district like Turkana. Indeed, at a meeting I attended at the end of 1983, officials from the Ministry of Agriculture and Livestock Development bluntly told the manager of the Turkana Rehabilitation Program (TRP), which had been established in 1980 to rehabilitate destitute Turkana, not to proceed with a planned expansion of irrigation schemes along the Turkwel and Kerio Rivers.

Along with a shift of interest back to the pastoral sector has come a growing realization of the need to involve pastoralists more fully in the planning of development and to build on their existing knowledge of the environment. The recent Turkana District Livestock Plan (1984) exemplifies this new approach to pastoral development. The plan calls for:

1. The maintenance of the present mobility of the Turkana pastoral system as making best use of the vegetation in an area of irregular rainfall
2. The avoidance of activities that could encourage settlement in the form of permanent or semipermanent camps with attached herds
3. The need to maximize the involvement and contribution of the district's inhabitants in all aspects and phases of livestock development and, consequently, to formulate this development at an appropriate level
4. The need to lay heavy emphasis on improving stock-owner/ institution contact through effective methods of extension, familiarization, and training.

As a result of the Turkana Livestock Plan, the British organization, Oxfam, has become involved in the implementation of three development projects in the district: a livestock restocking project, a water harvesting project, and a browse and fodder project. All three projects are intended ultimately for implementation and management by Turkana themselves, possibly through the establishment of "herders associations."

## Oxfam Restocking Project

One of the recommendations of the Turkana District Livestock Plan (TDLP) was for a pilot restocking project. The principal objectives of the project were:

1. To provide destitute families with the means (livestock, camping equipment, maize) to return to the pastoral sector
2. To experiment with different kinds and levels of livestock "packages"
3. To explore the possibility of establishing "herders associations" among restocked families, based on the traditional Turkana cooperative grazing community or *adekar* (see Government of Kenya 1984b:118–119).

An initial feasibility study was carried out in the Kerio River area in mid-1984. On the basis of this study Oxfam approved funding for a two-year period starting in early 1985. A manager and his assistant, both anthropologists, were recruited to manage the project (see Hogg 1985a). As of September 1986, over 300 families had been restocked, and a total of nearly 20,000 small stock distributed. Each family received between 50 and 70 small stock, one pack donkey and, in order to give the flock an opportunity to establish itself in the first year, a supplement of 540–720 kg of maize.

The Oxfam restocking project is not the first of its kind in the area. In 1963, just before independence, there had been an earlier attempt to distribute small stock to destitute families. Only 20 small stock were distributed per family, however, and no attempt was made to provide a comprehensive package—including maize, pack animals, camping equipment (water containers and cooking pots) and veterinary support— which would have allowed a family to return to the pastoral sector as a viable unit. As a result, most of the families that received stock were soon back on famine relief (see Brainard 1981:92).

In contrast, the Oxfam project is intended as a much more radical and comprehensive experiment to allow destitute Turkana who have fallen out of the pastoral sector through drought and livestock disease to reestablish themselves as nomadic pastoralists. As such it represents a significant departure from most previous development projects in the area, which were based on the assumption that destitution represented a "natural" process of adjustment to carrying capacity. As I argue below, this view of pastoral destitution is seriously open to question.

First, overstocking is more often than not asserted rather than proved. Information from anthropologists and ecologists working on the South Turkana Ecosystems Project (STEP)[9] indicates that there is no long-term range degradation except around permanent settlements, and that much of the area in the south of the district is completely deserted of both people and stock. In 1982 only half of the district was occupied, and within this half 45 percent of the population was living within 5 km of a permanent settlement (see Government of Kenya 1983).[10]

The pattern of range exploitation is therefore very uneven. While there are heavy concentrations of both people and stock near permanent settlements, large areas of the best grazing lands, especially near the borders of the district, are left unoccupied. The main reasons for this are, first, livestock raiding in border areas and the growth of permanent settlements—relief camps, administrative/trade centers, irrigation schemes—that have attracted an increasing number of poor pastoralists (see Hogg 1982).

Second, while droughts are a recurrent feature of marginal pastoral environments like Turkana, their consequences for the local population vary. These consequences are often most severe not as a result of the degree of livestock and population increase, but of the degree of external interventions that restrict mobility and create permanent settlements. Destitution, indeed, has often little to do with drought at all, but has been a direct consequence of national incorporation. There is, for example, historical evidence that the punitive campaigns the British mounted against the Turkana in the first quarter of this century created a large number of destitute Turkana. In one such campaign in 1915, 400 Turkana were killed and 20,000 cattle and over 100,000 small stock were seized (Barber 1968:180), and Lamphear estimates that between 1916 and 1918 a quarter million livestock were confiscated from Turkana (1976:241). Far from being overstocked, it is very likely that Turkana District was actually understocked in the early years of the colonial period.

Third, in most of the district there is no real economic alternative to livestock keeping for the majority of the population. Yet there is growing evidence, mainly reported by anthropologists (see Broche-Due and Storås 1983; Hogg 1985b, 1986),[11] of an increasing inequality in access to pastoral resources. The *maskini*, or poor Turkana, live in the peri-urban slums of towns like Lodwar and Kakuma, or in the irrigation schemes and relief camps, or along the lake shore. They eke out an existence as charcoal burners, distillers of illicit alcohol, prostitutes, odd-job men, food-for-work laborers, part-time farmers, and fishermen. Their chances of returning to the pastoral sector are increasingly remote. They are caught in a poverty trap, for even if they do manage to buy a few livestock, they cannot afford to maintain the extensive set of social relationships necessary for survival back in the pastoral sector (see Njeru 1984).

It is increasingly evident that impoverishment is becoming permanent for a large number of Turkana, and that this impoverishment has more to do with the particular structure of opportunities in the district than with questions of "carrying capacity."

There are good reasons, therefore, to reject any preconceived assumptions about pastoral development. While overstocking may be occurring, it cannot be assumed, and certainly should not be the basis of interventions in the pastoral sector to control livestock movements and shift people out of pastoralism. What is required is a clear identification of long-term trends in the pastoral economy, and in particular the increasing shift of resources into the hands of fewer and fewer people.[12]

## Anthropology and Development

Anthropological involvement in development in Turkana dates back to 1948, when Gulliver was appointed government sociologist.[13] His major contribution to the anthropology of the district, "A Preliminary Survey of the Turkana" (1951), a report to the Government of Kenya, remains the most complete and comprehensive record of Turkana society, although it has since been superseded by more detailed studies of particular facets of Turkana economic life, in particular of their pastoral economy (see McCabe 1984; Wienpahl 1984; Galvin 1985).

The extent to which Gulliver's work influenced policymakers in the district is difficult to know. The report was intended less as a comment on specific development projects than as a general social and economic survey. As such it was meant to provide an account of mainly traditional Turkana practices rather than directly address contemporary development issues. Nevertheless, the wealth of detail in the survey, across a wide range of topics, would have provided useful information to district officials. Indeed, the primary value of the report today lies in its holistic account of Turkana society and its early identification of an important trend in the economy toward the accumulation of wealth in the hands of government-appointed chiefs (Gulliver 1951:160).

After Gulliver there was a long hiatus as social science research fell out of favor with the government (see Grillo 1985:14–15). However, in the last ten years or so, partly as a result of the failure of conventional pastoral development projects and increasing uncertainty about the methods and purposes of pastoral development, there has been a burgeoning of anthropological research in the district. This research has been broadly of two kinds:

1. Research on traditional Turkana pastoralism, mainly studies carried out by the STEP project since 1980 on livestock movements, herd/flock management practices, and nutrition among Ngisonyoka pastoralists in the south of the district (see in particular the recent studies by Dyson-Hudson and McCabe 1982; McCabe 1984; Wienpahl 1984; Galvin 1985)
2. Research on pastoralists in change, mainly studies carried out by the University of Bergen's Turkana research project, funded by the Norwegian government (see in particular the works of Henriksen 1974; Broche-Due 1980, 1983; Jul-Larsen 1981; Broche-Due and Storås 1980, 1981, 1983), but including other studies and consultant reports (see J. Brown 1980; Hogg 1982, 1985b; Njeru 1984).

A large part of this recent research has focused on specific topics and/or development projects. For instance, most of the Norwegian-financed research has centered on the impact of fisheries and irrigation agriculture on Turkana, while the STEP project studied aspects of traditional Ngisonyoka pastoral adaptations. Much of the research is therefore relevant to the concerns of pastoral development planners in the district, but this relevancy has a price: what has been increasingly lost from contemporary anthropological research in the district is precisely the breadth and scope that distinguishes works like Gulliver's "A Preliminary Survey," which remains the only general account available of Turkana society. There is a clear danger that in the quest for "relevancy" (see Rew 1985) anthropologists will so narrow the focus of their research that they will lose sight of the complexity and range of social and economic interconnections that go to make up a society and its economy.

This is not to argue against policy- or development-oriented research. There is certainly a growing need for critical studies by anthropologists of development projects and programs: the works of Henriksen on problems of development in Turkana and of Broche-Due and Storås on the Katilu irrigation scheme have been particularly influential in this respect. There is also a need to deepen our understanding of traditional Turkana pastoral adaptations. These needs require as wide an interpretation of "relevancy" as possible, and long-term anthropological research. Only such research, carried out over months and years rather than weeks, can hope to identify long-term economic and social trends in the district.

## Notes

I am grateful to the British Overseas Development Administration for supporting my research in Northern Kenya (1982–84), and to Nikki Hogg for the map.

1. Dixey's "Hydrographic Survey of Turkana" and Edwards' "Report on the Grazing Areas of Turkana" were published in 1943 and 1944, respectively.

2. Dixey (1943) had recommended a limited borehole program to extend the area of dry-season grazing. Implementation of this program was constantly delayed for lack of money.

3. The marketing of small stock was also encouraged, but this was largely in the hands of Somali traders. In the 1950s auctions were established. In 1959 the estimated take-off of stock was 30,000 (Colony and Protectorate of Kenya 1959). For most of the period to date the export of cattle from the district has been banned.

4. *Epaka* comes from the Swahili word *mpaka*, meaning boundary.

5. Nowadays few Turkana use the traditional term *amaire*, preferring to use the word *epaka* to describe grazing reserves.

6. In the 1960s there were several attempts to establish water-spreading schemes for fodder production. The most notable was at Lorengipi. By the late 1960s, however, most of the schemes had been discontinued (see Brainard 1981).

7. Funding came largely from the United Nations Development Program (UNDP), with technical assistance from FAO.

8. For a similar story from Isiolo District see Hogg (1983).

9. The South Turkana Ecosystems Project is intended as an interdisciplinary study of the adaptation of the Ngisonyoka Turkana. The project is largely funded by the National Science Foundation. (See M. Little 1985; Wienpahl 1984; McCabe 1983, 1984; McCabe, Hart, and Ellis 1983; McCabe, Galvin, and Ellis 1985; McCabe, Dyson-Hudson, et al. 1985; and Galvin 1985).

10. In the latest aerial survey of the district, carried out in the March/April 1984 wet season, 45 percent of the district was unoccupied (Government of Kenya 1985).

11. See also the work of anthropologists working outside Turkana District, e.g., P. Little (1985a, 1985b), and Ensminger (1984).

12. Swift (1982) has recently written about some of these long-term trends in West African pastoralism.

13. There were, however, several earlier ethnographic accounts of Turkana (see Barton 1921; Rayne 1919; Emley 1927).

# References

Allan, W.
  1965    The African Husbandman. London: Oliver and Boyd, Ltd.
Anderson, D.
  1984    Depression, Dust Bowl, Demography and Drought: The Colonial State and Soil Conservation in East Africa during the 1930s. African Affairs 83:321–343.
Barber, J.
  1968    Imperial Frontier: A Study of Relations between the British and the Pastoral Tribes of Northeast Uganda. Nairobi: East Africa Publishing House.
Barton
  1921    Notes on the Turkana Tribe of British East Africa. Journal of the African Society 20:107–115, 204–211.
Brainard, J.
  1981    Herders to Farmers: The Effects of Settlement on the Demography of the Turkana Population of Kenya. Ph.D. dissertation, State University of New York, Binghamton.

Broche-Due, V.
  1980    Pastoral Women in a Process of Change from Pastoralism to Seden-
          tarization. Progress Report 2, Turkana Research Project, University of
          Bergen.
  1983    Women at the Backstage of Development: The Negative Impact on
          Project Realization by Neglecting the Crucial Roles of Turkana Women
          as Producers and Providers. A Socio-anthropological Case Study from
          Katilu Irrigation Scheme, Turkana. FAO consultancy GCP/KENEO48/
          NOD.
Broche-Due, V. and F. Storäs.
  1980    The Relationship between the Pastoral and Agricultural Sectors in
          Turkana. Progress Report 1, Turkana Research Project, University of
          Bergen.
  1981    The Relationship between Nomadic Adaptation and Alternative Eco-
          nomic Forms with Specific References to the Organization of Work
          and Productive Relations. Progress Report 5, Turkana Research Project,
          University of Bergen.
  1983    The Fields of the Foe: Factors Constraining Agricultural Output and
          Farmers' Capacity for Participation. A report to the Norwegian Aid
          Agency (NORAD) on Katilu Irrigation Scheme. Turkana, Kenya.
Brown, J.
  1980    A Socio-anthropological Survey of the Irrigation Schemes of the Turkana
          River. Rome: FAO.
Brown, L.
  1963    The Development of the Semi-arid Areas of Kenya. Nairobi: Ministry
          of Agriculture.
  1973    Conservation for Survival: Ethiopia's Choice. Addis Ababa: Haile
          Selassie University Press.
Colony and Protectorate of Kenya
  1943    Turkana District Documentation Center: District Annual Report.
  1959    Turkana District Documentation Center: District Annual Report.
Dixey, F.
  1943    Hydrographic Survey of Turkana. Nairobi: Colony and Protectorate of
          Kenya.
Dyson-Hudson, R., and T. McCabe
  1982    Final Report to the Norwegian Aid Agency (NORAD) on South Turkana
          Water Resources and Livestock Movements.
Edwards, R.
  1944    Report on the Grazing Areas of Turkana. Nairobi: Colony and Pro-
          tectorate of Kenya.
Emley, F. D.
  1927    The Turkana of Kalosia District. Journal of the Royal Anthropological
          Institute 57.
Ensminger, J.
  1984    Political Economy among the Pastoral Galole Orma: The Effects of
          Market Integration. Ph.D. dissertation, Northwestern University.

FAO (Food and Agriculture Organization)
  1964    Report on a Reconnaissance of the Agricultural Potential of the Turkana
          District of Kenya. CB-AG-010(22). Rome.

Galaty, J. G.
  1980    The Maasai Group-Ranch: Politics and Development in an African
          Pastoral Society. *In* When Nomads Settle. P. Saltzman, ed. New York,
          NY: Praeger.

Galvin, K.
  1985    Food Procurement, Diet, Activities and Nutrition in an Ecological and
          Social Context. Ph.D. dissertation, State University of New York,
          Binghamton.

Government of Kenya
  1980    Turkana District Development Plan, 1979–83. Nairobi: Government
          Printer.

  1983    Turkana District Resources Survey Draft Report. Vol. 11. Ministry of
          Energy and Regional Development.

  1984a   Evaluation Report on Turkana Cluster. Ministry of Agriculture and
          Livestock Development.

  1984b   Turkana District Documentation Center: Turkana District Livestock
          Plan (authorized by Turkana District Livestock Committee).

  1985    Turkana District Resources Survey, 1982–84: A Planner's Compendium.
          Nairobi: Ministry of Energy and Regional Development.

Grillo, R.
  1985    Applied Anthropology in the 1980s: Retrospect and Prospect. *In* Social
          Anthropology and Development Policy. R. Grillo and A. Rew, eds.
          Pp. 1–36. ASA Monograph 23. London: Tavistock Publications.

Gulliver, P.
  1951    A Preliminary Survey of the Turkana. A Report compiled for the
          Government of Kenya. Communications from the School of African
          Studies, University of Cape Town.

  1955    The Family Herds. London: Routledge and Kegan Paul.

Helland, J.
  1980    Five Essays on the Study of Pastoralists and Development of Pastoralism.
          Occasional Paper 12, Social Anthropology, University of Bergen.

Henriksen, G.
  1974    Economic Growth and Ecological Balance: Problems of Development
          in Turkana, N. W. Kenya. Occasional Paper 11, Social Anthropology,
          University of Bergen.

Hogg, R. S.
  1982    Destitution and Development: The Turkana of Northwest Kenya.
          Disasters 6(3):164–168.

  1983    Irrigation Agriculture and Pastoral Development: A Lesson from Kenya.
          Development and Change 14:577–591.

  1985a   Restocking Pastoralists in Kenya: A Strategy for Relief and Rehabili-
          tation. ODI Pastoral Development Network Paper 19c.

1985b   The Socio-Economic Responses of Nomadic Pastoralists to Permanent
        Settlement and Irrigation Agriculture. Overseas Development Admin-
        istration ESCOR Research Scheme R 3674.
1986    The New Pastoralism: Poverty and Dependency in Northern Kenya.
        Africa 56(3):319–333.
Horowitz, M.
1979    The Sociology of Pastoralism and African Livestock Projects. AID
        Program Evaluation Discussion Paper 6. Washington, DC: Office of
        Evaluation, Bureau for Program and Policy Coordination, Agency for
        International Development.
Jahnke, H.
1982    Livestock Production Systems and Livestock Development in Tropical
        Africa. Kiel: Kieler Wissenschafts-verlag Vauk.
Jul-Larsen, E.
1981    The Lake Is Our Shamba. Report to NORAD about certain socio-
        economic aspects regarding Lake Turkana Fishery Project.
Lamphear, J.
1976    Aspects of Turkana Leadership during the Era of Primary Resistance.
        Journal of African History 17(2):225–243.
Little, M.
1985    Multidisciplinary and Ecological Studies of Nomadic Turkana Pastor-
        alists. Biological International (IUBS, Paris) 11:11–16.
Little, P.
1985a   Social Differentiation and Pastoralist Sedentarization in Northern Kenya.
        Africa 55(3):243–261.
1985b   Absentee Herd Owners and Part-Time Pastoralists: The Political Econ-
        omy of Resource Use in Northern Kenya. Human Ecology 13(2):131–
        151.
McCabe, T.
1983    Land Use among the Pastoral Turkana. Rural Africana 15–16:109–126.
1984    Livestock Management among the Turkana: A Social and Ecological
        Analysis of Herding in an East African Pastoral Population. Ph.D
        dissertation, Department of Anthropology, State University of New
        York, Binghamton.
McCabe, T., T. C. Hart, and J. E. Ellis
1983    Road Impact Evaluation in Northern Kenya. A Case Study in South
        Turkana. Final report to NORAD.
McCabe, T., K. Galvin, and J. Ellis
1985    Coping with Drought in Pastoral Turkana. Interim Progress Report to
        NORAD.
McCabe, T., R. Dyson-Hudson, P. Leslie, P. Fry, N. Dyson-Hudson, and J.
Wienpahl
1985    Movement and Migration as Pastoral Responses to Limited and Un-
        predictable Resources. Paper presented to Ecology of Nomadic Pas-
        toralists Symposium, Tucson, AZ.

Njeru, E.
  1984   The Family Herders: Irrigation, Reciprocity and Marriage among the
         Turkana Pastoralists of Northwestern Kenya. Ph.D. dissertation, De-
         partment of Anthropology, University of California at Santa Barbara.

Pratt, D., and M. Gwynne
  1977   Rangeland Management and Ecology in East Africa. London: Hodder
         and Stoughton.

Raikes, P.
  1981   Livestock Development and Policy in East Africa. Uppsala: Scandinavian
         Institute of African Studies.

Rayne
  1919   Turkana. Journal of the African Society 18:25–65, 183–189.

Rew, A.
  1985   The Organizational Connection: Multi-disciplinary Practice and An-
         thropological Theory. *In* Social Anthropology and Development Policy.
         R. Grillo and A. Rew, eds. Pp. 185–197. ASA Monograph 23. London:
         Tavistock Publications.

Sandford, S.
  1983   Management of Pastoral Development in the Third World. London:
         John Wiley and Sons.

Swift, J.
  1982   The Future of African Hunter-Gatherer and Pastoral Peoples. Devel-
         opment and Change 13:159–181.

Talks, K.
  1983   Assistance to Irrigated Agriculture in Turkana/Pokot, Kenya. Final
         Report of Agro-economic consultant, GCP/KEN/048/NOD.

Wienpahl, J.
  1984   Livestock Production and Social Organization among the Turkana.
         Ph.D. dissertation, University of Arizona.

# 10

# Planning for Population Change in Kenya: An Anthropological Perspective

*Edward H. Greeley*

### Overview

Three of the most frequently recurring development errors can best be corrected by anthropologists: incorrect assumptions about the nature of the problem; over-reliance on modern technology as the solution to the development problem; and insufficient use of nongovernmental resources to initiate and sustain development interventions. In this chapter I examine these recurring errors from the vantage of experience gained in over a decade's residence in Kenya (1973–1984) and from field data collected in Kenya's central highlands during 1974–1975.[1] The chapter will illustrate how an anthropological perspective can contribute to the solving of key problems in the population sector.

Kenya is a particularly appropriate country for a population case study, as it has the highest recorded population growth rate in the world—close to 4 percent—and it has been the recipient of an exceptional number of programs aimed at slowing the rate. While recognizing the many shortcomings in programs to date, the chapter focuses on successful developmental efforts in the population sector. By so doing, it endorses the pragmatic view that the development process is so complex, and our knowledge of it so incomplete, that we gain more by finding what works and replicating it than by analyzing unsuccessful efforts.[2]

The lessons learned, based as they are on the unusually long and extensive field studies and development efforts in Kenya, can be applied to population problems in other countries of sub-Saharan Africa. In most of these, experience in population planning is limited, and development trends are resulting in alarmingly high rates of population growth, similar to that in Kenya.

The chapter is organized around the three errors listed above. Discussion will be based primarily on historical and contemporary data derived from the author's research in the Kenya Highlands, and on subsequent development experience working as a United States Agency for International Development (USAID) staff member—first in AID's Regional Office for East and Southern Africa based in Nairobi, and then in the AID Mission to Kenya. Some of the basic points to be covered are:

- *Incorrect assumptions.* Lack of attention among development planners to Kenyan ideas and practices of child spacing and birth limitation has led to the misconception that fertility regulation is an alien, foreigners' concept, and thereby hindered in its acceptance by Kenyans.
- *Choice of technology.* Promotion of family planning through modern contraceptive methods has received overriding attention, although the indigenous practice of breastfeeding (for improved child health and nutrition purposes) offers a highly effective and socially appropriate complement to modern contraceptive methods.
- *Role of nongovernmental organizations and firms in implementing change.* Government often takes on too much responsibility in implementing change, particularly in such sensitive areas as health care and the provision of family-planning services. This results in neglect of other socially sound, self-sustaining, community-based approaches, such as those that can be supported by nongovernmental private and voluntary organizations (PVOs), including profit-making industries and agricultural cooperatives located in rural areas.

## Incorrect Assumptions

Historical data on the dynamics of population change among the Meru of the central highlands dramatically illustrate the problems created and opportunities lost through planning under false assumptions. The most serious assumption is the most basic in this case: the idea that child spacing and family-size limitation are long-standing ideas of foreigners and aliens, and that local Kenyan ideas and practices contradict and do not support these "alien" ideas. In fact, the reverse is true. During the colonial period, the outsiders were pronatal both in attitude and in practice. The insiders, the Meru, although deeply pronatal, had a fully elaborated system of indigenous fertility regulation that has not been adequately exploited by development planners.

The Meru constitute a series of subgroups speaking the East Central Bantu language Kimeru. They live and farm on the Eastern slopes of

Mt. Kenya. Traditionally they practiced shifting cultivation and lived in village settlements. Each subgroup occupied and protected from its neighbors a pie-shaped piece of the Mt. Kenya slopes, typically formed by the banks of two rivers starting on the upper slopes of the mountain and flowing out and down to the lower and broader semiarid lands beyond the base of the mountain. At the center of each settlement was the *gaaru*, a warrior's barracks where the younger married men and the uncircumcised men of the settlement lived as a kind of permanent militia, prepared for the intergroup skirmishing that was, according to informants, a common feature of traditional life.[3]

Meru ideas and practices related to fertility regulation were strongly developed and often connected to the need to survive in an environment of fairly regular threat of attack from neighbors. Child spacing of up to three or four years was practiced, and clearly tied to the need for a woman to be mobile in time of attack. With two "babes in arms" a mother could not flee quickly and safely. Warriors married at a relatively late age, and after marriage continued to live and sleep in the all male gaaru. Intercourse was considered mainly as an instrumental endeavor for warriors: in some cases a warrior who wished to visit and sleep with his wife "to seek a child" (*gwikira mwana rukooro*) even needed the consent of the barracks chief.

Concepts and practices of fertility regulation were present throughout the life cycle of the Meru. Circumcision of girls was practiced, and was delayed until several years after onset of puberty. Circumcision of boys was later, occurring in the mid-twenties. There was a strong tabu against intercourse and pregnancy before circumcision for boys and girls. A guilty couple would be severely beaten if caught having intercourse. If the uncircumcised girl had the misfortune to become pregnant, she and her uncircumcised lover were loathed. They were staked one on top of the other at a crossroads—he over her in the standard position for intercourse—beaten, and left in the sun to die. At the least, if the pregnant girl was unsuccessful in an abortion attempt, both offenders would flee or be banished from the community. After circumcision but prior to marriage, only partial intercourse was sanctioned: coitus interruptus and coitus intra cura (with the girl protecting herself by a tight leather undergarment, *ng'athi*).

A circumcised girl proudly wore a string of bark (*mitungo*) around her neck as a sign of purity. It was removed by her husband when she finally came to sleep in the new home in her husband's homestead. Child spacing, as in many East African groups, was attained primarily through the effects of a lactation tabu. Among the Meru, this tabu lasted as long as three years. The sperm of the man was believed to be dangerous to the health of the mother and baby; the child would probably die. The time when a man could return to "look for a child" and sleep in his wife's hut was a community-recognized event signified by the mother's sending her youngest to the gaaru with porridge for her husband, or by other signs described by informants, such as when the last born could "talk and run," had begun to lose milk teeth, or was old enough to drive the sheep and goats into hiding in times of attack.

Further prohibition of pregnancy occurred in the later years of a life cycle, when the oldest child of a mother was circumcised. This marked the end of her child-bearing years, and she would not be expected to become pregnant again.

The policies and practices of the British colonial government regarding population dynamics stand in sharp contrast to those of the Meru. Essentially through most of the colonial period, starting with the arrival of the British in Meru in 1913, the British saw an increasing Meru population as an increasing source of cheap labor for coffee plantations and other economic activities. In the early years, such pronatalism was expressed in justifications for health expenditures in areas like Meru in the so-called "native reserves." The attitude is exemplified in the Meru District Report of 1915, in which the District Officer, G. S. W. Orde-Brown, writes of a successful vaccination campaign to combat an outbreak of smallpox followed by an epidemic of spinal meningitis:

[It is] . . . worst in lower Mwimbe, where the mortality was most serious, the young people of both sexes being principally affected: so many deaths occurred that the amount of labour was severely reduced, while the destruction of the huts of those that had died, also had an appreciable effect on the hut tax (Colony and Protectorate of Kenya 1915:35).

The pronatal effect of early British practices was seen in many aspects of Meru life. The coming of Pax Britannica led to the gradual decline of the barracks life for men organized around the gaaru. Collection of the hut tax, for example, speeded this dissolution as Meru men learned to avoid the gaaru as a spot that tax collectors usually visited first and most frequently. This dissolution in turn was associated with a breakdown in the effectiveness of the tabu against giving birth before circumcision. As warriors became less occupied and constrained by local systems of social control, the rate of pregnancies of uncircumcised girls increased greatly. One result was an increase in attempted abortions and complications resulting from them.

Abortions were further increased by the reluctance of mothers to allow downward adjustment of the age of their daughter's eligibility for circumcision. In the words of a Meru District Officer:

According to Meru custom, if a son or daughter is circumcised the mother is not allowed to bear another child; if she does the circumcised child will die. This custom tends to delay the circumcising of girls until they are considerably over the marriageable age and incidentally is the reason for the very numerous abortions that are caused since it is a very serious offence for an uncircumcised girl to give birth to a child (Colony and Protectorate of Kenya 1924:3).

This problem continued for over a decade; the Meru District Annual Report of 1933 shows abortion to be the most serious social problem in the district. At the height of the problem, there were 77 convictions of abortion specialists in Meru (Colony and Protectorate of Kenya 1933:2). To curtail the rapid spread of this dangerous practice (abortions were usually performed by forcefully kneading the lower abdomen) and the less usual practice of infanticide, the British Administration finally succeeded in lowering the circumcision age of boys and girls. This innovation (when accompanied by a gradual decline in the observance by these women of the rule that they must cease bearing children as soon as their eldest child was circumcised) effectively resulted in a longer period of childbearing.

The other important early outside force for change in Meru was missionary activity. The first Protestant mission, established in 1922 by the Church of Scotland, was run by a medical doctor who spearheaded the building of schools, a rural health center, and, over time, a network of dispensaries. Conversion to Scottish Protestantism required radical change in behavior and outlook, most of which resulted in the dissolution of the indigenous system of fertility regulation and the promotion of practices that increased fertility and family size.

Families who accepted the teaching of the church were required to reject traditional tabus, including those supporting birth spacing. The church encouraged husbands and wives to live and sleep together, and perhaps most traumatic, required families publicly to reject women's circumcision. Early converts were shunned, and in fact lost their identity as Meru people. Over time, however, their status in the rapidly changing society reversed itself. Supported by the significant improvements in health and family welfare brought about by the introduction of education, coffee as a cash crop, and health services, the followers of the Church of Scotland became some of the largest and most powerful families in the changing economy and society of the district.

To summarize, the case of the Meru shows a reverse of the usual assumptions of population planners. The insiders were organized to achieve a desired small family size, and spacing. The outsiders were to a certain degree in favor of increased population growth and introduced many practices that had a widesweeping pronatal effect. The coming of the second major missionary group in the 1930s, the Consolata Catholic Mission of Italy, accelerated the pronatal impact, as it gradually assumed a similarly innovative role (although less intrusive regarding the traditional living practices mentioned above) in establishing schools and dispensaries in areas mainly not served by the Church of Scotland mission.

All too often the assumptions of the present overlook the realities of the past, and thus opportunities are lost for generating support of population programs by emphasizing the extent to which they fit a number of indigenous patterns among Kenya's ethnic groups.[4] Population planners have been highly critical of what they see among Kenyan leadership as lethargy and even resistance to concerted efforts to reduce population growth. The planners' attitude is fueled by the knowledge that strong leadership and political support are among the most important determinants of the effectiveness of family-planning programs (Simmons and Lapham 1986:38). They often fail to realize the extent of indigenous practices that support fertility regulation, and overlook the fact that an earlier generation of outsiders introduced policies and practices that promoted population growth.

## Modern and Indigenous Technologies

The clearest example of the failure of population planners to take indigenous solutions into account in the population sector is found in the limited extent to which breastfeeding is promoted (for child health and nutrition purposes) given its enormous potential for depressing fertility at the societal level. Breastfeeding reduces the probability of conception because it extends the postpartum anovulatory period and reduces the likelihood of conception once ovulation has occurred. The period of anovulation closely corresponds to the period of amenorrhea (absence of menstruation). Typically, for each additional month in the average duration of breastfeeding, there is an increase in the average birth interval of 0.25 to 0.5 months (Huffman 1986:3). As recently as ten years ago, breastfeeding accounted for more protection in 28 of 29 countries reported by the World Bank than did family-planning programs in the five sub-Saharan African countries of the study, where contraception contributed "virtually nothing" (World Bank 1984:113 and 116). Breast-feeding is cited as a "major factor depressing fertility" in the Kenya Contraceptive Prevalence Survey (Government of Kenya 1984:119).

Recent analysis of Kenyan data shows the relative importance of breastfeeding and contraceptive use in providing protection. Assuming a theoretical maximum total of 17 babies per mother, Kenya's actual fertility rate is less than half—7.4. Widespread breastfeeding in Kenya contributed significantly to Kenya's lower actual fertility rate—an average of 4.22 births (per woman). Modern contraceptive use, on the other hand, accounted for only 0.67 of a birth in determining the difference between Kenya's potential and actual fertility rate (World Bank 1984:114).

In the highlands of Kenya, the importance of breastfeeding in providing protection from pregnancy was noted early in the colonial period. In 1932, for example, the anthropologist (and renowned archeologist) Louis Leakey explained the reason for the increased population growth he observed among the educated "Christian" Kikuyu near the city of Nairobi as follows:

> The reason for the great overcrowding today, in my mind, is that the last fourteen or fifteen years have seen a tremendous change in native custom as it affects birth and population. Formerly no Kikuyu woman was allowed to conceive a second child until the first child had stopped suckling, which was usually not until the end of the second year, so there were generally intervals of about three years between children. That has been broken down entirely . . . and children are now being born—according to figures from the Kabete mission—about one every one-and-a-half years (Leakey before the Land Commission in 1932, quoted in Herz 1974:49).

The effects of the extensive practices promoting breastfeeding and of modern contraceptive use among the major Kenya ethnic groups, including the Meru, are seen in Table 10.1.

The powerful effect of breastfeeding should receive greater attention, especially given the relatively low cost of breastfeeding-promotion programs in relation to the intended impact on fertility, and its potential for multiple benefits in nutrition and health. This is not to argue, however, that breastfeeding should be promoted at the family level primarily as a contraceptive technique; it is too unreliable for that. Nor should support for providing modern contraceptives receive any less attention. The key point is that breastfeeding, while being advocated primarily for its health and nutrition benefits, has an impact on fertility, and can be promoted in conjunction with the promotion of modern contraceptive methods. For example, advising exclusive breastfeeding (without supplemental foods) in the first six months may serve as a highly effective complement to promoting contraception after the first six-month period (Huffman 1986:6).

## "Home-grown" Nongovernment Approaches

A third all-too-common practice of development planners is the tendency to look to governments for sponsorship and financial support

TABLE 10.1
Months of Fertility Protection from Breastfeeding and
Modern Contraception Compared for Eight Kenyan Ethnic Groups

|  | LBI | BF | A | M | %C |
|---|---|---|---|---|---|
| Mijikenda | 41 | 23 | 17 | 8 | 2 |
| Luo | 31 | 17 | 12 | 2 | 2 |
| Kamba | 30 | 18 | 11 | 8 | 4 |
| Meru/Embu | 29 | 18 | 11 | 7 | 9 |
| Luhya | 28 | 16 | 10 | 6 | 3 |
| Kikuyu | 30 | 14 | 10 | 8 | 8 |
| Gusii | 28 | 17 | 13 | 5 | 1 |
| Kalenjin | 27 | 16 | 9 | 6 | 2 |
| Kenya Mean | 30 | 17 | 11 | 8 | 4 |
| (n = 5,159) |  |  |  |  |  |

LBI = Estimated mean live birth interval in months. BF = Estimated mean duration of
breastfeeding. A = Estimated mean duration of postpartum amenorrhea. M = Estimated
mean duration of the menstruating interval. %C = Percent using "effective" contraception
(pill, IUD, condom, sterilization, and other female scientific methods).

Source: Adapted from Mosley, Werner, and Becker 1981:632; based on the Kenya
Fertility Survey 1977–1978.

of family-planning interventions. Outside organizations and donor countries, lacking the knowledge of local conditions to identify and fund
nongovernment programs, turn to government organizations. This dependence on government sanctioned and supported programs results in
the host government's trying to exercise control in a politically sensitive
area—provision of health and family-planning services. In Kenya, for
example, governmental medical policies and laws introduced during the
period of British colonial rule to protect the population from unsound
or unscrupulous medical practices unnecessarily restricted initiatives
taken by nongovernmental organizations to provide health and family
planning.

Nongovernmental organizations, including both PVOs and private
industry, offer an excellent alternative to community-based, family-
planning programs sponsored and run by the host government. Church-
based hospitals and privately owned tea and coffee plantations, for
example, may serve a wide population in an area where government
health coverage is minimal. The fees often charged for health services
in church-based hospitals generally increase the likelihood of self-
sustainability of the service, and thus the service may be seen in favorable
terms by donors who are reluctant to fund new activities without assurance
of self-sustainability. Private firms often run health clinics licensed by
the government as part of the services they provide to employees. If

there is commitment from management, and the firm is viable, such clinics offer high promise of self-sustainability. Nongovernmental organizations may also offer other advantages: for example, they may serve a segment of the rural population most likely to want and seek family planning—be it progressive farmers (and members of a progressive church that provides services) or wage earners who live on company land and have high demands on the family wages and little access to land to grow food.

The potential of such organizations can be illustrated with reference to the Kenya highlands. The Church of Scotland Presbyterian Mission in Southern Meru District, referred to above, is an example. Based at Chogoria on the lower slopes of Mt. Kenya, this former mission enclave (now the Presbyterian Church of East Africa) operates a community-based family-planning program, providing services in tandem with the Ministry of Health, which also has clinics in the area. Currently about 27 percent of the couples in this rural area (population 200,000) use modern contraceptives, compared with 8 percent in the country as a whole (World Bank 1986:47).[5]

This rate is one of the highest in a rural, agricultural area in sub-Saharan Africa. The experience of Chogoria exemplifies the advantages of a strongly established, church-based organization in supporting modern family-planning methods. Some of the advantages follow:

*Long and Close Involvement in the Family Life of Several Generations of a Changing Society.* Instruction on deeply personal matters such as circumcision and polygyny can be included here. A popular book written by the head of the Chogoria Mission further illustrates the highly interventionist role played by missionaries that is still acceptable among church followers today. Entitled *How to Behave: Some Manners and Customs of Civilized People*, it promotes westernized roles for Meru men and women and provides additional support for the acceptability of modern contraceptive methods for church members (Irvine 1958).

*Well-established Role as Introducer of Western Technologies.* For example, in the 1920s, missionaries initially faced difficulties introducing the latrine, as Meru men were believed not to need to defecate and hence rejected its use. Latrines were more readily adopted when their importance as a means to promote cleanliness was associated with the teachings of the Ten Commandments. In recent years, church ministers have been encouraged to speak out for family planning from the pulpit.

*Long Involvement in Changing, and in Many Ways Improving, the Status of Meru Women.* In the 1930s, for example, a third of the students at mission schools were women; often graduates were recruited for school teaching and hospital work.

*High Probability of Self-sustainability.* The Chogoria Church mission introduced coffee on a smallholder basis in Southern Meru, as a means for church families to earn cash and meet family and church needs, including church capital development and ongoing support of mission education and health services. An arrangement linking the church financial office to the local coffee cooperative made payment of fees for schools and health care an efficient process. The cooperative paid the fees a family owed for services directly to the school and hospital first, and then paid the remaining coffee payout to the family. This system of guaranteed collection of fees applied to all coffee growers using the church health services, not just to church members.

*Ability to Be Experimental.* Restrictive government regulations in the health field, many of them legacies of the colonial period, were mentioned above as a deterrent to initiating improved programs. As a relatively remote but fairly well staffed rural hospital, Chogoria has been in an excellent position to experiment with new ways of providing community-based, family-planning services by paraprofessionals, for example, without incurring the wrath of the Ministry of Health for violating regulations restricting such practices. Although such practices have alarmed some government medical specialists, the mission hospital has been seen by others as a relatively safe environment for testing new approaches. When evaluated as safe, pilot programs (e.g., broadening the use of para-professionals in providing contraceptives) can provide the basis for improvements to more conservative, outmoded national regulations and policies (such as those limiting provision of contraceptives to physicians).

*Position As Guardian of Community Wellbeing.* As well-established institutions in rapidly changing rural areas, church organizations can serve as protectors as well as experimenters. The introduction of an experimental, commercial, marketing program to sell condoms "like soap" in local shops throughout Meru District in the mid-1970s illustrates how a church can play the familiar guardian role.[6] Although evaluated as a success (Rogers 1973), the program was in fact very poorly received by community leadership in Meru, and was soon phased down with government assistance. In this particular case, an important drawback to the experimental program was the aggressive style in which it was introduced. Church and medical leadership at Chogoria, among other Meru leaders, outspokenly condemned this program to market Kinga (Kiswahili for protection) condoms. It was considered insulting and offensive to Meru morals, and as irresponsible in the way it was aggressively implemented by outsiders.

In the case of the Kinga condom marketing program, the private sector fared poorly as an agent for change in the family-planning arena. More recent efforts, however, demonstrate the strong potential of the private sector as an organizational framework to introduce and maintain effective programs to deliver family-planning service. Kenya Canners, with a force of 5,000 women employed to process pineapple, is an example of a Kenyan firm successfully involved in a self-sustaining program that delivers family-planning service. Another large firm offering family-planning services is the Brooke Bond Company, which employs 26,000 workers in its tea, sisal, and flower estates throughout the country.

The extent of the promise of nongovernmental voluntary and profit-making organizations in promoting family planning can be seen in the very rapid progress of a "Private Sector Family-Planning Project" funded by AID in conjunction with the Kenya government. Designed in 1983 to explore and demonstrate the potential of nongovernmental organizations (mainly private firms) to provide family-planning services, the project entails a team of expatriate and Kenyan family-planning specialists whose main task is to identify, design, and fund a wide range of subprojects. The project's purpose is to help establish self-sustaining, fully equipped, family-planning programs in nongovernment health facilities (United States Agency for International Development 1983).

The project has met 90 percent of its targets in less than three years of operation. It has initiated 50 subprojects throughout Kenya and reached over 27,000 new accepters (as of June 1987). It has established 119 new service-delivery points, stimulated a high level of interest from nongovernmental organizations and companies, and leveraged a significant portion of start-up costs for programs from participating organizations. Both Kenyan and AID leadership have hailed it as an outstanding example of family-planning program design. Nevertheless, it was met with significant resistance from staff of the Kenya Ministry of Health, as it challenged their interpretation of government regulations regarding the role of nongovernmental organizations in family-planning service delivery. Favorable experience with the project has reduced resistance and demonstrated the applicability of the approach in other African countries as well.[7]

Subsequent to completion of the design of this project for implementation in Kenya, AID has approved a far larger project of similar concept and design for implementation on a worldwide basis. The project was designed with extensive anthropological input (the author was design officer, and there was significant involvement of Kenyan as well as expatriate anthropological expertise). As a replicable model with high potential for soundness and appropriateness in many contexts, such a project design could be classified as the kind of operationally useful "methodology for social action" that Michael Cernea, sociologist at the World Bank, calls for in *Putting People First: Sociological Variables in Rural Development*.[8]

## Conclusion

Using experience from Kenya, this chapter has undertaken to demonstrate the benefit to be gained by analyzing the population-growth problem in Africa from an anthropological perspective. Such an approach can improve the assumptions on which planning is based; it can identify existing local solutions to problems often overlooked by planners, who tend to focus narrowly on the transfer of modern technologies from industrialized countries; and it can also help move planners beyond conventional government-based solutions to other, more innovative approaches designed to mobilize local resources to solve problems in a self-sustaining way.

In the case of the population sector, analysis reveals that planners can refine their assumptions about the dynamics of population change by understanding better the prevalence of fertility regulation practices within indigenous cultures. They can more effectively promote child spacing and birth limitation by supporting breastfeeding, in conjunction with the use of modern family-plannning methods. They can increase the availability of self-sustaining family-planning programs by supporting service delivery through nongovernmental organizations, particularly private companies and church-based institutions located in rural areas. These kinds of approaches—promising more effective use of local resources through improved knowledge—are seriously needed in Africa if population problems are to be effectively and efficiently solved in the short and long term.

## Notes

The content and views in this article are solely the responsibility of the author, and are in no way intended to be taken as a statement or reflection of USAID views or policies.

1. Methodology for data collected is described in Greeley (1977).

2. In fact, Kenya has a far better record for promoting the economic and social development of its peoples than have most of its neighbors, and it has been a pioneer among African nations in grappling with the means to slow population growth. The government extended official sanction to the promotion of family planning in 1966, although a national program was not implemented until the early 1980s. Documents for the 1974–79 program claimed that despite a growing fertility rate in the early 1970s, Kenya would achieve a decline in population growth rate from 3.3 in 1974 to 3.0 percent in 1979 (World Bank 1982:17).

The actual population growth rate in 1981 was estimated to be over 4.0 percent per year, however, despite the nationwide program and nongovernmental efforts. Early 1981 studies showed that the ideal and actual completed family size was roughly similar for men and women. Both wanted eight children—a number that was in fact the average completed size (Dow and Werner 1983:84). This rate is especially significant given that the country is endowed with relatively little arable land (about 20 percent of the total land area) and meager productive resources.

Recent analysis in Kenya, however, indicates that the effects of rapid change, including a concerted effort over a number of years to slow the increasing population growth, has led to a turndown from over 4 percent per year population increase to about 3.8 percent (Gary Merritt, cited in Harden [1986]). In addition, the use of contraceptives among couples doubled over the six-year period 1978 to 1984, from almost 7 percent to 15 percent, with about 8.1 percent using modern methods (Government of Kenya 1984:83).

3. See Jeffrey Fadiman (1973) and Stanley Mwaniki (1972) for descriptions of warfare among the Meru.

4. See Angela Molnos (1972, 1973) for a description of such practices in a number of East African cultures.

5. A more recent estimate in mid-1987 for Chogoria puts the acceptance rate at 45 percent in a population of 350,000 (personal communication, Dr. Gary Merritt of USAID).

6. For a description of the rationale of this program, see Black (1973).

7. In passing, it may be instructive to consider other development-related problems for which nongovernmental organizations (like the Chogoria church-based organization described here) have special applicability. Combating and coping with Acquired Immune Deficiency Syndrome (AIDS) is one such problem.

Church-based health delivery systems may come to play a pivotal role in dealing with AIDS over the long haul, as a complement to government-supported efforts (especially in hard-hit areas), for the following reasons.

1) Church hospitals and clinics provide relatively efficient and effective curative (and to an increasing extent preventive) health care to a large proportion of rural populations.

- For example, in Kenya over 30 percent of the rural population is served by church-based health systems. The proportion is probably higher in Zaire, Uganda, and Rwanda.
- These systems are often staffed with relatively low-cost, experienced medical staff (e.g., missionaries), charge fees for drugs and services, and put strong emphasis on self-sustainability.
- Many have favorable track records for adopting and maintaining health equipment.

2) Church-based health systems are well suited to introducing a technological package for combating AIDS—information, education, and communication (IE&C), condoms, and, eventually, blood tests—efficiently and effectively at the community level.

- The package can be introduced to rural families in a context that maximizes both initial acceptance and long-term sustained benefit, when supported by the credibility and commitment of the church/hospital community.
- This approach directly addresses a potentially significant *barrier* to rapid introduction of such technology: the resistance of local religious communities to dealing with the spread, effects, and technology for combating a sexually transmitted disease. The significant role of Christian organizations in ameliorating the effects of the devastating (but—significantly—less often fatal) diseases in medieval times in Europe is described in McNeill (1976:107–109).
- As well as having their own forums for communication (pulpits, parish groups), churches typically are linked with other institutions appropriate for combating AIDS (schools, women's groups, clinics).
- Church organizations include committees well suited to address previously unanticipated ethical and related issues created by AIDS and its impact. For example, the hospital board should be involved in resolving community issues related to testing for AIDS, and for policies of treatment.

3) The church-based hospital system provides enormous scope for rapid and effective *spread* of the intervention package to combat AIDS.

- Church-hospital systems are often linked to a nation-wide church organization, and so can use existing lines of communication to share experiences and knowledge gained at the community level.
- They can accelerate introduction of "combating AIDS" technical packages in rural areas through the auspices of the national church organization.
- They can operate under the sanction of a national decision-making "board" in addressing ethically difficult (and previously undefined) problems related to AIDS.

4) Targeting the church-based systems has related benefits.

- Church congregations often have a disproportionate number of the relatively better educated, productive, and influential members of a community, those who provide leadership in the economy and society and can influence others.
- As institutions and the population undergo increasingly unprecedented stress from the effects of AIDS, church-based systems may provide important support and guidance to the local social structure and population (including survivors and orphans) as well as to persons with AIDS.

8. See the opening chapter of Michael Cernea's *Putting People First: Sociological Variables in Rural Development.* "What sociologists and anthropologists can offer will largely determine the extent to which they will change their current marginal position in development work. The key lies in addressing the core issues head on: showing how to do development and how socially to translate objectives into reality, rather than discussing endlessly what these objectives should be.

Without downgrading the importance of contributing to defining policies and objectives, we have to recognize that sociology has an overdue debt: an obligation to provide methodologies for action. . . . [Social scientists' claim to relevance] will remain hollow and unconvincing if their contributions to policy formulation are not supported by sociologically designed operational strategies to translate these policies into real life" (Cernea 1985:9–10).

# References

Black, Timothy
   1973   Rationale for the Involvement of Private Sector Marketing Institutions in Family Planning in Africa. *In* Studies in Family Planning 4:25–32.
Cernea, Michael M.
   1985   Sociological Knowledge for Development Projects. *In* Putting People First: Sociological Variables in Rural Development. Michael M. Cernea, ed. Pp. 3–21. Published for the World Bank. New York, NY: Oxford.
Colony and Protectorate of Kenya
   1915   Meru District Annual Report, Kenya National Archives (DC/MRU).
   1924   Meru District Annual Report, Kenya National Archives (DC/MRU).
   1933   Meru District Annual Report, Kenya National Archives (DC/MRU).
Dow, Thomas E., and Linda H. Werner
   1983   Prospects for Fertility Decline in Rural Kenya. Population and Development Review 9:77–98.
Fadiman, Jeffrey
   1973   Early History of the Meru of Mt. Kenya. Journal of African History 14:9–27.
Greeley, Edward H.
   1977   Men and Fertility Regulation in Southern Meru: A Case Study from the Kenya Highlands. Ph.D. dissertation, Anthropology Department, The Catholic University of America.
Government of Kenya
   1984   Kenya Contraceptive Prevalence Survey. First Report. Central Bureau of Statistics: Ministry of Planning and National Development. December.
Harden, Blaine
   1986   Birth Control Raises Scare in Kenya—Children Warned Against School Milk. Washington Post. 8 March.
Herz, Barbara
   1974   Demographic Pressure and Economic Change: The Case of Kenya Land Reforms. Ph.D. dissertation, Yale University.
Huffman, Sandra L.
   1986   Promotion of Breastfeeding: Can It Really Decrease Fertility? American Public Health Association.

Irvine, Clive
  1958   How to Behave: Some Manners and Customs of Civilized People.
         Nairobi: The Highway Press.
McNeill, William H.
  1976   Plagues and Peoples. Garden City, NY: Anchor Press/Doubleday.
Molnos, Angela, ed.
  1972   Cultural Source Materials for Population Planning in East Africa.
         Nairobi: East Africa Publishing House, Vols. 1 & 2.
  1973   Cultural Source Materials for Population Planning in East Africa.
         Nairobi: East Africa Publishing House, Vols. 3 & 4.
Mosley, W. Henry, Linda H. Werner, and S. Becker
  1981   The Dynamics of Birth Spacing and Marital Fertility in Kenya. Inter-
         national Population Conference, Manila. Proceedings, 1981 International
         Union for the Scientific Study of Population. Pp. 611–648.
Mwaniki, H. S. K.
  1972   The Chuka: Struggle for Survival in the Traditional Days to 1908.
         Mila 3:13–21.
Rogers, Everett
  1973   Communications Strategies for Family Planning. New York, NY: The
         Free Press.
Simmons, George B., and Robert J. Lapham
  1986   Family Planning Program Effectiveness. Paper prepared for the National
         Research Council's Committee on Population, Working Group on Family
         Planning Effectiveness. Delivered at the Conference on Population
         Growth, Economic Development, and the Role of Family Planning,
         March 6.
United States Agency for International Development
  1983   Kenya: Private Sector Family Planning (615:0223). Project Paper. Wash-
         ington, DC: USAID.
World Bank
  1982   Staff Appraisal of a Joint Rural Health and Family Planning Project.
         Report of a Joint Appraisal Mission. Washington, DC: World Bank.
  1984   World Development Report. New York, NY: Oxford University Press.
  1986   Population Growth and Policies in Sub-Saharan Africa: A World Bank
         Policy Study. Washington, DC: The World Bank.

# 11

# Women's Groups Near the Kenyan Coast: Patron-Clientship in the Development Arena

*Monica Udvardy*

*Women's groups are the backbone of Kenya's* harambee *self-help movement, and hence catalysts for rural development.*

(Women's Bureau 1985)[1]

Women's groups,[2] those self-help, voluntary associations ubiquitous in rural Kenya, contribute substantially to raising standards of living and to bringing infrastructure to rural areas. This chapter examines some causes of and constraints to the success of women's groups in Kaloleni Division, Coast Province, Kenya. I argue that a patron-client relationship can be found between women's groups and certain males, and that these relations affect the independence and success of women's groups' projects. The dominance of males in such a predominantly female arena of development can be traced to a number of factors, including indigenous beliefs about gender, differential access to education between the sexes, and the impingement of national administrative and nongovernmental organizations.

## The Mijikenda and Gender Relations

The present study is based on a sample of 12 women's groups in Kaloleni Division in the coastal Kenyan hinterland.[3] Kaloleni town is situated in the palm belt, approximately 30 km directly west of the Indian Ocean at the edge of a gently rising north/south-running range of hills (elevation: 200–300 m) that separates the coastal strip from the Taru Desert. Temperatures average between 25 and 29 degrees Centigrade and rainfall reaches an average of 1000 mm per year, distributed in a

TABLE 11.1
The Administrative Decision-making Process for Rural Development to the District Level

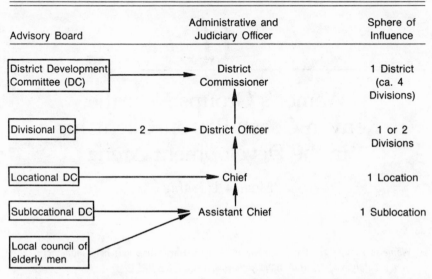

| Advisory Board | Administrative and Judiciary Officer | Sphere of Influence |
|---|---|---|
| District Development Committee (DC) | District Commissioner | 1 District (ca. 4 Divisions) |
| Divisional DC —— 2 —— | District Officer | 1 or 2 Divisions |
| Locational DC —— | Chief | 1 Location |
| Sublocational DC —— | Assistant Chief | 1 Sublocation |
| Local council of elderly men | | |

Note: Vertical arrows indicate increasing and inclusive hierarchical responsibility. Horizontal arrows indicate direction of advice. The corresponding administrative office appoints the members of the advisory board.

*Source:* District Focus Circular 1985 and oral interviews with representatives of the District Officer's Office, Kaloleni Division, and Ministry of Culture and Social Services, Kilifi District.

long and short rainy season. Despite abundant annual precipitation, rainfall distribution is unreliable, and the porous limestone sediment of the coastal range makes water catchment problematic without technical innovations.

Kaloleni Division encompasses eight of the nine culturally and historically related Mijikenda peoples,[4] who had a total population of 732,820 in 1979. The northernmost Mijikenda groups have noncorporate, dispersed patriclans and lineages, with the indigenous political structure based on local councils of elderly men. Today, remnants of this structure exist and operate independently, as well as being partially integrated into an overlying, national administrative apparatus (see Table 11.1).[5]

The palm belt Mijikenda cultivate maize as staple food and rice as a wet-season alternative; they intercrop various kinds of legumes and spinach-like, green leafy vegetables. The women's groups studied are located in areas where the coconut palm is the most important cash crop. The major income from palms comes from the sale of copra and illicit palm wine. These earnings accrue to men, because they monopolize ownership of the palm trees. But a third product of the palm is the manufacture of roof tiles, known locally as *makuti*, for sale and home use. Makuti are made by tying palm fronds around sticks cut from the stalks of palm branches. While the time-consuming production and sale of makuti roof-tiles is not exclusively women's work, virtually all adult women engage in it. Although these earnings are small in relation to copra or palm wine incomes, makuti making is the most important income-generating activity for women and women's groups in the palm belt.

Gender stratification among the northern Mijikenda is similar to other East African agricultural societies in that gender defines access to power, authority, prestige, and resources. Thus, women are today excluded from all indigenous authoritative judicial bodies. Legal title to land is fixed in the name of one or more patriclan or patrilineage males. Important economic resources such as palm and cashew nut trees are either individually owned by males, or corporately owned by the patrilineage. Women do, however, have usufructory rights to specific tree crops, and they do have complete control over the incomes gained from those products. While women can thus own some economic resources outright, an unusual occurrence within East African Bantu groups (see Hay 1982), this right is limited, and does not in any way make a woman equal to her male peers in controlling economic resources. Ideologically, women are viewed as quasi members of the patrilineage: either as daughters who will marry out, wives who are necessarily of different descent, or widows who are potentially polluting.

The above examples demonstrate the systematic gender inequality in these patrilineal, northern Mijikenda groups: according to customary law, women are not legal persons, have no positions of judicial authority, have circumscribed economic rights, and occupy an inferior and potentially dangerous position within the local belief system.

## The Composition and Activities of Women's Groups in Kaloleni Division

Contemporary Kenyan women's groups stem both from a transformation of indigenous cooperative groups, based on rural women's needs to mobilize assistance, and from a model introduced by European women to teach African women about Western health and home economics (Monsted 1978; Riria-Ouko 1985; Wipper 1975). The growth in women's groups occurred during the 1970s, and following the establishment of the Women's Bureau in 1975, their numbers more than doubled between

1976 and 1980. Today the rapid expansion in numbers of women's groups has subsided, although a steady annual increase is maintained.

The past four decades have seen a gradual change in orientation, so that groups today have such commercial goals as income generation and infrastructural development. Although there is wide variation between districts nationwide, most current groups (90 percent of total) conduct farming or livestock-rearing activities, with handicrafts of secondary importance (Business and Economic Research Co. 1984).

In 1984 there were approximately 202 registered self-help groups in Kilifi District. Of those, 192 were women's groups. The most common projects undertaken by them were farming or livestock-rearing for commercial sales, and infrastructural water pipeline development (Ministry of Culture and Social Services 1985). These were the main projects of the approximately 60 women's groups in Kaloleni Division in 1984 as well. Other project goals included owning a local restaurant, hotel, rental house, or bakery.

Most women's groups in the coastal hinterland were begun around 1982, although the earliest groups date to 1974, and new ones are constantly being formed. Group size ranges between 15 and 150 members, with most groups having 30–40 active members. Women's groups typically draw their membership from the same neighborhood, and while adult women of the same compound sometimes join the same women's group, it is unusual for one woman to hold multiple membership in various groups.

Group members live in households typical of the rural hinterland in their subsistence-farming orientation: limited presence of material goods and lack of cash surplus.[6] Few members receive any monetary or material aid from their employed children, but most have at least one child in school, requiring cash outlays for tuition.

The women themselves are mostly over 30 years old, but otherwise representative of adult females in the general population. Most are married or widowed, and fully two-thirds are illiterate. Twice as many women over 30 join women's groups than would be expected if a random sample were drawn from the overall, adult female population. In addition, unusually many of these women are in their 50s. Members form and participate in women's groups in order to create a potential pool of assistance for monetary or collective work aid in emergencies, and as a possibility for themselves as individuals to affect infrastructural improvements in their communities. Instigation of women's groups by males also occurs and will be described in detail below. All groups have a nine-member executive committee; weekly dues (usually US $0.13 per member per week or the equivalent in makuti roof tiles) that are deposited in the group's bank account; and a jointly selected group project.

Virtually all groups undertake farming, with varying degrees of success, and most have owning a plot of land as a goal for the group. Two of the 12 groups studied had indeed succeeded in becoming landowners, and 4 others grew crops for sale on borrowed land. Despite limited success in achieving their goals, groups continue because they see the many achievements of a few highly progressive groups in the division, and because group activities give nonmaterial benefits that are valuable to members: a chance to be together with other women, to exchange ideas, and to learn new skills.

### The Women's Groups Within the District Administration and the Role of Nongovernmental Organizations (NGOs)

*The Ministry of Culture and Social Services (MCSS)*

Since the formation of the Women's Bureau within the MCSS in 1975, that governmental department has had administrative responsibility for these and other self-help projects. But until recently, neither the MCSS nor the local-level government administration provided any specific guidelines for women's groups to follow. The task of the MCSS is to coordinate, advise, keep records, and provide funds to self-help groups in order to boost the development of their projects. Its greatest impact on women's groups is in the area of funding distribution. In 1984 it had KSh 75,000 (US $5,000) to distribute to all types of self-help groups, and KSh 100,000 (US $6,700) to give to women's groups alone. Together with locational, divisional, and district officials and committees, and staff members of the many NGOs operating in Coast Province, the MCSS selects deserving women's groups for cash awards of KSh 10,000 or KSh 15,000 each. Predictably, more groups are nominated for grants than there are funds available. Thus, the MCSS has ultimate district responsibility for coordinating all organizations aiding women's groups, to ensure an equitable distribution of all available funds and expertise.[7]

*The Governmental Administrative Hierarchy*

Contact between government personnel and women's groups typically begins after a group's membership has stabilized and its existence is common knowledge in the community. Then, local elected or administrative officials and technical extension personnel, of their own initiative, usually pay a visit to the group. They will advise the group of its requirement to register and pay a fee to the MCSS; and agricultural, health, and family planning officers will give brief lectures on their subject specialities. Thereafter, extension officers usually do not pay any further visits except at the rare invitation of the group. Local-level administration officers do, however, keep in close contact with groups, as will be described in detail below.

But while women's groups are closely involved with locational administrative and elected officers, above this level their relationship to divisional and district personnel is much more circumscribed. Women's-group chairpersons should be appointed to advisory development committees, but until recently, their participation was minimal.

### Maendeleo ya Wanawake *Organization (MYWO: Swahili, Progress of Women) and other NGOs*

MYWO is a national, independent organization committed to improving the economic, social, and political status of Kenyan women, particularly in the rural areas (MYWO 1985:7). Its funding comes from the Kenyan government, together with a host of foreign aid organizations. It also gives funding as well as advice and training to local women's groups. Until recently, the role of MYWO in the rural areas of Kilifi District was weak. In addition to the Kenyan MYWO, at least three other foreign-aided NGOs[8] are involved with training and other forms of assisting rural women's groups. Ideally, all NGOs should interact with each other, with the district administration, and with the MCSS.

### Patrons and Clients: The Dynamics of Women's Group Activities in the Local Arena

The pattern of gender-based, patron-client relationships may begin when either one man or a group of men encourage or insist upon the formation of a women's group. Of the 12 groups studied, 4 were created at the instigation of a locally prominent man. In one unusual case, a women's group was initiated by several males. It is described first because it illuminates an important reason for male involvement with groups: the greater access that women's groups have to development aid.

In this case, a group of neighboring men wanted to establish a health dispensary in their locality. After meeting to discuss funding possibilities, they decided that forming a women's group would be the most expedient means of achieving their goal. The following excerpt from my field notes reflects the irony of their insistence on the establishment of a local women's group.

> These men summoned the political representative of locational women and requested her to organize a women's group. When she questioned her ability to do so without a single woman present, they promised to

assemble their wives. These 30+ wives were all dutifully present at the next meeting, and a new women's group was launched. The next few meetings were conducted with both sexes present, the men discoursing from their circle of stools under the cool shade of a solitary mango tree; the women busily tying makuti for group benefit, while seated straight-legged upon the ground in the hot sun.

Neighborhood men understand the potential access of female self-help groups to national-level aid. Without knowing the processes involved, they have accurately observed that women's groups have strong possibilities of attracting outside funds and assistance. While the MCSS has funds available to award to any qualified self-help group, grants or training specifically directed to women's groups constitute a fund some four times as large in Kilifi District. In this case, a group of men initiated a women's group as a tool to accomplish their own development project. The women constituted necessary components, as well as a convenient labor force.

## Individual Males as Women's-Group Patrons

In the above case, the intentions of the men concerning formation of the women's group were openly stated. Reasons for the involvement of individual neighborhood men in particular women's groups are more disguised. All but one of the groups studied had a close relationship to a male community member. Typically, he was the husband or another close relative of the women's-group leader, but nearly as often a respected elder within the traditional cultural and judicial affairs of the community. This male associate was usually mentioned to me early in my contact with a group, but upon questioning, women were unable clearly to define his group status. The most lucid terms applied to such men were that they were the "guardian" or "eye" of the group. They were not considered regular members, since they did not pay the regular weekly dues or participate in mandatory labor inputs or other regular group activities, but it became clear that they were instrumental in the group's dealings with the surrounding community.

The definition of their role as that of guardian is fitting, because it was indeed the group's welfare that these men protected. But the significant trait, held in common by all these guardians or sponsors, is that they were men; and we have seen that among the gender-stratified Mijikenda, men comprise the superordinate stratum. By this criterion, as well as by the nature of his duties toward the group, I believe his role befits that of patron.[9]

In which ways, then, does the patron of a women's group serve his client? In all cases but one, groups' access to farming plots had been arranged by the male patron. Plots belonged either to the patron himself or to his close male associate; to a group member's male relative; or, in one case, to a church committee member. These plots were either given free of charge, or lent, or sold to women's groups for a small fee. In the one case where a group had solicited a plot independently of its patron, it was charged a high rental fee. Agriculture is an important and sustaining activity of district women's groups in which their male patrons play an instrumental role.

There are many other resources to which Mijikenda men have access and women do not. Patrons, with their considerable social networks and knowledge of the extra-local scene, advise their respective groups on how to initiate and implement such projects as water development, brick making, or poultry keeping. They arrange for government surveyors to plan and design group water projects, buy cement and hire local masons for concrete work, and advise women on the construction of poultry sheds. In an unusual case, one women's group was composed of wives of local administrative personnel. Despite the group's weak organization and lack of project focus, it was soon awarded a government grant. These examples illustrate the greater knowledge of and access to government and technical services and procedures that Mijikenda male patrons have in comparison to their clients.

The following cases show that male patrons are a crucial element in the operation of groups within the matrix of Mijikenda gender relations. The one group that had no male patron had been formed before the 1983 nationwide party elections by one of the few active female politicians in the division, and illustrates the risks of proceeding without male patronage:

> The group attempted numerous innovative fund-raising activities, but due to inexperience and high initial costs, it failed to raise any funds and, on the contrary, depleted its entire savings.
>
> At the time, its leader was running for local political office against a handful of male candidates. During the campaign, her opponents accused her of having usurped her group's entire revenue and of having squandered it on her political aspirations. Although she had male political backers, the candidate had no patron for her women's group. Due to the suspicions raised by these accusations, she was unable to mobilize further funds for her group, and it rapidly dissipated during the course of the elections (summary of author's 1985 field notes).

Had this group had a male patron, it is unlikely that the charges leveled could have had such severe effects, and it is doubtful whether they would have been made at all. With his male links to the political arena, a patron probably would have heard about the charges and might conceivably have thwarted them before they became public.

The second example points to the hidden framework of patron-clientship under which women's groups operate:

> The leader was locally renowned for her determination and charisma, and despite being completely illiterate, her group was one of the oldest and most successful in the division. Formed in 1974, it had established a water development project, despite its lack of technical knowledge or contacts. The leader had acquired necessary permits, pipes, and taps through direct contact with relevant ministries, rather than in the accepted, indeed expected, manner of working upward through the administrative hierarchy.
>
> After the group's water-selling stalls opened, numerous visitors came to examine this unusual group's achievements. The leader claims that during the height of this success, local-level officials twice tried to assassinate her. She relates that "the trouble started after the surveying for the water project. People from Mombasa and Nairobi and overseas came to see because such things were unusual back then. Many famous people came to see me and didn't go to see [the local officials] so they thought if they killed me, those people would come to see them instead." Only after she contacted the high court in Mombasa did these attempts on her life cease. In the interim, "fire was put in my house and it was burned to ashes. My parents wanted me to stop with the group, but I [refused]" (summary of author's field notes 1985).

Regardless of whether these accusations are true, the account demonstrates this woman's awareness of the danger incurred when she bypassed the patronage of low-ranking, male authorities in her determination to accomplish the group's goal. The same theme occurs again in her rationalization of their assassination attempts: that important visitors came to see her, rather than them.

Consistent with what is known about patron-client relationships elsewhere, the favors with which Mijikenda women's groups as clients repay their male patrons are not as direct or tangible as those of patrons to clients. Nevertheless, a variety of benefits accrues to the patrons.

First, any returns to members from their group efforts indirectly benefit husbands, households, and the local community. Second, even though material benefits to most groups are negligible when calculated on the basis of time and energy invested, and loans or labor assistance to individual members are rare, small but impressive monetary dividends to members are usually made soon after a group's formation. Leaders assured me that an allocation of only Ksh 15 (US $1) per member, distributed before an important holiday, would be appreciated by the members' husbands, since a wife usually handed the money over to her husband, or spent it on her family. He thus gained some spare cash and, more importantly, immediate incentive for allowing his wife's continued group participation.

For the few highly successful groups, the returns to members and indirectly to husbands can be many, including development of a permanent local water supply or household water storage tanks; scholarships to local schoolchildren; or periodic gifts of seed or small portions of groups' seasonal crop harvests. One group annually distributed large monetary payments to members, a significant return to low-income farmers, whose possibility of saving is difficult in the face of constant alternative demands on cash.

The male patron stands to gain concrete, if somewhat disguised, benefits in return for his favors. For example, one patron, the husband of a women's-group leader, granted to the group the use of a simple building that had long stood empty. This seemingly unselfish act emerges in a somewhat different light upon closer scrutiny. The building had been intended to serve as a small grocery shop but had been abandoned with only the foundation and mud walls constructed when his funds ran out. In order for the group to use it, they completed the walls and erected a roof, all at their own cost.

Other diffuse but nevertheless lucrative benefits accrued to another women's-group husband who through his contacts arranged cement for their brick-making project. He owned a general goods store in a trading center that had at least three other competitors. Members gladly confined their purchases to his store in return for his help to the group.

Finally, I was able to confirm at least one case of a patron who illicitly extracted a return from his client group:

> This man controlled an impressive array of locally valued objects, but it was apparent that he could no longer afford to maintain his holdings properly, for his cattle were thin, his land reverted to bush, and his buildings dilapidated. Although it was generally acknowledged that this wizened elder was a sorcerer, he nonetheless helped the women's group by lending his palm trees to them to harvest, and by linking them to administrative authorities who might assist their project. Early in the group's formation, one of his wives, upon his own nomination, was elected group treasurer. A year later, strong rumors were circulating that the elder was embezzling group funds for improvement of his buildings. Simple calculation confirmed that the current balance of group savings did not correspond to the group's accumulated weekly contributions, and his buildings were indeed being repaired. But not a single member of the group had the courage to demand a record of accounts from the treasurer, for they feared that her husband, their patron, would retaliate with acts of sorcery.

These examples illustrate that while returns to patrons are usually more indirect than are the favors they themselves grant, their efforts are nevertheless rewarded.

## Local Officials as Women's-Group Patrons

So far, patrons have been described who, simply by virtue of their structurally superior status as men, have access to resources that women cannot easily obtain. The second type of patron has authority over groups both through his male status and through the formal office he holds. These are the low-level government officials who are in closest contact with women's groups. Their official positions give them considerable local authority, for they grant the permits to women's groups that allow them to hold public functions. They are an important link between groups and the MCSS in that they are among those who will recommend groups to be awarded grants. In addition, they approve all infrastructural improvements to be carried out in their location. Other government staff members often label them as "obstacles" to women's-group development.

Each of the women's groups studied could relate at least one case where it had been exploited by local authorities. These incidents often involved the extraction of fees or donations from groups. For example, local officials might offer to take a group's registration fee to the district headquarters and never return with the required certificate. Or, after one official had solicited donations from a group for local, public holiday preparations, another official would later solicit the same contribution, thus resulting in a double donation by the group. Such deception is easily carried out against members of a stratum of society who are unfamiliar with receipts because they can neither read nor write, are uneducated in the workings of bureaucracy, and are uninformed of their rights and obligations vis-à-vis the local community.

Women's groups were easy objects for other fund-raisers as well, who could collect in one visit to the group what would otherwise take several hours of local canvassing. Although women complained that these constant community requests for donations were a drain on group funds targeted for its own projects, they could hardly take the matter to the local administrator whose favor it was crucial to maintain.

Other demands were made upon groups without any compensation. One group describes a local authority's request for them to retrieve and carry bricks from a distance of about 4 km for a school construction project. All members, including pregnant and older women, were expected to help. Officials also asked women's groups to provide food, to cook, to clean, and to entertain visiting dignitaries during national holiday celebrations, without any direct compensation.

The approval required of local authorities for various kinds of women's-group activities sometimes results in the unfair extraction of favors from the groups. Their socially sanctioned authority as men and their government-sanctioned authority as officials make them powerful figures indeed within the governing politics of the local arena.

## Politicians as Women's-Group Patrons

[The] nucleus of development in our societies is women's groups. They are initiating all development projects. . . . Most initiative is taken by women. So their presence at [administrative] rallies is vital (locational political chairperson [male], Kaloleni, October 1985.)

A third kind of patron impinges upon the operation and outcome of women's-group activities. This category of patronage encompasses the regional party politicians. These patrons need not always be male, for recently a few women were elected to their ranks.

Although women's-group members had not yet realized their political potential at the time of this study, these prospects were not lost on aspiring party officers. Thus, political candidates would use local women's-group meetings to campaign, wooing single votes by giving monetary "gifts" to individual group members, or soliciting the promise of a group's entire support in return for a monetary contribution to the women's group as a whole or assurances of future assistance to group projects.

One recently elected female politician had plans to run for higher office in the next election, three years hence, and had already begun to use her current post to assist women's groups in her constituency. She helped neighborhood women to form groups, actively sought to link established groups to foreign nongovernmental organizations operating from Mombasa, and also actively petitioned for greater female presence in district administrative meetings. Her assistance and outspoken acts in defense of women stemmed from an honest desire to help, but were simultaneously acts of political patronage, calculated to yield returns from her corporate clients in her future campaign.

The quotation above indicates the increasing importance that politicians are attaching to the role of women's groups in community development. With the growing awareness of the potential of women's groups, many male party officers, and the few female ones as well, are seeking to establish their political patronage.

## Breaking out of the Patron-Client Syndrome

How do clients break out of their situation of dependency on patrons? Studies of patron-clientship find that the relationship weakens when clients can directly attain the goods and services traditionally supplied by the patron. This may occur when:

- clients collectively organize, e.g., by forming unions, cooperatives, or by revolting against patrons;
- reforms are introduced allowing new patrons to emerge; or
- new channels are created that allow clients to bypass patrons to attain their goals.

Elements of all three of these transformations were being introduced into Kaloleni Division and were being acted upon by Mijikenda women during the course of this study.

Since 1984, new guidelines and directives, emanating from several different sources and apparently not coordinated, suggest that the role of grass-roots women's organizations in local development in Kenya is at a turning point. First, since late 1984, the MCSS has attempted to coordinate regular district women's-group meetings, and tightened their registration and reporting requirements. Second, in the July 1985 nationwide ruling-party elections, women were voted into newly created posts, three per district, as political representatives of district women. Third, in August 1985, one month after the U.N. End of Decade for Women and Forum '85 conferences were held in Nairobi, the new District Focus for Rural Development of the Kenyan government directed that the "District Development Committee should ensure that women's organizations are adequately represented in the District Development Committees and the lower-level committees" (District Focus Circular 1985). These measures indicate a new and serious national interest in local women's groups as instruments of development.

The measure to have the most direct impact upon the regular, grassroots members of the groups is the increased presence in the rural areas of district women's-groups representatives, and officers of MYWO. Since late 1984, division-wide meetings have been established, at which committee members of all local women's groups gather regularly under one roof. New regulations that were announced in 1985, uniformly applicable to all groups, had an immediate effect upon the relationship of groups as clients to their male patrons.

One is a requirement of MCSS and MYWO that monthly reports, including financial accounts, be a criterion for women's-group eligibility for donor funds. The locational administrator, who used to receive the reports, is now bypassed, and his role reduced in the affairs of women's groups.

Second, district women's-group representatives announced that groups may not be singled out for local fund-raising activities because of their ease of access and ready funds. It is the responsibility of all households to contribute equally to local development projects. Subsequently, many women's-group leaders refused local authorities' demands for monetary or labor contributions. One group promptly complained to the divisional district officer about labor and food provided to a local official for a visiting dignitary, and was compensated through a community collection.

New recommendations concerning women's-group finances, including a minimum sum to be accumulated, after which a bank account with three cosigners should be opened, may act as an additional safeguard against the siphoning off of these savings by male patrons.

The new District Focus for Rural Development, with its requirement of greater direct participation of women's leaders in the local-development decision-making process, opens up another channel with potential for women's groups to escape their dependence both on private male patrons and on local administrative authorities. If women indeed become members of all development committees affecting the district, then they should be able to present and negotiate for their needs directly, rather than through locally prominent men or officials.

The new female representatives of the ruling political party are already working to establish potentially powerful group patronage. After a meeting with Kenya's president in Nairobi subsequent to their elections, one of the three officers for Kilifi District summarized the incipient influence of their new role by declaring: "Within five years, all women's groups in Kenya will be organized under [the political party]." If so, women's groups will indeed become an important voting bloc in future campaigns.

In early 1986, fully three umbrella organizations—MYWO, the ruling political party, and Kilifi District—were acting in the interest of women or their self-help groups. From the loose supervisory structure of MCSS prior to 1985, Kaloleni Division women only a little more than a year later had several authoritative bodies claiming to serve their interests. The very multiplicity of these organizations threatened to rupture the new and fragile solidarity that they had created between the women's groups. After only four months in office, factionalism of political women's leaders against the nonpolitical district representatives was already becoming apparent. At a January 1986 division-wide meeting, the vice chairperson's pointed statement that women's groups should remain nonpolitical did not augur well with those women holding political office. Only the compact meeting agenda prevented a heated public exchange.

## Conclusions

While intragroup dynamics are part of the reason for the limited achievements of women's groups, this chapter focuses on the considerable constraints within the local arena, the surrounding community, the division, and the district.

Women's groups in Kaloleni Division are embedded in a social context of gender inequality that has forced them to operate through males in a manner that may loosely be described as a patron-client system: the alliance of two parties of unequal status or access to resources. Three kinds of patrons were identified that operate with varying degrees of contact and of balanced reciprocity with the individual women's groups of the division. Almost all groups have a man whom they recognize as their sponsor or guardian, who works closely with them in a more or less amiable relationship to provide the capital or to establish contacts that facilitate the group's attainment of its goals. This kind of patron fulfills his position through the single criterion of maleness, with its attendant greater knowledge of and access to resources.

The second kind of patron exercises influence both by his status as male and by holding administrative office. The local official approves the public activities and projects of women's groups, and sometimes makes this authorization contingent upon excessive demands on the labor and monetary contributions of the groups. Until recently, the groups were exploited in many ways through their participation in this relationship.

The third kind of women's-group patron is the politician. He or she solicits groups' political support in return for helping them to receive monetary or training aid. The reciprocity between group and political patron is therefore more equal than with the two other kinds of patrons. The politician's patronage is primarily based upon the powers of political office rather than upon gender, even though almost all politicians are male.

While recent changes in directives, regulations, and recommendations weaken male patrons' hold on women's groups, it is the newly created female political offices that offer the first structural opportunities for women to break through the gender barrier. Within the mode of structural inequality and dependence presented here, the authority of these new posts offers a direct challenge to power and influence hitherto monop-olized by men. In entering the ranks of those able to grant favors, these new female political party officers offer competition as rivals to a hitherto exclusively male world of patronage.

The following are some recommendations for further improving the role of women's groups, and are adapted from analyses of factors that weaken the patron-client relationship, and from the structural dynamics, described here, of the rural Kenyan development arena:

1. The MCSS, with its overall responsibility for women's groups, should reduce the number of umbrella organizations currently representing women's groups, or allocate specific and complementing tasks to each. Three such organizations provide an unnecessary and unwieldy bureaucracy, and there is a real risk of factionalism impeding their efforts.
2. Increase the flow of information to local women's-group leaders concerning the district-wide resources available to women's groups. There are several persons whose responsibility it could be regularly to inform women's groups. These include the representatives of the umbrella organizations, the MCSS officer, the assistant social development officer, and lower-level officials or politicians.
3. Advise women's-group leaders to do as much of the bureaucratic footwork themselves as they can. Encourage leaders themselves to register with the MCSS in Kilifi and to make the necessary contact with water surveyors, bank officials, technical assistants, and the like, rather than relying on their male patrons to perform these tasks.
4. Form rural producers' cooperatives for women's groups. Marketing problems are a considerable constraint not only for makuti sales in Kaloleni Division, but for women's groups everywhere in Kenya. Cooperatives could regulate prices by maintaining proper store-houses, pay individuals or groups on the spot, and provide trained personnel to market products.

Despite such improvements, the structure of gender inequality itself will require much more far-reaching measures to change. Kenyan women are shouldering an ever-increasing share of development, as they are simultaneously overburdened with more domestic and child-rearing responsibilities. At the same time, men's share of labor and domestic responsibilities is shrinking. The national impact of women's groups demonstrates clearly that men's efforts are not significantly being channeled into development. Future development policy in Kenya will have to address this basic structural inequality. The measures that follow will then have to be designed so that they both facilitate the energetic, voluntary efforts of rural women, and motivate men to greater grass-roots participation in development.

## Notes

The author gratefully acknowledges the sponsorship of the Swedish Research Council in the Humanities and Social Sciences (H.S.F.R.); the Swedish Institute; and the African Studies Programme, Department of Cultural Anthropology, University of Uppsala, Sweden.

I would like to thank the Mijikenda women's-group members for their warm reception; Alvina Kazungu, women's leader, research assistant, and friend; Mohamed Salim Baya and Mohamed Mashin. I am also grateful to N. Thomas Håkansson for his critical comments on this chapter.

1. *Harambee*, meaning "pull together" (Swahili) was a rallying cry used by Jomo Kenyatta in the early years of Kenya's independence. Since then, it has become the Kenyan term for any community-based, self-help project (Miller 1984).

2. I have chosen to call these organizations "women's groups" rather than the more precise "women's associations" because the former is the term Kenyans most often use for them.

3. Fieldwork was conducted in Kaloleni Division for a total of 12 months during 1985 and 1986. Research on women's groups was part of a larger study of the power and authority of Giriama women at different stages of the life cycle. The main methods used in the study of women's groups was participant observation in 12 representative groups; attendance at all divisional women's group and development committee meetings; open-ended interviewing of group leaders, representatives, and administrative heads; and a survey of a random sample of 85 members of six women's groups.

4. They are Giriama, Kauma, Jibana, Chonyi, Kambe, Ribe, Rabai, and Duruma.

5. Kenya is divided into 40 districts, which are further subdivided into divisions, locations, and sublocations.

6. The overwhelming majority of members' homes are constructed of mud walls and makuti roof thatch. A wealth index, adapted from Castro, Håkansson, and Brokensha (1981), revealed that more than half of these women own no cash-purchase items other than such basic necessities as a plastic water-storage container, kerosene lantern, or flashlight.

7. Interviews with representatives of MCSS, October 1985.

8. Tototo Home Industries, Y.W.C.A., and World Vision.

9. "A patron-client relationship is a vertical dyadic alliance, i.e., an alliance between two persons of unequal status, power, or resources, each of whom finds it useful to have as an ally someone superior or inferior to himself" (Landé 1977:xx). The relationship is direct and voluntary, involving the exchange of favors and mutual assurances of aid. Each partner can, upon demand, supply the other with favors that the other partner has difficulty in gaining access to.

The nature of the relationship is, however, more fundamentally asymmetrical than symmetrical.

The patron, has, by definition, more wealth, power, status, authority, or influence than the client. The nature of the favors provided by the patron are usually either material, e.g., providing goods for the clients, or political, e.g., acting as the clients' advocate or protector, or representing the clients' interest to a higher or outside authority. Clients, in turn, usually provide favors that are less tangible, involving, e.g., the expenditure of labor, the provision of information or votes, or the display of esteem or loyalty to the patron (Wolf 1966). Patrons' favors to clients are provided at more or less regular intervals, but the aid of clients to patrons is held in reserve to be exercised at the will of the patron. This leads to the potentially exploitative character of patron-clientship, wherein the patron in his/her superior position can increase the demand for favors to the point where repression of clients may become institutionalized.

Underlying the relationship is the principle of inequality between layers of society: landowners and landless, saints and religious followers, politicians and voters (see, e.g., Foster 1961; Boissevain 1964; Graziano 1973). This same principle applies to gender relations in East Africa, where men everywhere are in positions of power and authority relative to women, who generally lack access to economic, political, or administrative resources.

## References

Boissevain, Jeremy
  1964    Factions, Parties, and Politics in a Maltese Village. American Anthropologist 66:1275–1287.
Business and Economic Research Company, Ltd.
  1984    Study on the Production and Marketing of Women's Groups Products in Kenya. Draft. Submitted to S.I.D.A. Vol. 1. Main Report. Nairobi: Business and Economic Research Co., Ltd.
Castro, Alfonso P., N. Thomas Håkansson and David Brokensha
  1981    Indicators of Rural Inequality. World Development 9:401–427.
District Focus Circular
  1985    District Focus for Rural Development Circular. Nairobi: Office of the President.
Foster, George M.
  1961    The Dyadic Contract: A Model for the Social Structure of a Mexican Peasant Village. American Anthropologist 63:1173–1192.
Graziano, Luigi
  1973    Patron-Client Relationships in Southern Italy. European Journal of Political Research 1:3–34.
Hay, Margaret J.
  1982    Women as Owners, Occupants, and Managers of Property in Colonial Western Kenya. In African Women and the Law: Historical Perspectives. Margaret J. Hay and Marcia Wright, eds. Pp. 110–124. Boston, MA: Boston University.

Landé, Carl H.
   1977   Introduction: The Dyadic Basis of Clientelism. *In* Friends, Followers,
         and Factions. A Reader in Political Clientelism. Steffen W. Schmidt et
         al., eds. Pp. xiii–xxxvii. Berkeley, CA: University of California Press.
MYWO (Maendeleo ya Wanawake Organisation)
   1985   Projects: A Profile in Development. Nairobi: Maendeleo ya Wanawake
         Organisation.
Miller, Norman N.
   1984   Kenya: The Quest for Prosperity. Boulder, CO.: Westview Press.
Ministry of Culture and Social Services
   1985   List of Women [sic] Groups in Kilifi District by Division. Kilifi: Ministry
         of Culture and Social Services District Headquarters.
Monsted, Mette
   1978   Women's Groups in Rural Kenya and Their Role in Development. CDR
         Paper A.78.2. Copenhagen: Centre for Development Research.
Riria-Ouko, J. V. N.
   1985   Women's Organizations in Kenya. Journal of Eastern African Research
         and Development 15:188–197.
Wipper, Audrey
   1975   The Maendeleo ya Wanawake Movement in the Colonial Period: The
         Canadian Connection, Mau Mau, Embroidery and Agriculture. *In* Rural
         Women: Development or Under-development? Rural Africana 29. Au-
         drey Wipper, ed. Pp. 195–214. East Lansing, MI: African Studies Center,
         Michigan State University.
Wolf, Eric R.
   1966   Kinship, Friendship and Patron-Client Relations in Complex Societies.
         *In* The Social Anthropology of Complex Societies. Michael Banton,
         ed. Pp. 1–22. New York, NY: Frederick A. Praeger Publishers.
Women's Bureau, Ministry of Culture and Social Services
   1985   Women of Kenya. Review and Evaluation of Progress. Nairobi: Kenya
         Literature Bureau.

# 12

## Anthropology, Nutrition, and the Design of a Health Intervention Program in Western Kenya

*Miriam S. Chaiken*

### Introduction

South Nyanza District in Western Kenya has the highest rate of childhood mortality in Kenya (216 of every 1,000 children die before age two), as well as very high rates of malnutrition and malaria. The standard of living is lower than in other agricultural areas of Kenya, as measured by such indicators as sewage facilities, the rate of female literacy, and access to piped water.[1] In response to these facts, a socioeconomic and nutritional study was initiated in Mbita Division, South Nyanza, with the support of UNICEF. The study was intended to help identify the key factors that contribute to infant mortality and malnutrition in order to modify health-intervention programs to suit local conditions. The ultimate goal is to improve child survival and welfare by implementing more effective and locally relevant development programs. Its information will also serve as a baseline for monitoring the impact of future development projects.

### Research Site

Mbita Division, South Nyanza District, borders Lake Victoria in western Kenya. The low and unpredictable rainfall (averaging 750–1,050 mm per year distributed over two rainy seasons), in combination with infertile and eroded soils in much of the district, results in generally poor agricultural yields, but farming, at least for subsistence, remains an important economic activity, with maize and sorghum as the most common crops. Lake Victoria is also a major economic resource, providing the least expensive source of protein in the lakeshore area, as men fish and women process and market fish. Many of Mbita Division's residents, especially young men, migrate out of the area for wage labor in the cities.

The majority of the people are ethnic Luo who live in traditional rural compounds composed of individual houses each linked to the cluster through a male member of the household. Each cluster, or patrilocal compound, is in turn a member of a patrilineal landholding clan. These people with a rural orientation rely primarily on farming and fishing for their livelihoods. Most of the houses are mud wall with thatch roofs; only about 20 percent of the households have a corrugated metal roof, and only 4 percent have cement walls. A small but growing number of people have a more urban orientation. They live in rented housing and engage in trade, wage labor, or local manufacturing in one of the several towns within Mbita Division that serve as market and administrative centers for the region. Work opportunities in these towns include civil service jobs and casual labor at the agricultural research station. Local entrepreneurs include skilled craftsmen (carpenters, tinkers), market vendors, shopkeepers, charcoal makers, and wholesale traders in fish and grains.

Most households combine several economic activities to meet their needs for cash and subsistence. For example, a husband may fish and do the land clearing for the agricultural season, while the wife cultivates, plants, weeds, and harvests the agricultural field. At the same time she may sell charcoal and dried fish as a secondary economic activity. The specific combination of activities of the members of any given household is influenced by the size and quality of landholdings, proximity to the lake, educational backgrounds, and, to some extent, age of the household heads.

## Research Methods

Data were collected during field research conducted in 1984 and 1985. The information reported in this paper is derived primarily from a series of detailed interviews (n = 85) with residents of five sample communities representing the range of environmental and economic conditions found within Mbita Division. Supplemental information was collected by a team of ten enumerators and extracted from records kept by two local mission health centers.

The interviews examined the socioeconomic status of the family: income levels; intrahousehold allocation of resources; occupational and educational backgrounds; food production, preparation, and consumption patterns; health care facilities; child-rearing practices; and fertility and mortality. All children under five were weighed and measured and then compared with an international standard to determine whether they exhibited signs of malnutrition or were within the range of normal height for age (Waterlow et al. 1977; World Health Organization 1983).

The data collected during the interviews were analyzed on a woman-focused basis, with a woman and her children viewed as the minimal social group, and a woman's own income plus any remittances from the husband computed as the household operating budget (rather than father's income or combined income). We had several reasons for this. First, women are primarily responsible for the provision of food and basic necessities for children (Hay 1976; Pala Okeyo 1979). Second, 47 percent of the women interviewed were married polygynously, which complicates attempts to analyze the production and income of the entire household. It is the available income of the mother that primarily determines whether the child receives the proper foods, health care, and preschool education.

## Program Concerns and Intervention Design

Data on health, welfare, and social dimensions were compiled to identify major problems and to design interventions appropriate to Mbita Division. Most families in the rural areas do not have pit latrines (ranging from 60 to 80 percent of households, with the higher figure found in the more isolated communities). Water is drawn from unprotected sources, either from Lake Victoria or, farther inland, from streams, rivers, or springs. More than half of the households indicated that they did not treat drinking water, either by boiling or filtering. Many of the most serious and debilitating tropical diseases such as malaria, schistosomiasis (bilharzia), and water-borne gastrointestinal parasites are common in Mbita Division. Diseases such as leprosy, sleeping sickness (trypano-somiasis), cholera, polio, and measles, which are eradicated or under control elsewhere, are still prevalent in the area. Their effect is exacerbated by malnutrition, poor sanitation, and difficult access to health care.

While the program's ultimate goal—increasing the rate of survival and improving the welfare of children under five—can only be achieved through comprehensive programs aimed at increasing household food security, protecting children from disease and malnutrition, and easing the labor burdens on women, this paper focuses only on nutrition, sanitation, and public health.

### Nutrition

As illustrated in Table 12.1, the results of our nutritional testing showed that one in four children under five was stunted. An indicator

TABLE 12.1
Incidence of Stunting, Mbita Division Sample

|  | Normal: Height for Age ≥ 90% Standard | | Stunted: Height for Age < 90% Standard | |
| --- | --- | --- | --- | --- |
|  | Number | Percent | Number | Percent |
| First Testing (n = 99)[a] | 72 | 72.7 | 27 | 27.3 |
| Second Testing (n = 85)[b] | 65 | 76.5 | 20 | 23.5 |
| All Observations (n = 184)[c] | 137 | 74.5 | 47 | 25.5 |

[a]Testing conducted at the end of 1983–1984 drought, which had resulted in a nearly complete crop failure for 1984.
[b]Testing conducted during August and September 1985, which was three months after the beginning of the 1985 long rains harvest.
[c]Combined results.

*Source:* Chaiken (1985).

of malnutrition, stunting is the measure of height for age below 90 percent of normal. It reflects long-term nutritional history, indicating that the child has had persistently inadequate food to sustain normal growth.

The significance of stunting is not simply that the child will be too small, for the growth and development of the body mirror growth, strength, and development of the internal organs, the brain, and the mental capacity of the child. Many studies have demonstrated that malnourished children do poorly in school and lack the mental potential of healthy children, even if they recover from the nutritional stress (Cravioto and De Licardie 1973; Galler and Ramsey 1985). Further, children with poor nutritional status are more likely to die from illnesses that would not be fatal to well-nourished children (especially malaria and measles) (Scrimshaw et al. 1968; Scrimshaw 1971; Wenlock 1980, 1981).

Virtually all Mbita babies are breastfed from birth, frequently until 18 to 24 months of age, a practice recommended by many health organizations. Women may be away from home for many hours every day, however, working in their fields or engaging in business, especially in the peak labor periods. Children, even infants, are generally left at home when the mother is away, in the care either of a grandmother or, more often, an older sibling (frequently only four to eight years old).[2] As a response to the mother's long absence during the day, many babies nurse repeatedly at night. Over 60 percent of the women sampled say their babies breastfeed more at night, when the mother is close, than during the day, but it is not clear whether this is sufficient to make up for infrequent breastfeeding during the day.

Most health professionals recommend that babies receive supplemental food after four to six months of age, as the calories supplied by breastfeeding are not sufficient for a growing child. In Mbita, however, most children under 18 months receive little to eat other than *nyuka* (a gruel made of water and maize, sorghum, or millet flour about the consistency of milk), or perhaps sweetened tea. Children who are old enough to eat the foods prepared for the whole family will generally receive two meals each day of a stiff, bulky, maizemeal porridge (*kuon* or *ugali*) served with a cooked vegetable or fish soup. Breakfast for older children and adults is generally no more than a cup of nyuka or tea, and between-meal snacks are not the norm. Thus in general the diet of small children, like that of their parents, relies heavily on bulky, starchy foods consumed two or three times a day. These foods provide a feeling of fullness, but the caloric content is low and the diet lacks variety, providing insufficient protein, vitamins, and minerals. The result is that given the small stomachs of children and the infrequent feeding, it is generally not possible for children to consume enough of these starchy foods to satisfy their nutritional needs. This tendency, in combination with infrequent breastfeeding, contributes to the high rate of malnutrition found in Mbita's children.

Discussions concerning changing food patterns indicate that in the past, babies' traditional diet was superior to that of today. The keeping of cattle was common, with men primarily responsible for cattle care and women for agriculture. Milk from the cows, ghee (clarified butter), and fresh or dried blood were all regular parts of the diet, reportedly added to the infants' porridge and thus increasing the nutritional quality. Because of shrinking land holdings and a consequent decline in animal grazing area, an increase of male migrant labor, and the increasing commercial value of dairy products, the amount of milk available to families has decreased, and the presence of these foods in local diets has reportedly declined (Ayot 1979:159).

One way of improving the diet is to resume this traditional pattern of adding high caloric density foods to the children's porridge. As milk is now often too expensive and cow's blood rare, an alternative food that could be used for supplementing porridge is dried fish. Lake Victoria is a productive fishery and many local people are involved in the fishing industry. A common fish harvested from the lake is the sardine-like *omena*, which is dried and sold by the sackful in the local markets. Omena is already a common food in local diets and the least expensive source of protein. Dried, whole omena fish can be ground together with grains (either by hand or power mill), resulting in a flour with nutritional quality superior to ordinary maize or sorghum flour. The porridge can then be prepared in the usual manner, or optimally with a spoonful of cooking fat and sugar added. This necessitates little extra labor on the part of women and no alteration in feeding patterns, as porridge would still be the food of choice.

Some local women who have already adopted this practice report that their children find the porridge quite palatable. Despite skepticism voiced by other women, when we prepared the improved porridge at cooking demonstrations, most women found that their children would eat the omena porridge readily. Though the storage quality of this enriched flour is unknown, preservation problems should not be severe. As the climate tends to be dry and the flour is ground frequently, the processed flour would not be sitting in a store for long periods of time.[3]

Elsewhere attempts have been made to manufacture improved baby foods for commercial sales using local resources (Gibbons and Griffiths 1984; Easterbrook 1986), but this approach is not appropriate for Mbita. Women have very small disposable incomes and rely heavily on foods produced on the farm or fish caught locally. Even if low-cost baby foods were available, it is doubtful that most women could justify using their scarce cash to purchase food that would be consumed by only one member of the family. The advantage of the porridge enriched with omena, in addition to its being consistent with traditional patterns of food preparation, is that it relies on resources that are already common in nearly every home, requires little extra labor, and utilizes a fish that is affordable by even poor families.

### Sanitation

While measures to improve water that are currently taught at local health centers (such as home water-treatment techniques and methods for preparing oral-rehydration fluids for treating diarrhea) are important, programs designed to improve sanitation should also be included in order to get at the root of the problem rather than only treating the symptoms.

Sanitation in Mbita Division could be improved by encouraging the construction and use of pit latrines. A number of organizations have developed prototype latrines intended for use in areas with scarce water. These new designs, generically referred to as ventilated improved pit (VIP) latrines, are devised to minimize offensive smells and insects and are sturdier than most locally constructed latrines. The construction of these prototypes on such public sites as marketplaces, churches, and meeting areas, can demonstrate the technology to local people. The opportunity to see and use the VIP latrines will increase local awareness and interest.

A major obstacle to the construction of VIP latrines is the cost of the cement slab and ventilation pipe. Even when relatively low-cost alternative materials are used, the cost of a latrine is prohibitive for many families, regardless of their inclination. If the two manufactured items necessary for the latrine could be provided at no cost, or highly subsidized, the technology would be much more accessible to the populace.

Latrine-building competitions between communities (or church congregations, school districts, or women's groups) would heighten public awareness and peer pressure to construct latrines by providing a goal for the group to attain. Similar competitions have been employed elsewhere with some success, such as contests aimed at improving child nutrition in the Philippines organized through "Mothers' Clubs." The district government (in conjunction with nongovernmental agencies) could sponsor a competition and offer awards (such as contributions toward school building funds, money or materials for the establishment of a women's group project, or contributions to churches) plus positive publicity to the group that completed the most new latrines in the time allotted. The advantage of the competition is that it provides positive incentives for latrine building rather than being coercive, and fosters open discussion of the problems created by poor sanitation while providing peer pressure to remedy the situation.

## Public Health

Local physicians report malaria (and associated anemia), diarrheal diseases, measles, and respiratory infections to be the most frequent causes of illness and death among children in Mbita. The Ministry of Health in Kenya recommends use of chloroquine for malaria prophylaxis up to age five, use of oral rehydration fluids for treatment of all types of diarrhea in children, and a series of childhood immunizations including a vaccination against measles. These services are available free in government health centers throughout South Nyanza and either free or at a nominal charge in a number of mission-based clinics. The combination of these techniques has been demonstrated elsewhere significantly to reduce child mortality, yet in South Nyanza children still die at an alarming rate from precisely these illnesses.

One factor in this situation is that many children have not received all of the recommended immunizations. Of the 86 sample children for whom records are available, 24 percent had not received any immunizations, 33 percent had partial immunization coverage, and only 42 percent had received all of the immunizations recommended for their age.[4] This incomplete immunization coverage is partly attributable to the long distances women must travel to attend health centers. Most women will take a sick child to a maternal/child health clinic (MCH) for treatment, but they are less likely to make the trip for preventive medical care such as immunizations, malaria prophylaxis,[5] or monitoring the child's growth progress. The older the child, the less regular are its visits to the MCH clinic: it becomes heavy to carry, the mother may be pregnant again, and/or the birth of a new baby may force the mother to leave the older sibling at home in favor of bringing the newborn to the clinic.

Steps can be taken to protect a greater number of children from common diseases. First, mobile clinics, which offer basic services such as immunizations, growth monitoring, malaria treatment and prophylaxis, and education, should be expanded to more areas. Approximately ten mobile clinics are currently held in remote areas of Mbita Division, each for one day per month, conducted by one of the mission health centers. The popularity of these clinics is growing, and attendance records indicate increasing numbers of children seen each month, but many parts of Mbita Division are still unserved by any health care. An expansion of the number of locations at which these MCH services are offered, through increasing the number of monthly mobile clinics, should greatly increase the percentage of children receiving protection.

A second measure involves additional training of health-center personnel. When children are brought into a health center because of illness, they should also be immunized (unless the illness is severe or accompanied by fever) and given malaria prophylaxis. This is the policy of the Ministry of Health, but it is only haphazardly followed. Although many of the staff of health centers are dedicated and hardworking, there are still inconsistencies in the day-to-day delivery of services. Repeated examples of improperly completed Child Health Cards, children who were not immunized despite visiting the health center, children who were not properly diagnosed as malnourished, and staff who did not know how to make or use oral rehydration fluids were witnessed in the course of fieldwork.

These lapses in service delivery can be explained by the varying degrees of training of staff and the inconsistent sharing of knowledge. The government ministries and various nongovernmental organizations have held numerous workshops and seminars that offer additional training to representatives of rural health centers on such topics as nutrition and immunization policies, but the people who most often attend these seminars, the clinical officers and community nurses, are not necessarily the same people who deliver MCH services in the health centers. Because of shortages of trained staff, many health centers use informally trained nurse assistants to deal with the MCH work, and the clinical officer who has attended the seminar may not be able or willing to spend time to instruct his staff on the material learned in a seminar or to follow up the implementation of improved practices at the MCH clinic.

An alternative step to the seminars, which might have even more impact on improving MCH services, would take the form of a traveling, intensive, one-day refresher course that would be taught to the whole staff in the health center. The intensive course would have the advantage of reaching the whole staff simultaneously, and would take place in the clinic with the trainers working alongside the staff to show how to put these lessons into practice.

All of the health problems discussed in this paper—malnutrition, poor immunization coverage, and poor sanitation facilities—are related to the issue of low public awareness of health issues. If local people learn to prevent disease through better sanitation, nutrition, and home treatment of common illnesses, then improved health and child survival will follow independently of other interventions in health care delivery, agriculture, or economics.

In Kenya, as in other countries, there have been recent efforts to introduce various systems of community-based health care (CBHC), which rely on community members to teach one another and to take increasing responsibility for their own health care. In many CBHC programs the local community health worker (CHW) is selected by community members for training, and then in turn becomes a motivator and teacher of his or her peers concerning issues of basic health, sanitation, and nutrition. Inclusion of some form of CBHC in Mbita will help add the necessary educational component to proposed health improvements. The CHW may also dispense simple medicines for common ailments, helping to reduce the burden of the health centers.

Like many rural communities in the developing world, Mbita has traditional health practitioners who regularly treat patients. In traditional Luo culture there are three types of these healers: a *nyamrerwa*, a woman who is a traditional birth attendant and who offers some pediatric and obstetric care; a *jayadh nyaluo*, a man or woman who is an herbalist; and an *ajuoga* (always male), a diviner. Their services, especially those of the nyamrerwa, are still commonly used. Over half of the children in our sample were born at home with a nyamrerwa in attendance, and more than a third of women interviewed reported that someone in the family had consulted a nyamrerwa within the last six months.

If the traditional medical practitioners could be more thoroughly incorporated into the overall health-care system, a greater number of people would be reached than through current programs. They can be trained in techniques of disease prevention and treatment, and their services as educators and motivators can be enlisted. Other components of community-based health care should be added as time goes on, but inclusion of the traditional health practitioners at the beginning seems to be the most viable and culturally relevant first step.

## Conclusion

This paper has described the status of health and nutrition in Mbita Division and has identified conditions that contribute to the high frequency of malnutrition and child mortality. The various interventions that have been discussed—improved weaning foods, the expansion of mobile clinics, additional training of health care personnel, programs to improve sanitation, and the establishment of community-based health care programs—are all intended directly to influence the factors that contribute to childhood mortality without requiring major technological or infrastructural inputs.

The recommendations of this paper represent only a portion of a comprehensive package of programs that was described in detail in a technical report (Chaiken 1985). The report has been distributed widely at the local level (to the district officer, divisional administrative and health staff, church leaders, etc.), at the district level, and at the national level to the funding agency and the Ministry of Health. While some of the recommendations will not be adopted, others have already been accepted. The district officer and various local health-center personnel have reportedly adopted a number of the recommendations as an action plan and have recently carried out planning meetings and nutrition-awareness workshops for women representing each sublocation within the area. Local health centers are also initiating their own campaigns to improve immunization coverage and expand nutritional testing and education programs. Representatives of local administration (chiefs, counselors, etc.) recently met to discuss the findings of the research and the implications, but it is premature to speculate about the consequences of their actions. In sum, it appears that the recommendations of the research program are being discussed at the local and district levels, and individual recommendations have been accepted as policy and program guidelines.

The solutions to the problems of childhood mortality and morbidity in Mbita will not be technological, but will come from improvements in health service delivery, educational programs, and in increased public awareness, motivation, and participation in prevention of disease. The solutions do not rely solely on medical advances, construction of new health facilities, or on increasing the number of medical practitioners, but rather on the optimal use of existing resources.

## Notes

The author would like to thank the United Nations Children's Fund (UNICEF)/ Kenya Programme Office for its support of this work. The views expressed in this paper are those of the author and not UNICEF.

The following people contributed to this work in various ways. For their help in the fieldwork, administration, analysis, or report reviewing I am indebted to: Peter Chege, W. Thomas Conelly, Diana Dissemond, Sultanali Kala, Sally Kellock, Karen Atieno Odede, Gawdensia Juma Odhiambo, Joyce Ouma, Victoria Quinn, Inge Sailer, and Karen Test. I am also grateful for the support of the District Officer, Mbita Division; the District Commissioner and District Development Council of South Nyanza District; and the staff of the Ministry of Health at the local and district levels.

For any errors or omissions that remain the author is solely responsible.

1. Third Rural Child Nutrition Survey (Central Bureau of Statistics 1983).

2. Many mothers report leaving a cup of porridge for the baby when they are away from home. It is difficult to determine, however, how conscientious a small child is about making certain the younger sibling is fed regularly. Casual observations during our fieldwork indicated that these older siblings may pay minimal attention to the baby. Additionally, we have witnessed cases of older children eating food intended for a younger sibling, which again calls into question the quality of care provided by these young caretakers.

3. Others have expressed concern that some toxicological problems may result from unhygienic treatment during long storage of the dried fish (Alnwick 1985). Local people recognize, however, that the omena should be eaten shortly after drying. They report that if the omena becomes too old the taste becomes bitter, so they tend to purchase omena only in quantities that can be used up quickly. This pattern will help reduce the risk of contamination of porridge flour, as the flour they would mix with omena for porridge would also be purchased and used in small quantities.

4. At the time of our work, the recommended immunizations included: BCG for protection against tuberculosis (to be given shortly after birth); DPT (for protection against diphtheria, whooping cough, and tetanus) and oral polio, both to be given in three dosages at three, four, and five months; and a single measles immunization to be given at eight months. Because the measles immunization is the last given, many children do not receive it, as their mothers discontinue bringing them to the maternal/child health clinics before this age.

5. The district hospital advises local health centers to administer weekly chloroquine for malaria prophylaxis to children under five. The risk of malaria in Mbita is great, and the consequences severe: malaria can result in anemia, loss of appetite (thus increasing risk of malnutrition), increased susceptibility to other infections, and potential brain damage in cases with high fevers. It is a common cause of death among small children. The chloroquine given for prophylaxis does not eliminate the risk of malaria, as chloroquine-resistant malaria (especially *Plasmodium falciparum*, which can cause cerebral malaria) is found in South Nyanza. The chloroquine may reduce the risk of malaria, or

decrease the number of cases a child might otherwise experience. Alternative drugs that might provide more complete prophylaxis (such as Maloprim or Fansidar) are not advisable to give for an extended duration, as potential long-term consequences of taking them are unknown. An additional concern is that if these drugs become widely used there will be an increased risk of Maloprim- and Fansidar-resistant strains of the malaria *plasmodia* developing, from which there would be no additional pharmaceutical line of defense.

# References

Alnwick, D.
  1985   Personal communication.

Ayot, Henry Okello
  1979   A History of the Luo-Abasuba of Western Kenya from AD 1760–1940. Nairobi: Kenya Literature Bureau.

Central Bureau of Statistics (CBS)
  1983   Third Rural Child Nutrition Survey. Nairobi: Ministry of Finance and Planning.

Chaiken, Miriam S.
  1985   Nutritional Surveillance and Intervention Programme, Mbita Division, South Nyanza, Kenya. Final Report. Nairobi: UNICEF.

Cravioto, J., and Elsa R. De Licardie
  1973   Nutrition and Behavior and Learning. World Review of Nutrition and Dietetics 16.

Easterbrook, Gregg
  1986   A Feeding Machine. Science '86 7(1):48–54.

Galler, Janina R., and Frank Ramsey
  1985   The Influence of Early Malnutrition on Subsequent Behavioral Development: VI. The Role of the Micro-environment of the Household. Nutrition and Behavior 2(3):161–173.

Gibbons, Gayle, and Marcia Griffiths
  1984   Program Activities for Improving Weaning Practices. Geneva: World Federation of Public Health Associations.

Hay, Margaret Jean
  1976   Luo Women and Economic Change During the Colonial Period. *In* Women in Africa. Nancy J. Hafkin and Edna G. Bay, eds. Pp. 87–109. Stanford, CA: Stanford University Press.

Pala Okeyo, Achola
  1979   Women in the Household Economy: Managing Multiple Roles. Studies in Family Planning 10(11/12):337–343.

Scrimshaw, Nevin S.
  1971   Environmental Factors in the Interrelationship of Nutrition and Infection. Proceedings of the First Asian Congress of Nutrition. Hyderabad: Nutrition Society of India.

Scrimshaw, N. S., C. E. Taylor, and J. E. Gordon
  1968   Interactions of Nutrition and Infection. Geneva: World Health Orga-
         nization Monograph No. 57.
Waterlow, J. C., et al.
  1977   The Presentation and Use of Height and Weight Data for Comparing
         the Nutritional Status of Groups of Children under the Age of 10
         Years. Bulletin of the World Health Organization 55(4):489–498.
Wenlock, R. W.
  1980   Nutritional Risk in the Family Environment in Zambia. Ecology of
         Food and Nutrition. 10:79–86.
  1981   Endemic Malaria, Malnutrition, and Child Deaths. Food Policy 6:105–
         112 (May).
World Health Organization (WHO)
  1983   Measuring Change in Nutritional Status. Geneva.

# Notes on Contributors

**Joshua Akong'a** received his Ph.D. in anthropology in 1979 from the University of California, San Diego. Since 1985 he has been a Senior Research Fellow/Lecturer at the Institute of African Studies (IAS), University of Nairobi. From 1979 to 1985 he was lecturer in the Department of Sociology, University of Nairobi. His Ph.D. thesis was a comparative study of social training, while his subsequent research on drought and famine in Eastern Kenya has resulted in several journal articles and a chapter in *The Impact of Climatic Variations on Agriculture* edited by M. Parry, T. Carter, and N. Konijn (Kluwer Academic Publishers 1988). He is currently the coordinator of the district sociocultural profiles project (Kenya) at IAS and has coedited several volumes of this series of publications.

**David W. Brokensha,** Professor of Anthropology at the University of California, Santa Barbara, also chairs that university's Environmental Studies Program and is a Director of the Institute for Development Anthropology. He has carried out research on social change and rural development, on ecological associations, and on minorities, in Ghana, Kenya, Tanzania, and California, and has been an adviser and consultant to the Food and Agriculture Organization of the United Nations, the World Bank, and the U.S. Agency for International Development. He has served on the Advisory Panel on Low Resource Agriculture in Developing Countries of the Office of Technology Assessment of the U.S. Congress, has directed several Peace Corps training programs, and been a consultant to the governments of Ghana, Kenya, and Nigeria. He has been an invited participant in workshops on energy and nontraditional energy sources—in the U.S. and Sierra Leone—for the National Academy of Sciences, and has published widely on indigenous knowledge systems, social forestry and fuelwood, farming systems, and other aspects of rural development and anthropology in the Third World, especially tropical Africa.

**Stephen G. Bunker** teaches sociology at the Johns Hopkins University in Baltimore. He wrote *Underdeveloping the Amazon* (University of Illinois Press 1985; University of Chicago Press 1988) and *Peasants against the State* (University of Illinois Press 1987). He is now working with Linda J. Seligmann toward a monograph on small-basin irrigation in the Peruvian Andes and conducting research on the environmental, demographic, and economic effects of a large iron mine in southeastern Amazonia.

**Miriam S. Chaiken** is an Assistant Professor of Anthropology at Indiana University of Pennsylvania. She completed her Ph.D. in anthropology in 1983 at the University of California, Santa Barbara, after conducting dissertation research in the Philippines on spontaneous settlers' adaptation to frontier conditions. She lived in Kenya from 1984 to 1987 during which time she completed extensive consultancies for UNICEF, the International Labor Organization, and the Rockefeller Foundation. Her primary research interests include new lands settlement, determinants of nutritional status in rural communities, and nutrition intervention program design.

**W. Thomas Conelly** is currently anthropologist on an interdisciplinary farming systems project (Small Ruminant CCRSP) based in western Kenya and is a Research Associate with the Department of Rural Sociology, University of Missouri, Columbia. He has a Ph.D. in anthropology (1983) from the University of California, Santa Barbara, based on dissertation research in the Philippines on the development of upland farming systems and shifting cultivation. In 1984–1985, as a Rockefeller Foundation Social Science Research Fellow, he studied indigenous pest management strategies and intercropping practices in Kenya. His other research interests include management strategies for intensive crop/livestock farming systems, household time allocation and labor use, and the impact of agricultural development on nutrition and food security.

**Anne Fleuret** is a Senior Research Fellow in the Institute of African Studies, University of Nairobi. She received her Ph.D. in anthropology from the University of California, Santa Barbara, and has taught at California State University, Los Angeles, and at the American University, Washington, DC. Dr. Fleuret has done extensive research in Kenya and Tanzania, most recently on the socioeconomic determinants of undernutrition in Taita District, Kenya, and has served as a consultant to the Office of Technology Assessment of the U.S. Congress, the Agency for International Development, the United Nations, and several private voluntary organizations. She has published in *Human Organization, Human Ecology, Ecology of Food and Nutrition*, and other journals, and is currently completing the manuscript of a book on the ecology of malnutrition in rural Kenya.

**Patrick C. Fleuret** is head of the social sciences branch in AID's Regional Economic Development Services Office for East and Southern Africa, located in Nairobi, Kenya. He has conducted long-term field research on marketing and social change in Tanzania (1975–1977) and on the agricultural and socioeconomic determinants of child nutrition in Kenya (1981–1982). He has worked for shorter periods of time in 13 countries throughout the region, focusing on policy and institutional issues arising in programs of agricultural and rural development. His professional publications are concerned with the social causes and consequences of agrarian change in Africa.

**Edward H. Greeley,** a career officer in the Agency for International Development, is Chief of the Policy Planning and Evaluation Division, Office of Development Planning in AID's Bureau for Africa. His previous AID assignments include Project Development Officer in the Kenya AID Office and Social Analyst for the Regional Economic Development Services Office, based in Nairobi, Kenya. Dr. Greeley received his Ph.D. in anthropology from The Catholic University of America in 1977. Data for the paper in this collection were drawn from his dissertation, "Men and Fertility Regulation in Southern Meru: A Case Study from the Kenya Highlands." Dr. Greeley's previous experience in Africa includes teaching in Uganda and serving as a Peace Corps volunteer in Nigeria (1966–1977).

**Angelique Haugerud** has been Assistant Professor of Anthropology at the University of Georgia, Athens, since 1986. She carried out doctoral research on rural political economy, agrarian change, and household dynamics in Kenya (with funding from the National Science Foundation and the Social Science Research Council). She received her Ph.D. in 1984 from Northwestern University and returned to Africa for two years under a postdoctoral fellowship from the Rockefeller Foundation to conduct agricultural research in Rwanda, Burundi, and Kenya. Recent publications in edited volumes and professional journals focus on land tenure, wealth, food production, the relationship between off-farm and on-farm investment and income, and the sociopolitical organization of agricultural production.

**Richard Hogg** is a Research Fellow in the Department of Social Anthropology, University of Manchester, England. Since receiving his Ph.D. in 1981 he has carried out extensive research among northern Kenyan pastoralists. He has served as a consultant to various international organizations, and in 1985–1986 managed a livestock restocking project in Turkana District, Kenya, for Oxfam. He has published articles on pastoralism and pastoral development in such journals as *Africa, African Affairs,* and *Development and Change.*

**Peter D. Little** received his Ph.D. in 1983 from Indiana University. He is a Senior Research Associate at the Institute for Development Anthropology (IDA) and an Adjunct Assistant Professor at SUNY-Binghamton. He has served as consultant to the United Nations, the World Bank, the Agency for International Development, and the Office of Technology Assessment of the U.S. Congress, and is a member of the Advisory Board for the Africa Program of Oxfam America. He has carried out research on pastoral ecology and production systems, regional marketing, and irrigated agriculture in Kenya and Pakistan, and is currently conducting research on livestock and milk marketing in Somalia. He coedited *Lands at Risk in the Third World* (Westview 1987) and has published widely in edited books and professional journals, including *Africa, American Ethnologist, Human Ecology,* and *Human Organization.*

**Benson C. Nindi,** whose Ph.D. is from the University of Hull, is an Associate Professor of Sociology at the University of Dar Es Salaam, now working at the Swedish University of Agricultural Sciences, Uppsala, Sweden. He has conducted extensive research on agricultural policies in Tanzania and Zambia. He was a visiting scholar at the University of Illinois, Urbana-Champaign, as a Fulbright Fellow in 1983–1984 and a Fellow at Queen Elizabeth House, Oxford, in 1985. He has published widely in professional journals and written chapters for a number of books, on agricultural policies and food in sub-Saharan Africa.

**Anita Spring** is Associate Dean of the College of Liberal Arts and Sciences and Associate Professor of Anthropology at the University of Florida. She has carried out research in Zambia, Malawi, Cameroon, and Somalia, and published widely on women in agriculture, farming systems research and extension, health care systems, and gender roles. She directed the Women in Agricultural Development Project in Malawi funded by USAID (1981–1983) and the Women in Agriculture Program at the University of Florida (1984–1986). She served on the Advisory Panel for Low Resource Agriculture in Africa for the Office of Technology Assessment of the U.S. Congress (1985–1987) and subsequently assisted in that agency's evaluation of the African Development Foundation in Botswana and Zimbabwe. She is the author of *Agricultural Development in Malawi: A Project for Women in Development* (Westview 1988) and coeditor of *Gender Issues in Farming Systems Research and Extension* (Westview 1988), *Women Creating Wealth: Transforming Economic Development* (Association for Women in Development 1985), and *Women in Ritual and Symbolic Roles* (Plenum 1978). She received her Ph.D. from Cornell University.

**Monica L. Udvardy,** a doctoral candidate in cultural anthropology at the University of Uppsala, Sweden, is a member of the five-year research project on *African Folk Models and Their Application,* sponsored by the Swedish Research Council in the Humanities and Social Sciences. Her chapter in this collection is based on data from her field research among the Giriama of the Kenyan coastal hinterland. Her doctoral dissertation, a life-cycle study focusing primarily on older women and men, combines Giriama cognition and symbols of gender with a study of the roles of the elderly in social organization, ritual, and indigenous medicine. Two articles are in press, one on Giriama protective medicines and one on a female fertility cult among the Giriama. She worked for three years in a Swedish interdisciplinary research project on the elderly in Swedish society and has served as consultant to the Swedish International Development Authority (SIDA) investigating women in development in Ethiopia, and to SIDA/SAREC (Swedish Agency for Research and Educational Cooperation) concerning behavioral aspects of AIDS in Africa. In addition to her fieldwork among the Giriama, she has conducted fieldwork on the aged among the Gusii of western Kenya.

# Index